Social Policy and the Ethic of Care

Olena Hankivsky

Social Policy and the Ethic of Care

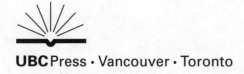

UBCPress · Vancouver · Toronto

15   14   13   12   11   10   09   08   07   06   05   04   5   4   3   2   1

Printed in Canada on acid-free paper

Library and Archives Canada Cataloguing in Publication

Hankivsky, Olena
    Social policy and the ethic of care / Olena Hankivsky.

    Includes bibliographical references and index.
    ISBN 0-7748-1070-X (bound); ISBN 0-7748-1071-8 (pbk.)

    1. Caring – Moral and ethical aspects. 2. Canada – Social policy.
3. Feminist ethics. I. Title.

HV108.H36 2004   361.6'12'0971   C2004-903587-8

Canadä

UBC Press gratefully acknowledges the financial support for our publishing program of the Government of Canada through the Book Publishing Industry Development Program (BPIDP), and of the Canada Council for the Arts, and the British Columbia Arts Council.

This book has been published with the help of a grant from the K.D. Srivastava Fund and from the University Publications Fund at Simon Fraser University.

UBC Press
The University of British Columbia
2029 West Mall
Vancouver, BC V6T 1Z2
604-822-5959 / Fax: 604-822-6083
www.ubcpress.ca

Contents

Preface and Acknowledgments

Research in the area of care ethics is proliferating rapidly and is becoming increasingly significant within moral philosophy, feminist theory, and gender, legal, and political studies. Much of the work tends to remain at the level of theory and relatively few works have sought to apply care ethics directly to social policy. Through its concrete application of care within specific Canadian social policies, this book explores the transformational potential of a care ethic. It represents the first project of its kind in the Canadian context.

In addition, despite the associated difficulties and complexities, interdisciplinary scholarship is essential for investigating the full potential of a care ethic to affect a plurality of policy issues. Because the discussions in this book reflect insights gleaned from integrating a number of disciplinary perspectives, I believe that it represents an important addition to the emerging literature on care ethics.

The project was made possible by a postdoctoral fellowship from the Social Sciences and Humanities Research Council of Canada. It also benefited tremendously from my affiliations with the Centre for Research on Violence Against Women in London, Ontario, and the British Columbia Centre of Excellence for Women's Health in Vancouver, British Columbia. These centres provided me with invaluable opportunities to engage with the policy areas used as case studies in the book.

My deepest gratitude goes to Barbara Arneil in the Department of Political Science at the University of British Columbia for her mentorship and encouragement. Her insights and suggestions helped to improve the first draft and to move this project forward to its completion.

I owe particular thanks to Emily Andrew, my editor at UBC Press, for her commitment and steadfast belief in this project from its very beginnings to the finish. I would also like to acknowledge the anonymous reviewers for their thoughtful comments and criticisms, which contributed significantly to the refining of ideas, sharpening of arguments, and overall improvement of the manuscript.

For their support and advice, special thanks to my colleagues and friends Marina Morrow, Colleen Varcoe, Jane Friesen, Rita Dhamoon, and Natalie Kos. In addition, I was fortunate enough to have two former students, Nyranne Martin and Lindsey Galvin, provide research assistance at different stages of the project. I am also grateful to my parents, Roma and Basyl Hankivsky, who were patient and reassuring and whose own values and priorities inspired the thinking in this book. And finally to Orest Klufas – to whom I dedicate this book, thank you for caring so well.

A slightly different version of Chapter 4 appeared in *Journal of Nursing Law* 8, 2 (2000): 31-53, under the title of "Enhancing Therapeutic Jurisprudence for Victims of Institutional Abuse: The Potential for an Ethic of Care."

Social Policy and the Ethic of Care

Introduction

The care of human life and happiness, and their destruction, is
the first and only legitimate object of good government.

– Thomas Jefferson, 1809

In our private lives, the need for care is generally expected and understood.
Political theory and social policy, however, have traditionally located care
both "beyond (or beneath) politics and the public sphere."[1] Public responsibility for care – care in the domain of impersonal relations – is not
widely recognized or accepted. In contrast, many feminist theorists have
attempted to demonstrate that care is publicly and politically relevant. As
a result of their work, the value of care is being increasingly recognized.
In the context of political theory, an ethic of care has brought to the
public fore dimensions of our lives that have been largely uninvestigated.
An ethic of care privileges networks of human interdependencies that challenge the public/private divide and the concomitant role that care plays
within such relations. It emphasizes that across our lifespan – at all stages
and in many situations – we need care to "sustain the best possible lives."[2]
From this foundation emerges a set of distinct values for guiding our social
lives and understanding the entire spectrum of human experiences and
human needs. The values can be considered essential to living a worth-
while, fulfilling, and balanced life.

Although the theory continues to develop, less attention has been paid
to care's practical implications. While a small number of feminist theorists have begun to seriously interrogate the implications of the care
ethic's distinct values for the public sphere,[3] to date there have been few
systematic investigations of how social policy could be transformed by a
care ethic. As Iris Marion Young has noted, "the ethics of care has done
little in terms of applying its insights to the pressing social policy issues
of justice and needs that face all societies in the world."[4] The explorations
of this book are meant to address the gap between theoretical and public policy analysis by considering the implications of an ethic of care for
a range of Canadian social policy issues.

The fundamental question that underpins the argument of *Social Policy
and the Ethic of Care* is "What are the consequences of the human need

for care in social policy?" In answering this question I consider the values that we currently prioritize in the public sphere to understand why we are making and justifying specific social policy choices. If we start with the assumption that the need for care should be taken seriously, then the status quo, developed in accordance with the values and priorities of a liberal justice orientation, is not acceptable. The limitations of our current vision become illuminated and the need to rethink our values in relation to society, citizenship, and future policy directions becomes clear. Arguably, the inclusion of a care ethic can lead to greater social justice in social policy because it opens up new ways of seeing human beings, their social problems, and their needs, and it enables us to analyze critically how government responds to these. Specifically, I intend to demonstrate how, from the perspective of the care ethic, the centrality of human interdependence and care is revealed.

From this basis, I attempt to show that an ethic of care prioritizes, with its very distinct normative framework, contextualizing the human condition, thereby giving new meaning and significance to human differences that arise from gender, class, race, ethnicity, sexuality, ability, and geographic location. Because of its sensitivity and responsiveness to other persons' individual differences, uniqueness, and whole particularity,[5] a care ethic opens new ways for understanding experiences of discrimination, suffering, and oppression. And, finally, because it rejects indifference to social consequences of actions and decisions, an ethic of care can provide valuable guidance for governments and social institutions to create more humane, effective, and robust social policies. In sum, a care ethic enhances our understanding of the moral complexities that are at the heart of any social policy issue.

Admittedly, policy change is often dependent on numerous political, social, and economic factors. However, as John Kingdon has argued elsewhere, politics and policy making are driven by ideas as much as or even more than by conventional political processes.[6] The fact remains that policies are about choosing between a range of options and alternatives. Values, which are at the heart of ethics, have been and will continue to be instrumental in directing these choices. They allow us to make reasoned arguments for why a particular course of action is preferable over another. When we consider what counts as a good reason in policy discourse we are inevitably drawn into principles of political thought.[7] All public policies therefore have implicit normative dimensions. A distinguishing feature of a care ethic is precisely that it is intended to be an alternative source for moral and political judgments. It can be instrumental in contributing to the kind of debate and discussion that often precipitate fundamental changes in social policy. If a care ethic and its associated values came to bear on social policy decision making, then the traditional policy paradigm would be replaced by one that brings into view the realities of our lives and aspects of policy choices that have been traditionally overlooked or ignored. A care ethic brings to our attention the need to contemplate how care fosters the necessary conditions for any society to flourish.

The Context of Canadian Social Policy

Canada has a reputation for being a country that cares. Historically, through its complex social welfare system, Canada has provided its citizens with a social safety net that promotes the welfare of its citizens. Security, redistribution, and social integration have been the goals of this system and its policies.[8] The promise of protection against the uncontrollable and unexpected contingencies of life reflected and reinforced the notions of caring that were once central to the Canadian identity.[9] Like many other welfare states, Canada acknowledged the importance of care in terms of citizens' well-being and overall social stability.[10] However, since the mid-1980s, and especially with the introduction of the Canada Health and Social Transfer in 1996, substantive social policy changes in the areas of health care, social programs, income support, employment insurance, and education have taken place. Total federal transfers to provinces have been dramatically reduced. For instance, cash transfers in the 2002/03 fiscal year were $2 billion less than they were in 1993/94.[11] Programs and services that have traditionally attended to the needs of Canadians and, in particular, the poor, the disabled, the physically and mentally ill, the elderly, and the vulnerable (e.g., victims of crime and sexual assault) have been contracted and transformed. There is a trend to make Canadians less dependent on their governments.

Canadian governments have been critiqued by the United Nations, among others, for not paying sufficient attention to the adverse consequences of cutting social expenditures for the population as a whole and for vulnerable and disadvantaged groups in particular.[12] In fact, statistics show a steady disintegration of the social fabric of Canadian society. In 1998 the National Council of Welfare reported that over 4.9 million Canadians, including 1.3 million children, were living in poverty.[13] Gaps between the rich and poor are widening.[14] In the last twenty years, homelessness has increased in Canada.[15] There are food banks in 465 communities spanning every province and territory.[16] Canadians have reported less confidence about being able to gain access to necessary health care services. Less than one-third of Canadians have faith in the country's social safety net.[17] Social policy, one could argue, no longer prioritizes attending to the needs of citizens, even though, in many cases, such needs are growing as assistance and state supports are diminishing in all their forms. The result is what Arlie Russell Hochschild has described as "care deficiencies"[18] in social policy.

Care deficiencies, however, have not gone completely unnoticed. Canadian politicians and policy makers have started the process of reconceptualizing the welfare state and related social policies. The discourse underpinning a new vision of governance has included a willingness to consider investing more effort into caring for people.[19] The 2003 federal budget, for example, noted the importance of building a society that enhances the well-being of all Canadians and that "puts people first."[20] The Canadian public has similarly expressed a renewed concern for others and a desire for the development of more generous and compassionate social policies.[21] The recognition of values associated with care is not limited to Canada. In preparation for the 2000 United Nations General Assembly on Governance Issues, a special commission made up of twenty-eight world leaders listed caring as a value that must be at the cornerstone of global governance.[22] In a somewhat parallel process, political philosophers have also interrogated the meaning and role of care within the public sphere of society. The convergence of these political and theoretical developments are part of a trend of reassessing what values should be prioritized in our public lives in terms of institutions, social structures, and policies. Indeed, there is a growing discourse regarding the need to re-evaluate the conceptual underpinnings of the current philosophy of social welfare.[23]

Here it is important to underscore that normative analyses of policy are not often undertaken; this is because the significance of the relationship between theory and policy is rarely acknowledged.[24] Ethics, however, are just as important in the "real world" of politics and policy as they are in the realm of ideas. This becomes clear when we investigate the normative framework that has informed Canadian social policy, determined how social problems are framed, and influenced how the state responds to affected people. The system of moral principles that has shaped the quality of life, the circumstances of living, and power and social relations needs to be interrogated.[25] Through such an exercise, there is an opportunity to scrutinize many of the unquestioned assumptions underpinning current government policy that are undermining the traditionally generous Canadian social policy orientation.

The Canadian welfare state has been operationalized within a liberal paradigm. Within the bounds of this paradigm, variances exist about the extent to which the state should respond to the needs of its citizens. For instance, in the first few decades after the Second World War, there was a commitment to maintain a minimum standard of living through redistribution to ensure equality of opportunity for all citizens. More recently, global and national pressures and the increasing visibility of a neoliberal ideology that is critical of much social dependency on the state have challenged the traditional approach to social welfare. Despite differences, both are derivatives of liberalism and its justice-centred ethical perspective, which reflect a set of assumptions and values that are not particularly oriented towards caring.

To begin with, liberal justice theory posits distinct assumptions about society and its members. At the very heart of this theory is the public/ private division. The public realm is the realm of focus. In this realm, society is viewed as a contract between rational, autonomous individuals who seek to maximize their own self-interests. According to the justice perspective, we are seen as independent, equal, moral agents who, through abstract reasoning, develop a set of rules for society that will best allow us to pursue our own interests (most commonly linked to economic interests). Liberal thinkers such as John Rawls suggest that we choose to model our political institutions on principles of justice that would be acceptable to free, rational, and impartial persons. Human separateness is a key feature of this realm, and impartiality is considered the ultimate form of moral reasoning.

The objective of this perspective is that we, as citizens, determine responsibilities and obligations towards others with as little interference with our own liberty, from others or from the state, as is possible. Our political obligations towards others are identified as rights. Rights are the means by which moral dilemmas are solved. Making morally just decisions typically involves the use of "objective" criteria of neutrality, impartiality, and abstraction. Justice is achieved when individual rights are equally protected and each member of society is treated fairly. Judith Squires summarizes the elements of a liberal model of citizenship: "the liberal model of citizenship, conceived as a set of rights enjoyed equally by every member of the society in question, embodies the ideal of justice as impartiality. Everyone has a common set of political entitlements whatever their social, cultural and economic status."[26]

The liberal model of citizenship assumes that, for the most part, autonomous individuals are able to attend to their own basic needs. Reliance on family and friends in the private sphere is acceptable, but individuals are expected to transcend dependency once they enter the public realm. Dependency on the state is considered to be the exception and not the norm. As I hope to demonstrate throughout *Social Policy and the Ethic of Care,* this is a narrow and incorrect view of the human condition. The norms of independence and self-sufficiency fail to grasp the realities of human interdependence and the need for caring mechanisms in both the private and public spheres of our lives. More often than not, human beings depend on others for some form of assistance and care. There may be extended periods of time when our need for support from others is minimal, but this does not render us solely autonomous. Joan Tronto puts it best: "since people are sometimes autonomous, sometimes dependent, sometimes providing care for those who are dependent, humans are best described as interdependent."[27] And yet this is not reflected in how social policy is conceptualized. Those who look to the state for support are often viewed as "lesser" or "inadequate" individuals. They become "morally suspect."[28] Janine Brodie explains: "we are all dependent in one way or another but the discourse on welfare dependency stigmatizes those who depend on the state to meet their basic needs."[29]

A further assumption built into the liberal perspective is that human needs are essentially universal. For the most part, this leads to impartial regard for all persons. We are not, however, all the same. We are not equally situated or equally empowered. We have a range of needs that correspond to our particular situations in society. Moreover, people have different capacities and abilities to attend to their needs. Thus, governing the public sphere in accordance with the liberal tradition results in social policy that is limited in its capacity to capture and respond to issues of diversity and difference. When important information is screened out, the process of developing, implementing, and evaluating policy is compromised. The resulting social policy obscures and reinforces various forms of disadvantage and discrimination, and, for this reason, the welfare state has been referred to as "inadequate, patriarchal, classist, and racist."[30] This may also help to explain why, despite promises of a universal social safety net, Canadian social policy has not always been sufficiently directed to those who require assistance. It may also explain why, despite the renewed levels of social spending, social problems in Canada are seen as predominantly personal failures.[31] We need, as Joan Tronto suggests, to face head-on the inadequacy of the liberal tradition as it relates to justice. She argues that, despite its prescriptive power, it cannot alter conditions of remarkable social injustice.[32]

In sum, politics within the liberal framework of justice have been largely concerned with the autonomous individual as the appropriate unit of political analysis, impartial universalism as the desirable form of moral reasoning, and rights as measurements of fairness required for the realization of social justice. Liberalism has not recognized care as an essential dimension of citizenship or social policy. Care has therefore seemed irrelevant to public life.[33] As Lawrence Blum has observed, contemporary moral philosophy has paid little attention to the morally significant phenomena of sympathy, compassion, and human concern.[34] Not only has the significance of care been overlooked, the care ethic has been marginalized by the liberal perspective. Concern for care is a sign of weakness or failure. Defining citizenship and developing policy without recognizing the primacy of care has considerable repercussions. It distorts and truncates public practices of justice, equality, freedom, responsibility, and community that claim to comprehend the full range of human needs and aspirations.[35]

Given the parameters of liberal theory, it is highly unlikely that this normative stance can respond effectively to Canada's care deficiencies in social policy. What is required is a theoretical framework that explicitly acknowledges and values care. Our attention needs to be drawn to the central roles that care plays in both our public and private lives. Deborah Stone's description of the moral and public value of care is illustrative: "caring for each other is the most basic form of civil participation. We learn to care in families, and we enlarge our communities of concern as we mature. Caring is the essential democratic act, the prerequisite to voting, joining associations, attending meetings, holding office and all other ways we sustain democracy. Care, the noun, requires families and workers who care, the verb. Caring, the activity, breeds caring the attitude, and caring, the attitude, seeds caring, the politics."[36] The relationships between the state and its citizens and between citizens themselves need to be interrogated. We need to examine the far-reaching consequences of not prioritizing care and its values in the construction of our polity, its institutions, and in the content of our policies. And we need an alternative standpoint from which to rethink the Canadian welfare state and its social policies. But, as Leslie Pal has rightly concluded, a clear philosophy or ideology to provide guidance for change is lacking.[37] The ethic of care can provide us with such guidance as well as with a different perspective through which to look at social problems and approaches to social policy. It departs from the assumptions of liberal theory because it explicitly recognizes the interdependencies of human beings, acknowledges that these interdependencies cut across the public and private spheres of our lives, and grasps the central role that care has in sustaining us within these connective relations.

Origins and Developments of a Care Ethic

The work of care theorists has done much to help us to think about how the public sphere may be transformed if we take care seriously. Care is not an altogether new concept in the classic canon of Western political philosophy. Though certainly not part of the mainstream, elements associated with a caring ethic have been embraced by a number of political philosophers.[38] Nor are the values associated with care exclusive to Western philosophy.[39] However, it has been the work of feminist theorists over the last twenty years that has brought care to the forefront of Western political philosophy. The ethic of care is most often linked to Carol Gilligan's *In a Different Voice: Psychological Theory and Women's Development*.[40] In this work, Gilligan challenges Lawrence Kohlberg's influential theory of moral development. His framework is dominated by an ethic of justice and measures moral maturity by an individual's ability to adhere to rules and universal principles of rights and justice.

In her research, Gilligan claims to have revealed a different, albeit con-
ventionally unrecognized, voice of moral reasoning that she maintains
Kohlberg's psychological measures of moral development fail to acknowledge properly. Gilligan labels this "different voice" as a voice of care,
responsibility, and concern for others. Those who exemplify the "different voice" see themselves as defined by a context of relationships with
others. She elaborates on what it means to reason in a different voice:
"in this conception, the moral problem arises from conflicting responsibilities rather than from competing rights and requires for its resolution
a mode of thinking that is contextual and narrative rather than formal
and abstract. This conception of morality as concerned with the activity
of care centers moral development around the understanding of responsibility and relationships, just as the conception of morality as fairness
ties moral development to the understanding of rights and rules."[41]

Gilligan explains that those who reason in a "different voice" distrust
"a morality of rights" because of "its potential justification of indifference
and unconcern."[42] Unlike justice and rights thinkers who employ abstract
and impersonal decision-making styles, she argues that care-based problem solvers often question the hypothetical in order to gather more relevant information so as to better understand the full scope of problems and
the practical, material consequences of any decision. In other words, she
maintains that such thinkers are concerned with the social consequences
of action.

In situating her "different" voice in moral reasoning, Gilligan specifically states that her "focus is on a problem of interpretation rather than
[on] represent[ing] a generalization about either sex."[43] Indeed, there is
an explicit attempt on the part of Gilligan to defend her work against providing any sweeping generalizations about the sexes.[44] Instead, by revealing a new voice of moral reasoning, Gilligan hopes to "potentially yield
a more encompassing view of the lives of both sexes."[45] Although she
interprets the ethic of justice and the ethic of care as representing two
different moral orientations, Gilligan nevertheless argues in her conclusion
that any tension between care and justice can be resolved in a comple-
mentary fashion. She explains: "to understand how the tension between
responsibilities and rights sustains the dialectic of human development is
to see the integrity of the two disparate modes of experience that are in
the end connected."[46]

Ethics of care, inspired by Gilligan's work in moral psychology, have
been studied and cited in other fields including sociology, education, the-
ology, business, law, medicine, nursing, environmental studies, politics, and
public policy. In extending Gilligan's work, feminist care theorists have
attempted to validate care as a distinct theoretical ethic. Political theorists
representing a diverse range of traditions are beginning to consider more

seriously the challenges that the ethics of care pose to traditional normative philosophy. Not only is the ethic of care gaining theoretical promi-
nence but it is also the ethic most frequently contrasted with the ethic of
justice. The relationship between the two ethics has been widely debated.
Some theorists, like Jeremy Waldron and James Sterba,[47] reject the values
associated with an ethic of care; liberal theorists such as Will Kymlicka
and Susan Moller Okin[48] have attempted to accommodate care's values and
priorities within existing theories of justice. Joan Tronto, Grace Clement,
and Selma Sevenhuijsen[49] and others have interrogated how care and justice relate. When compared to the justice ethic, the public potential of a
care ethic has been undertheorized and, consequently, not explored fully
in practice.

Social Policy and the Ethic of Care seeks to contribute to the literature
in applied care ethics by demonstrating why a liberal theory of social justice is inadequate and why an ethic of care is essential for guiding social
policy. As such, it begins with an exploration of the basic formulation of
care theory, including its core concepts, values, and relationship with an
ethic of justice. Chapters 1 and 2 pay specific attention to the substantial
growth and revision of the care ethic since it was first popularized through
the work of Carol Gilligan. To this end I distinguish between what I refer
to as the "first generation" and "second generation" of care theorists. After
detailing the shortcomings of early conceptualizations of a care ethic, I
move on to explore the work and promise of "second-generation" care
theorists. Drawing on more recent articulations I examine in detail how
a care orientation differs from a justice orientation. I then develop a normative framework, based on the distinct aims and values of a care ethic,
for enhancing the interpretation, understanding, and evaluation of social
policy.

My purpose, however, is not to engage in a purely theoretical discussion of an ethic of care but, rather, to transcend the confines of typical
philosophical approaches by grounding the principles of an ethic of care
in social policy. In this way, I am engaging in a different kind of project;
namely, in showing how an ethic of care, if properly applied, may change
specific public policies in Canada and in determining what lessons might
be learned about the theory of care from such a focused application. I
consider, in a preliminary and often speculative way, the extent to which
including an ethic of care can directly affect a number of current and pressing policy issues in law, health, and economics. Although work of this
nature has been undertaken in other jurisdictions, a practical application
of care is largely uninvestigated in the Canadian social policy context.

In my investigations I understand social policy to be "an intervention
by governments or other public institutions designed to promote the well-
being of its members or intended to rectify social problems."[50] I feature

issues that are closely associated with traditional priorities in the liberal welfare state, matters over which the state and its institutions exert indirect power in shaping social policy, and different forms of social policy (such as key court decisions).[51] The topics cover such key themes as equality, government responsibility for past wrongdoings, appropriate methods for decision making, and caring work. The subject of the case studies includes equality rights interpretation under the Canadian Charter of Rights and Freedoms, Canadian redress and compensation schemes for victims of institutional abuse, dominant economic methods used for developing and evaluating social policies, and home care policies (including the roles and responsibilities of informal caregivers). These case studies are selective and are not intended to represent the entire spectrum of social policy, nor are they altogether consistent with a more narrow interpretation of social policy as welfare policy. The particular examples in this book were chosen precisely because they extend to a broad range of issues to which a care ethic can apply. They deal with a diversity of social problems that affect a wide range of citizens and, in many instances, those Canadians who are most disadvantaged and vulnerable.

The case studies also reflect the research and analyses that I have undertaken in these specific areas of social policy. Here I am in full agreement with Martin Rein who argues: "when we think about the limits of what we do or about what we ought to do (policy analysis) we work from examples of policies in action."[52] As a result of my own policy research, I have come to two interrelated conclusions: (1) the inherent limitations in efficacy of many social policies are linked to the normative framework of liberalism within which they are operationalized, and (2) these limitations are also linked to the absence of values associated with the care ethic – namely, contextual sensitivity, responsiveness, and attention to the consequence of choice. The case studies in which my analysis is grounded are thus intended to demonstrate a broad range of social needs that require the inclusion of a care perspective. They also further the value of a care ethic by illustrating what transformations could come about if the principles of care were to be systematically institutionalized within social policy. Applying care principles to concrete policy is key because, as Joseph Carens explains, "We do not really understand what general principles and theoretical principles *mean* until we see them interpreted and applied in a variety of ... contexts" (emphasis added).[53] My goal is to *show* what caring social policy might look like.

1

First-Generation Care Theorists and Liberal Assessments of Care

To understand how we can have caring social policy, we need to understand what exactly an ethic of care *is*, and why it has political value and policy relevance. To be sure, there have been numerous iterations of a care ethic. An important distinction exists, however, between care theorists who have linked an ethic of care (either explicitly or implicitly) to gender and those who propose that care is central to all human life. These differences can be categorized as representing the "first" and "second" generation of care theorists. One of the purposes of this chapter is to provide a critical overview of the first-generation care theorists and to demonstrate the limitations in their nascent conceptualizations – limitations that second-generation care theorists have attempted to overcome.

In addition to being able to identify and assess various "ethics of care," we also need to understand how the values and priorities of care can be distinguished from those of a liberal justice ethic that have dominated public sphere political discourses. Prominent theorists such as Will Kymlicka and Susan Moller Okin have attempted to challenge the theoretical distinction between justice and care by proposing that the more salient concerns of an ethic of care will fit into a liberal framework. Much of the focus of this chapter is dedicated to carefully examining and challenging the assimilationist stance put forward by Kymlicka and Okin and its distortion of the care ethic. Revealing the limitations of this stance is essential for two reasons: (1) it provides a contrast to the second-generation care theorists (who have more precisely understood the relationship between care and justice), and (2) it distinguishes the two ethics, thus enabling us to recognize the inherent worth of a care ethic (which is key to any meaningful exploration of how this ethic can inform and guide social policy).

First-Generation Care Theorists

The earliest "post-Gilligan" articulations of care were based on women's conventional activities and practices. Care was seen as a form of moral reasoning that emerged from the experiences of mothering, caring, and nurturing. Drawing on this perspective, a number of feminist theorists argued for the refocusing of ethical priorities in the public sphere. Included in such explorations is the work of Nel Noddings,[1] who has argued that natural caring is the foundation from which all other caring arises. She interprets natural caring as including a mother's caretaking efforts as well as our memory of being cared for. Natural caring, Noddings has maintained, inspires us to respond to others in caring ways. Even in her more recent work she furthers her line of thinking by considering how care, which she sees as rooted specifically in family life, can be transferred to the wider world in order to guide social policy.[2] Like Noddings, Sara Ruddick[3] has argued that an ethic of care develops from maternal work and offers a critical perspective that illuminates both the destructiveness of war and the requirements of peace. According to Ruddick, maternal work, which prioritizes the preservation, growth, and acceptability of one's children, leads to the development of the virtues of scrutiny, cheerfulness, humility, and commitment to the context of the realities of life. She maintains that such virtues lead naturally to pacifism: "a commitment to avoid battle whenever possible, to fight battles nonviolently, and to take, as the aim of battle, reconciliation between opponents and restoration of connection and community."[4] In a similar vein, Virginia Held has explored the possibilities of replacing traditional contractual views of human relations with moral characteristics derived from mother-child relationships.[5]

While most of the first generation of care theorists state that their ethic is not exclusively feminine, they nevertheless assume that women are more likely and more suited for the maternal role than are men. For example, Ruddick has written that "many women are, or expect to become, mothers, and more important, throughout most of the world, the majority of mothers are and have been women. It is, therefore, now impossible to separate, intellectually or practically, the female from the maternal condition."[6] Likewise Held argues that there is a link between biological facts and women's social attitudes towards mothering. She states, "since men ... do not give birth, and do not experience the responsibility, the pain, and momentousness of childbirth, they lack the particular motives to value the child that may spring from this capacity and this fact."[7]

The specific limitations inherent in these conceptions of care are well established in the literature. First, although caring labour has been the traditional domain of women, critics have noted that there is nothing distinctively female about caring. Numerous theorists have argued that no empirical correlation exists between women and the ethic of care.[8] Second, feminist attempts to provide the women's point of view also risk contributing to women's marginalization.[9] Maternal, nurturing-based defences of the ethic of care have been charged with contributing to women's oppression by reinforcing dangerous stereotypes about women in society. The "reification of femininity"[10] risks glorifying the often oppressive conditions under which caring is done.[11] This leads to what many critics have concluded is a patriarchal concept of care that requires women to engage in self-sacrificing caretaking activities for others, an illustration of the female desire to maintain relationships and gain male approval.[12] Third, in essentializing women and their caregiving activities, maternal care theorists have also been accused of contributing to race, class, and ethnicity biases regarding women[13] and of not properly identifying differences among women.[14]

A fourth criticism is that early care theorists favoured an ethic of care over an ethic of justice. Some tended to dismiss justice while others insisted that an ethic of care should be more basic and central than an ethic of justice with regard to deliberations within the public sphere. For example, Noddings has expressed her preference for care over justice because the former allows us to transcend the abstract quality of reasoning associated with the latter. She maintains that, when using an ethic of care, a moral situation is made concrete by considering how the introduction of facts, feelings, and personal histories can affect a decision.[15] Similarly, Sara Ruddick states that she is interested in ensuring care's dominance in all spheres of society – both private and public. She argues that the question for different voice theory is how to "conceptualize, recognize and focus on the demands of justice from the perspective of care."[16] And, like Sara Ruddick, Virginia Held has also put forward the argument supporting the primacy of care in public philosophy by maintaining that "care is the wider moral framework into which justice should be fitted."[17] For Held, it is within a network of caring relations that one can require justice, equality, fairness, and rights.

The significance of nascent articulations of care is that they made visible an alternative form of moral reasoning and its potential to affect the public realm. At the same time, articulations of care put forward by the first generation of care theorists essentialized women and, as a consequence, essentialized care. Without doubt, a gendered ethic based largely on the dynamics of mother-child relations is difficult to import into the mediation of public life. First-generation care theorists were not able to demonstrate persuasively how a care ethic can be relevant and applicable to the public sphere and its institutions (e.g., the basis for political or legal reform). For a time, beyond the boundaries of intimate relations, relational ideas associated with care triggered resistance.[18] In response, more recent theoretical works on care contain an understanding that, in order to be publicly viable, the care ethic must be distanced from the "uni-directional" conceptualizations arising from first-generation theorists.[19] To avoid the "strategic traps that have ... doomed this approach,"[20] care theorists have had to disentangle care from its traditional interpretations.

The most recent theoretical discussions of care include the assertion that care is not a superior form of morality and that there are dangers in excluding justice considerations in deliberations about care.[21] Care ethicists now converge in their shared commitment to finding a meaningful relationship between justice and care. At the same time, they are most concerned to resist assimilation. Indeed, assimilation does little to challenge the subordinate position care tends to occupy in the interplay of the two ethics, and it tends to gloss over their fundamental differences. The ethic of care does not make focal issues that are already implicitly contained in an ethic of justice.[22] Assimilating care into a justice ethic can only result in the marginalization of the care ethic. It does not allow for the full potential of a care ethic to be investigated. Grace Clement accurately cautions: "assimilating care into the ethic of justice *cannot* be done in a way that gives care equal status to justice. It can only be done by interpreting care through the perspective of justice, thereby devaluing and marginalizing it. By maintaining the standard focal points of an ethic of justice, we lose the benefits offered by the focal points of the ethic of care and by the interaction between the ethics' different focal principles."[23]

Liberal Assessments of a Care Ethic

In contrast with these recent care theorists, the position taken by liberal theorists Will Kymlicka[24] and Susan Moller Okin[25] falls into the trap of the assimilationist position. While their investigations demonstrate some commonalities between the two ethics, both fail to recognize fully how the demands of care are distinguishable and inherently valuable. As a result, they do not grasp either the extent to which care challenges justice or the radical transformations that would be realized if both care and justice were accommodated with equal respect and consideration in the public realm. Each theorist maintains that differences between the ethic of justice and the ethic of care have been exaggerated. They assume that, for the most part, the existing framework of the ethic of justice can be interpreted in a manner that satisfies the most essential demands of the ethic of care.

John Rawls and a Liberal Ethic of Justice

Both Kymlicka and Okin draw heavily upon the work of John Rawls,[26] including his *A Theory of Justice*[27] (the paradigm of justice thinking), to make their arguments. For Rawls, the primary subject of justice is the basic structure of society and, moreover, the ways that social institutions "distribute fundamental rights and duties and determine the division of advantages from social co-operation."[28] The objective of Rawls's theory is to demonstrate an impartial procedure for determining principles of justice for the regulation of society and its basic institutions, including a political constitution, principal economic and social arrangements, and the "monogamous family." To this end, Rawls proposes a hypothetical situation that he refers to as an "original position." The original position, for Rawls, is a "point of view, removed from and not distorted by the particular features and circumstances of the all-encompassing background framework from which a fair agreement between free and equal persons can be realized."[29] Persons in the original position are representative parties (typically, male heads of families) and are "symmetrically situated, and subject to a veil of ignorance."[30]

The veil of ignorance is a powerful mechanism for not only does it eliminate any particular knowledge available to individuals about themselves and their lives but it also renders them, in Rawls's opinion, free and equal in the process of making decisions. Under the veil of ignorance, no one knows their status or place in society or what their natural abilities might be. They have no knowledge of sex, race, or conception of the good. Individuals are void of all knowledge about themselves as particular human beings. They are privy only to general information about political affairs, economics, social organizations, and laws of human psychology.[31] In the process of developing principles of justice, normative reasoners are thus required to follow strict procedures. As Friedman explains, "they must ... first, suppress knowledge of their own subjective particulars; second ... suppose themselves possessed of all necessary general knowledge about persons and society; and third, ... abide by certain motivational constraints, most notably mutual disinterest and lack of envy."[32]

The result is that contracting parties cannot differentiate among themselves. There are no bargaining advantages or biases towards particular outcomes. For Rawls, the objective of the abstraction under such a veil is to ensure that "no one is advantaged or disadvantaged in the choice of principles by the outcome of natural chance or the contingency of social circumstances."[33] Those in the original position are linked entirely by their common public identity. Rawls asserts that only through this bias-free, prejudice-free process can humans be assured of justice for all or, in short, "justice as fairness." He further explains, "since all are similarly situated and no one is able to design principles to favour his particular condition, the principles of justice are the result of a fair agreement or bargain."[34] The resultant principles allow for social and economic inequalities only if they benefit the least well-off in society.

Instituted in the basic structure of society, these principles of justice determine how social institutions distribute what Rawls refers to as "primary goods." These are, according to Rawls, "things that any rational person wants and will want regardless of his plan of life or his place in the social schemes. No one of them is dispensable."[35] These goods are a range of political, civil, and social rights and include "i) the basic liberties (freedom of thought and liberty of conscience), ii) freedom of movement and free choice of occupation against a background of diverse opportunities ... as well as[the ability] to give effect to a decision to revise and change them, iii) power and prerogatives of offices and positions of responsibility, iv) income and wealth and finally v) the social bases of self-respect."[36] In sum, the principles of justice specify the proper distribution of basic liberties, opportunities, and goods in society and, in turn, outline the rights and duties that citizens have with respect to these social goods.[37]

Justice vs. Care

Using Rawls as a point of reference, Kymlicka starts his investigation by asking "whether we can identify a care-based approach to political questions that competes with justice, and, if there is [one], whether it is a superior approach."[38] To facilitate his exploration, he begins by identifying three possible categories within which justice and care can be distinguished:

- moral capacities: learning principles (justice) vs. developing moral dispositions (care);
- moral reasoning: solving problems by seeking principles that have universal applicability (justice) vs. seeking responses that are appropriate to the particular case (care); and
- moral concepts: attending to rights and fairness (justice) vs. attending to responsibilities and relationships (care).

It is the last distinction – differences in moral concepts – that Kymlicka understands to be at the heart of the justice-care debate.

Kymlicka begins with moral capacities. He argues that, even though justice theorists are more focused on principles than are care theorists, this does not preclude the moral dispositions of a care ethic. Determining correct principles leads to being equipped to act morally. To substantiate his position, he maintains that "moral sensitivities" that go beyond capacities for abstract reasoning are required for jurors to decide whether someone used "reasonable precautions" in negligence cases or to decide when pay differentials between traditionally male and female jobs are discriminatory. He explains that, in order to act justly in these circumstances, sensitivity to historical factors and current possibilities is as important as is the intellectual task of generating or discovering a principle. For him, any "sense of justice" is dependent upon a broad range of moral capacities, including the disposition to recognize and to respond to people's needs as espoused by the care ethic. Kymlicka should be challenged on this point. While justice principles may not exclude considerations that are consistent with a care ethic, at the same time they do not explicitly necessitate such considerations. Friedman has also made a similar observation: "to uphold ...

justice principles, however, it is not necessary to respond with emotion, feeling, passion, or compassion to other persons. A commitment to justice does not require the full range of mutual human responsiveness which is possible between persons."[39]

Further, Kymlicka tackles moral reasoning by discussing how both ethics respond to moral principles. He asserts that care theorists, preoccupied with developing broad moral capacities that allow responsiveness to the complexities of any given situation, "render principles unnecessary and counterproductive."[40] It is true that one of the criticisms of an ethic of care has been that it is not helpful in concrete dilemmas because it supplies no principles or end for orienting or guiding our deliberations.[41] While some care theorists, such as Gilligan and Noddings, maintain that a caring ethic is opposed to fixed rules or principles, this cannot be said of all care theorists. Care can be understood as a principle in so far as care is a requirement for human life. Similarly, Grace Clement maintains that an ethic of care requires general principles but explains that "principles of care are generally unexpressed and unrecognized as principles."[42] In the final analysis I agree with Kymlicka that the question is, therefore, "not whether we need principles, but rather what sort of principles [we need]."[43] And once he makes this statement, he moves on to explore the different ways that justice principles of "rights and fairness" contrast with care principles of "responsibilities and relationships."

Universality vs. Preserving Relationships
The first basic distinction that Kymlicka challenges is that justice aims at universality or impartiality while care is concerned with particular relationships. He argues that the distinction is overdrawn since care theorists are also committed to a principle of universality because they maintain that each person is connected to us "by virtue of being another person." However, Kymlicka does question the extent to which care theorists can reconcile maintaining connections that attend to the particularities of individuals with a commitment to universality. Quoting Blum, Kymlicka says, "how this extension to all persons is to be accomplished is not made clear."[44] He claims that theorists have not adequately dealt with how care can be extended to all persons.

Several care theorists do maintain that care is applicable only to the private spheres of our lives. For example, Noddings has argued that care is not simply a matter of feeling favourably disposed towards others or even of being concerned about people with whom we have no relations or connections. Genuine care requires actual encounters with others.[45] There is therefore a legitimate question as to how we can respond to those outside our existing circle of interpersonal relations. At first glance, there appear to be many obstacles associated with caring for those who are not known to us. For example, caring for those outside our immediate circles, communities, or nations can be hampered by the difficulty many of us have relating to or feeling a connection to those who are different from us. It is not hard to understand why we may be more favourably disposed to those with whom we share certain characteristics such as gender, ethnicity, or class.

The question of whether we can or even should care for others has been tackled by a number of theorists. For the most part, their discussions of why we should care for others stem from the explanation that human beings are vulnerable and dependent on others both in the private and public realms of society. Several care theorists have relied upon the arguments of Robert Goodin in this regard. He maintains that "the same considerations of vulnerability that make our obligations to our families, friends, clients, and compatriots especially strong can also give rise to similar responsibilities toward a much larger group of people who stand in none of the standard special relationships to us."[46] It may be true that caring needs, actions, and behaviours (as well as their antitheses) can be more easily understood in our most intimate circles of interaction. Proximity often allows us to observe the effects of our actions. But, as Goodin points out, it is our *particular obligations* that too often blind us to our larger social responsibilities. Moreover, Goodin also points out that each of us has the capacity to make choices and to produce consequences that matter to others. For him, vulnerability amounts to one person having the capacity to produce consequences that matter to another. In particular, he argues that policy decision makers have a special responsibility in this regard because their decisions directly affect how social institutions are structured.

If one considers how a change in government can lead to changes in policies, programs, and services that directly affect citizens, then we can see how the actions of politicians and policy makers affect those beyond their immediate and intimate circles. With the advent of globalization, it is also becoming increasingly clear how decisions by a few people in one state can have profound consequences for so-called strangers in another. Such examples include the consequences of making a policy choice to provide (or withhold) foreign aid to deal with poverty, HIV/AIDS, and other diseases. An ethic of care makes us more aware of the social responsibilities that come with human interconnection and interdependencies, and it leads us to seriously contemplate such policy choices. Other care theorists have made similar arguments. Grace Clement has written that, although we cannot care for strangers in the same manner that we care for our intimates, this does not preclude us from connecting with, and taking an active interest in, those we will never know personally.[47] Iris Marion Young argues that "the values of an ethic of care ... can and should be extended beyond face-to-face personal relations, to the interconnections of strangers in the public world of social policy and its implementation."[48] Similarly, Fiona Robinson has argued that "the transformatory potential of an ethics focus extends beyond the personal to the political, and ultimately, to the global context of social life."[49]

Respect for Common Humanity vs. Respect for Distinct Individuality

Another commonly held difference between justice and care that Kymlicka attempts to dispel is that justice responds solely to people's common humanity rather than to people's distinct individuality. He argues that theories of justice are not limited to respect for the "generalized other." Both Kymlicka and Okin use the theoretical mechanism of the original position in Rawls's theory of justice to substantiate their positions. By referring to the deliberations of individuals in the original position, Kymlicka contends that, although moral reasoning in Rawls's theory occurs in abstraction from particular preferences, talents, and social positions, this does not mean that these human characteristics are ignored: "the fact that people are asked to reason in abstraction from their own social position, natural talents, and personal preferences when thinking about others does not mean that they must ignore the particular preferences, talents, and social position of others."[50] Kymlicka therefore argues that care and concern are already incorporated in the empirical facts known about people and are reflected in how principles of justice are developed for the public sphere and its institutions.

To support his position, he refers to Okin's argument that Rawls's theory of justice is itself centrally dependent upon the capacity of moral persons to be concerned about and to demonstrate care for others, especially those others who are most different from themselves. Okin argues that an ethic of care, although not explicitly stated, is already implicit in the ethic of justice found in Rawls's liberal framework. She argues that "feelings such as empathy and benevolence are at the very foundation of his [Rawls's] principles of justice."[51] She notes that at the centre of the original position are feelings of responsibility, care, and concern for others because each person has to take the good of others into account when formulating principles of justice. Feminists, Okin maintains, have exaggerated the shortfalls of justice and the transformational effects of an ethic of care: "unfortunately, much feminist intellectual energy ... has gone into the claim that 'justice' and 'rights' are masculinist ways of thinking about morality that feminists should eschew or radically revise, advocating a morality of care."[52]

Both Kymlicka and Okin emphasize that a proper application of an ethic of justice in moral decision making should include some of the values we normally associate with care, such as attention to contextual details and sensitivity to particularity and concrete human differences. Most liberal theorists would in fact argue that justice reasoning should incorporate certain levels of contextuality. As Marilyn Friedman explains, "in reasoning about justice and rights, it is ... inappropriate to draw conclusions from highly abbreviated descriptions of situations."[53] However, allowing for such considerations is not the same as requiring them. Kymlicka and Okin fail to understand how very differently care and justice prioritize the need for context and the processes that they propose for discovering context.

To begin with, in the original position context is undermined by the lack of a real plurality of perspectives. One cannot reach a contextual understanding of the other because the other does not exist. We are required, as Benhabib has explained, to take the "standpoint of the generalized other" – a process in which we "abstract from the individuality and concrete identity of the other."[54] The standpoint of the generalized other requires us to view each and every individual as a rational being entitled to the same rights and duties we would want to ascribe to ourselves. Indeed, the standpoint of impartiality is the exact opposite of the standpoint of care.[55] Care's concern for context is fundamental, not a desirable addition. In this regard, both Kymlicka and Okin have exaggerated the extent to which the abstraction and impartial standpoint of Rawls's original position can automatically meet the standards of an ethic of care.

Kymlicka argues that the veil of ignorance forces him (the rational contractor) to "reason as if he were any one of them,"[56] and Okin assumes that our sense of benevolence will lead to an understanding of others' interests. This does not, however, capture the process that an ethic of care would deem as essential for including the standpoint of another. If we begin to deconstruct Rawls's theory carefully, we find that the procedure for deliberation under the original position is essentially antithetical to the one proposed by the care ethic. Rawls himself asserts that, behind this veil, men are not interested in each other, in their ends or their destinies. They are rational, yet mutually disinterested, individuals who "take no interest in another's interest."[57]

Even if, however, we were to accept Okin's contention that the original position requires a great deal of empathy on the part of all individuals, this is not necessarily congruent with an ethic of care. An ethic of care compels us to provide the space and opportunity to engage in dialogue, to allow others to "to speak and be heard, to tell one's own life-story, to press one's claims and point of view in one's own voice."[58] A sense of empathy is not the same as allowing those who are different to articulate their own situations and needs. We should reject, as Julie Anne White notes, "the notion that through empathy we can know what others need without engaging them as particular others."[59] From the perspective of care, awareness of human differences emerges out of a process of ongoing interactions and reflection rather than something that is known in advance from the fixed position of an original position. Shane O'Neil has similarly critiqued Okin for this shortcoming: "Despite Okin's optimism, we cannot simply trust that empathy and benevolence will guarantee that the interests of all are adequately taken into account. We need to listen and to reflect in ways that allow us to take into account what it would really be like to occupy a different position in society, to be a woman rather than a man, to be black rather than white, to be unemployed rather than a managing director of a large company."[60]

Claiming Rights vs. Accepting Responsibilities

The last distinction that Kymlicka tackles is that which he considers to be at the very heart of the justice-care debate – the extent to which we accept responsibility for others. He establishes that both ethics involve some form of moral responsibility. However, he also claims that the care ethic is flawed because of its grounds for moral claims – the expectation and responsibility to attend to and ameliorate "subjective hurts." Subjective hurts are claims of wrongdoing and identification of resultant needs that emerge in the process of dialogue with others. To make his point, Kymlicka contrasts subjective-hurts moral claims of the ethic of care to the "objective-unfairness" moral claims of the ethic of justice. He argues that, under a liberal ethic of justice, our rights and obligations are fixed in advance by abstract rules rather than by context-sensitive assessments of the needs of those around us. For Kymlicka, "if we are to have genuine autonomy, we must know in advance what our responsibilities are, and these assignments of responsibility must be insulated to some extent from context-sensitive assessments of particular desires."[61]

Indeed, according to the liberal standpoint, making morally just decisions typically entails treating everyone according to the criteria of neutrality, impartiality, abstraction, and objectivity. Justice is achieved when individual rights are equally protected and each member of society is treated fairly. The objective of this form of reasoning is to see others and ourselves in "universal," or general, terms. It also requires us to view others as having similar needs, rights, and duties. Not surprisingly, working within the liberal paradigm, Kymlicka asserts that those who suffer as a result of abstract rules have only themselves to blame: "the people who will suffer from the application of abstract rules are those who, through extravagance or carelessness, have formed desires which cannot be met within their rightfully allotted means."[62] Kymlicka therefore argues that the imprudent should pay for their choices. In sum, he argues that a care ethic, with its emphasis on subjective hurts and disappointments, leads citizens to take too little responsibility for their own well-being and, in turn, demands of them too great a responsibility for others. For Kymlicka, the ethic of justice rejects the emphasis on subjective hurts because these hurts represent an abdication of moral responsibility. Attending to such "hurts" threatens fairness and autonomy.

Kymlicka also claims that care theorists have not said much about the connection between subjective hurt, objective unfairness, and moral claims.[63] This, however, is not true. Care theorists have pointed out that, without some checks upon the care ethic, pathological forms of care can emerge. These include maternalism, parochialism, and colonialism.[64] Without doubt, any viable theory of care must take into account the oppressive conditions under which caring practices take place. It is critical, as Sevenhuijsen observes, to distinguish between an ethic of care and compulsory altruism.[65] Often caregivers have no choice about whether or not to undertake caring labour. Care theorists acknowledge the negative implications of unconditional care for both caregivers and care recipients. There also needs to be an acknowledgment of the oppressive conditions that caring practices can create. For example, Uma Nayaran has pointed out that "caring for" signifies how colonizers justify the subjection of foreigners.[66] Care needs to be balanced with justice because, as Friedman accurately observes, "the complex reality of social life encompasses the human potential for helping, caring for, and nurturing others *as well as* the potential for harming, exploiting, and oppressing others."[67]

Moreover, Kymlicka's claim that care theorists do not pay much attention to autonomy (which male justice theorists discuss at length) is only partially accurate. Although care theorists critique the "abstract autonomy" prioritized by justice theorists, they do not reject autonomy per se. Their concerns with abstract autonomy are twofold: it overlooks the facts that (1) humans are, by nature, connected to one another and (2) that they are embedded in a range of involuntary and voluntary social relations through which they are defined, structured, sustained, and limited.[68] Most important, abstract autonomy blinds us to the notion that we, as individuals *in relation to* one another, need care in the course of our daily lives. As Sevenhuijsen explains: "abstract autonomy overlooks what it is that makes care an element of the human condition; i.e. the recognition that all people are vulnerable, dependent, and finite, and that we all have to find ways of dealing with this in our daily existence and in the values which guide our individual and collective behaviour."[69] An ethic of care inspires a reconceptualization of autonomy – one that reflects the importance of human relations while, at the same time, challenging the inequalities of power within these relations. This approach, as Ruth Lister notes, is "a pre-condition for genuine, non-exploitative interdependence."[70] As Young explains, the autonomous self is established only within a caring and supportive context.[71] Moore has similarly noted that emotional autonomy can be realized through self-esteem, which can develop only through an adequate sense of caring.[72]

So while care theorists discuss the limitations and dangers of a care ethic and acknowledge the importance of autonomy, they also make persuasive arguments as to why we need to broaden our responsibilities to others. Responsibility goes beyond what has typically been associated with the liberal measurement of objective fairness operationalized through rules and rights. It is not that all care theorists reject rights. Indeed, many would agree with Jeremy Waldron's assertion that, in a human world, the limits of our affections for others may sometimes necessitate a structure of rights to which people can turn.[73] Rights have been and continue to be important tools for challenging sex and gender inequalities. As I outline in Chapter 3, with a care ethic we can even reconceptualize rights so that they accommodate more effectively the differing experiences and needs of those seeking equality. Feminist care theorists do argue, however, that our political obligations and expectations towards others should not always be reduced to abstract rules and rights. Even Waldron himself acknowledges that rights should not be paraded as the most desirable basis for social action.[74]

A care ethic challenges the limitations of objective fairness for a number of reasons. First, abstract rules and rights that assume equality and sameness obscure human differences and their significance to the legitimacy of moral claims. It is not difficult to see how the outcome of impartial reasoning congruent with objective fairness can lead to indifference towards others' needs. And yet, for theorists like Kymlicka, this inattention to the needs and expectations of others is a non-moral failing.[75] For care theorists, it is precisely such an outcome that demonstrates that "not all problems of oppression are problems of unfairness or the violation of rights."[76] There are important responsibilities that arise between human beings in the course of their lives – responsibilities that transcend the objective fairness of the justice paradigm. A traditional justice perspective, for instance, does not consistently consider how our judgments or actions affect concrete others.

Indeed, the whole point of the care ethic is to reveal a range of injustices that may otherwise be ignored. These may include the "subjective hurts," as Kymlicka labels them, that result from forces and circumstances beyond an individual's control. We cannot always be blamed for our so-called "choices" because not all of us have the power to control them when there are no alternatives from which to select. And to deny such a reality, to claim instead that people are "extravagant" or "careless," is to deny the social context of systemic discrimination. Care opens the door to the proper identification and critical understanding of those wider structures that create relations that result in exclusion, marginalization, suffering, and harm. Understanding people's lives, but, significantly, being able to honestly appraise and recognize conditions of inequality, disadvantage, and discrimination, can be especially beneficial for responding adequately and responsively to gender, racial, ethnic, cultural, and class differences and oppression.

Most important, an ethic of care requires a proactive stance in relation to others. It requires more than just an orientation towards, or motivation for, caring. It requires explicitly acknowledging the centrality of care in our lives. The question that is posed by Tronto – "How can we best meet our caring responsibilities?" – becomes central. An ethic of care broadens our moral landscape so that we are able to recognize that not all those things we need make sense within the context of a contractual ethics of rights.[77] As Iris Marion Young argues, we cannot simply respond to issues of violence, discrimination, racism, and sexism using a traditional liberal model of distributive justice.[78] Beyond rights are the caring responsibilities that arise between human beings in the course of their lives. An ethic of care encourages responsiveness to the needs of others. In the realm of social policy this entails, whenever possible, the promotion of the welfare of the citizenry and the prevention of harm, suffering, unjust burdens, and hurt.

In the end, Kymlicka does acknowledge that the justice and care models have been developed with different sorts of cases in mind. He also acknowledges that "neither seems well suited to deal with the full range of our moral obligations."[79] And, in his opinion, the ethic of justice and the requirement of objective fairness are better suited to interactions between "competent" and "autonomous" adult beings: "if the world was solely composed of able-bodied adults, there might be strong reasons for endorsing the justice approach."[80] The fact that justice reasoning "not only presupposes that we are autonomous adults" but, moreover, "that we are adults *who are not care-givers for dependants*,"[81] is for him a noteworthy limitation.

In fact, Kymlicka goes so far as to say that those justice theorists, "by continuing the centuries old neglect of the basic issues of child-rearing and care for dependants, are resting their theories on 'unexamined and perilously shaky ground.'"[82] Rawls's list of primary goods is one such example. These goods, which apparently all persons require to seek out their own conception of the good life, do not include any considerations of care. There is no mention of the "good" of being cared for or, alternatively, of the "good" we require to care for another. The centrality of human interdependency and care in human relationships is simply absent from Rawls's list of primary goods.[83] In Linda McLain's words, Rawls's version of political liberalism does not "make explicit enough the fact of human dependency and the importance of caregiving and caring relations to human development."[84]

While Kymlicka acknowledges the failings of justice in regards to care for dependants, his critical analysis is underdeveloped. He fails to fully grasp how central care is in all of our lives. His analysis still assumes that most adults are competent, able-bodied, and autonomous, and that dependants are, for the most part, children. This is an extremely limited interpretation of human beings, dependency, and the care ethic. In our lives we are all cared for, and in most cases, we also care for others. The type of care that we require may vary over the course of our lifetime according to age, illness, disease, and differing periods of physical abilities and mental capacities. Care, however, is a constant requirement for the well-being of all persons. This is true for persons who are in a state of utter dependency or vulnerability as much as it is for persons who appear to be, from the perspective of justice, fully autonomous. It is also equally true for both the private and public spheres of life.

If liberal theorists such as Kymlicka and Okin took this reality seriously, then dependency needs would be normalized. It would be widely accepted that such needs require appropriate responses during the entire course of our lives. Kymlicka himself acknowledges that "once people are responsible for attending to the (unpredictable) demands of dependants, they are no longer capable of their own predictability."[85] This concession about dependency undermines the legitimacy of not only objective fairness and autonomy but, arguably, of the entire justice model. In turn, it substantiates the strength of a care ethic vis-à-vis the ethic of justice. And while justice theories such as Rawls's continue to have widespread appeal and acceptance, especially for informing social policy within liberal democratic states such as Canada, this should not deter us from asserting that care must be taken seriously. This point is made clearly by Charles Taylor: "The power of procedural liberalism is enormous for it carries the force of our major institutions, the force of our major moral ideals, and the force of our scientific intellectual ideals. It is a powerful adversary, but we who are concerned with the crisis of care within our society know it must be fought."[86]

The objective is therefore to recognize the value and uniqueness of the care ethic. Only then can it be combined in a respectful way with the values of justice to ensure a balanced and reasoned resolution of practical issues and social problems. The work of the second generation of care theorists responds directly to this challenge. Their approach to conceptualizing care overcomes the limitations of the first generation of care theorists. In addition, they confront the subordination of care within the typical pairing of justice and care[87] and, in so doing, undermine Kymlicka's and Okin's position that care is a kind of moral "fill-in" for pre-existing frameworks of liberal justice. Current care theorists acknowledge the worth and priorities of a care ethic – namely, human interdependency, care, and the complexity of social problems and human needs. As is illustrated in the next chapter, their work provides the necessary foundation for arguing why a care ethic should be fully integrated into all aspects of social policy development, implementation, and evaluation.

2
Second-Generation Care Theorists and the Moral Principles of Care

In this chapter I briefly review recent conceptualizations and preliminary policy applications of a care ethic and consider their relevance for the Canadian political context. Building upon the promising work of second-generation care theorists, I also formulate a normative framework, which I employ in the following case study investigations in order to demonstrate the value of introducing a care ethic into Canadian social policy. While the framework outlined in this chapter reflects the assumptions and perspectives of the most promising theoretical developments, it nevertheless represents my own interpretation of the salient priorities and values of a care ethic, organized coherently into a set of principles suitable and effectual for social policy application.

In general, the formulation of alternative, progressive forms of care ethics have been successful for two main reasons. First, second-generation care theorists have established the centrality of care to all human life and activities. Care is now generally accepted as "a species activity that includes everything that we do to maintain, continue and repair our 'world' so that we can live in it as well as possible. That world includes our bodies, our environments, all of which we seek to interweave in a complex, life-sustaining web."[1] Second, these theorists have furthered our understanding of how an ethic of care and an ethic of justice can interact respectfully with one another. Emerging approaches are characterized by their commitment to the moral distinction and significance of care and an openness to exploring the potential synergy between care and justice.[2] Current articulations have also established a firm basis from which to argue that a care ethic should legitimately lead us to contemplate what we value in our public lives, including social policy actions and decisions.

Leading the way, Joan Tronto has taken the position that "care is only viable as a political ideal in the context of liberal, pluralistic, democratic institutions."[3] Tronto identifies four ethical elements of care: attentiveness, responsibility, competence, and responsiveness. Attentiveness involves recognizing the needs of others; responsibility is contrasted with the traditional concept of political obligation, the former being seen as a more flexible form of understanding what people should do for each other than the latter; competence relates to the quality of caring work; and responsiveness entails "a different way to understand the needs of others[.] [R]ather than put[ting] ourselves into their position ... it suggests that we consider the other's position as that other expresses it."[4] Tronto believes strongly that even connected to a theory of justice, an ethic of care can significantly affect public philosophy and public sphere institutions: "even conventional liberal thought will be transformed if we take care seriously."[5] Including the value of care with commitments to other liberal values (such as a commitment to people's rights) makes citizens more thoughtful, more attentive to the needs of others, and, therefore, better democratic citizens. Tronto's efforts are largely aimed at contributing to a renewed normative understanding of care. She does not provide any detailed case studies of how institutions or policies in the public sphere may be transformed, other than stating that care is "a way of framing political issues that makes their impact, and concern with human lives, direct and immediate."[6]

Expanding upon Tronto's efforts, Grace Clement has a slightly different perspective on the relationship of care and justice. In Clement's opinion, both ethics should be given equal status and should, therefore, "jointly determine deliberations in public."[7] For Clement, the two ethics are independently inadequate and therefore mutually interdependent.[8] To demonstrate how the care and justice ethics can be integrated, she turns to the examples of political pacifism and public funding of long-term care in the United States. With these case studies she attempts to show that care can be publicly applied and that it can also effectively interact with an ethic of justice without resulting in the devaluation of care. Clement argues that her public applications of care "offer ... a model of how one might evaluate any proposed public version of care."[9] Her model consists of asking whether a public policy takes on a contextual approach, whether it is based on a social conception of the self, and whether it prioritizes maintaining relationships and individual needs.[10] After considering case studies of political pacifism as well as the case study of social welfare programs, Clement concludes that Sara Ruddick's version of contextual pacifism and publicly funded elder care can be interpreted as consistent with her model of a public version of care.

In addition to the work of Tronto and Clement, Julie Anne White has extended the examination of the traditional care/justice interface by considering those institutional contexts that facilitate the work of care. Using two case studies of social services in the United States, she identifies the inadequacies and paternalistic practices of care in the public sphere before moving on to examine alternative models based on more mutual practices of care. Her investigation focuses on the "critical disparity between the needs of recipients as defined by professionals and the needs as articulated by recipients themselves."[11] In the final analysis, she contributes to the understanding of care ethics by offering a framework for public care that is modelled on dialogical and discursive democracy.

Applications of care ethics have reached beyond the United States. For example, the work of Selma Sevenhuijsen has been instrumental in understanding further the relationship between care and social policy. Sevenhuijsen has explored numerous ways of placing care within conceptions of democratic citizenship that would enable us to "judge with care." Like both Tronto and Clement, she places her discussion of care within a liberal framework of politics and citizenship: "In my opinion, the feminist ethics of care employs a moral epistemology which forms a radical break from epistemic rules of liberal political philosophy. On the other hand, this does not imply that I argue for a definitive farewell to liberal concepts such as equality, justice and autonomy ... on the contrary, it simply means that they need to be rethought from the perspective of the ethics of care."[12] To this end she has investigated how an ethic of care can provide new perspectives for two policy areas in the Netherlands: the legal regulation of child custody and the reform of public health care policies. In the case of child custody, she argues that care's focus on dealing with dependency, vulnerability, and responsibility in specific situations "has the capacity to provide a fuller and richer moral idiom that is better attuned to the manifold and often complicated moral dilemmas that people experience in their intimate relations."[13] In the realm of health policy, Sevenhuijsen maintains that an ethics of care can improve our understanding of public provisions of health care in terms of availability and access.

More recently, Sevenhuijsen has extended her application of the theoretical model of care to South Africa. In reviewing the design of new social policies since the fall of apartheid she points out that the "ethic of care has become a serious candidate as a guideline for policy making."[14] Citing South Africa's ten-point action program for social development, she notes that the first point of the plan prioritizes the "restoration of the ethics of care and human development into all our programs. This requires the urgent rebuilding of family, community, and social relations in order to promote social integration."[15] Sevenhuijsen maintains that, if a "justice-into-care" framework were to be adopted by South Africa, then care would be made into an issue of citizenship and, in the process, contribute "towards building a South African society that considers both justice and care as hallmarks of this new century."[16] And finally, she has developed a method called "Trace," which analyzes policy documents with regard to how they deal with care and which she has applied in the European context.[17]

As these examples illustrate, the theoretical and practical utility of an ethic of care is great. Despite the often striking differences in social policy, an ethic of care is a valuable normative guide to decision making in a variety of liberal democratic contexts. While similar investigations have not been undertaken in Canada, in any country where the welfare of citizens is considered to be a priority, care is a relevant issue for political analysis.[18] It is for this reason that care is especially pertinent to Canada. Known for its generous social policies, there has been a marked decrease in what can be interpreted as a caring social policy orientation. As criticism of policy restructuring and its implications increases, new frameworks and rationales for understanding the relationship between the state and citizens are needed. The application of an ethic of care is thus both timely and important: it has the potential to lead to unique policy analyses and to direct the ongoing process of Canadian social policy reform.

Significantly, applying a care ethic to social policy challenges how we think about and assess social justice in public decision making. Social justice is based on the idea that all members of society have equal access to the various features, benefits, and opportunities of that society, regardless of their position or station in life.[19] The project of reconceptualizing social justice is inspired by the work of Sevenhuijsen. She emphasizes the need to rethink concepts traditionally developed within the confines of an ethic of justice without altogether rejecting them. In a sense, my argument may seem paradoxical. On the one hand, I appear to be accepting the traditional liberal framework by working within its confines. To the extent that I rely upon concepts associated with liberalism, this is true. However, on the other hand, I reject the incomplete manner in which social justice has been developed; instead, I explore the potential of an ethic of care to transform the assumptions, content, concepts, and meaning of social justice.

The choice of social justice is appropriate for a number of reasons. Liberal theorists have always been preoccupied with questions such as "What is social justice?" and "How do we measure social justice?" In public decision making generally and in the area of social policy specifically, considerations of social justice remain of *crucial* importance.[20] Moreover, the commitment to social justice is shared by both the ethic of care and the ethic of justice: both support creating a society with fewer inequalities. For most contemporary liberals, this has been understood as enhancing welfare through the redistribution of resources.[21] For care theorists, this has been interpreted as preventing harm or relieving the burdens, hurt, or suffering (physical or psychological) of others.[22] So, while there is an overlap in goals, there is a difference in methodology and focus as to how these goals can be realized.

From the perspective of care, the traditional understanding of social justice is profoundly inadequate and morally impoverished. Social justice as it is presently understood does not generate a polity that is attentive to the expanse of injustices and their societal manifestations. By adhering to a homogenous notion of humanity, and prioritizing impartiality, this understanding falls short of asking important questions regarding the experiences of humans and their need for care. Uninformed by a care ethic, the conception of social justice will remain lacking – akin to an outline of a painting that has yet to be filled in. Care adds colour, dimension, texture, and perspective to the canvas. It reveals aspects of our public lives that have not been properly understood. It reveals the causes and solutions of human needs. It reveals the limited way in which care has been understood and the way in which society has approached the responsibility of caring for its citizens. Reasons for the welfare state and its various social policies and programs are looked at very differently from the perspective of care than they are from the perspective of justice. Infused with a care perspective, the method for attaining and measuring social justice is altered.

The objective of adding a care ethic to the concept of social justice is not to erase the outline of the painting. The outline is a critical, albeit incomplete, component of a finished piece of work. It represents those parts of the liberal theory of justice that are essential to checking the limitations and shortcomings of the ethic of care. So while there is a danger that relying upon conventional liberal categories may entail succumbing to them, as Peta Bowden effectively argues, "the alternative of ignoring or setting them aside risks losing the space and power they command, as well as the shared insights they provide."[23] The broader implication of this is that the current framework of social justice may be transformed without rejecting its currency in both theory and practice. The objective is to combine values of care with values of justice to ensure a balanced and reasoned resolution of practical issues and problems. What develops as a result is a more nuanced and comprehensive approach to social policy, or, as Tronto has put it, we "get closer to the fundamental questions of justice."[24]

Finally, it is important to note that the promise of care for social policy is based on the assumption that, either explicitly or implicitly, values always drive public policy. Moskowitz, for example, argues that the influence of values on policies is evidenced "when policy decision makers knowingly articulate the societal and cultural norms that root and shape government action" or, conversely, when "the moral underpinnings of policies seem so accepted and familiar that officials act without describing the normative ends that motivate their conduct."[25] Thus, values direct the questions that we ask, determine what information we consider to be important, select the actors that we see as integral to the policy process, and determine the consequences of choosing to react or not to react to a specific social problem or issue. Accordingly, the absence of a care ethic and its values has, without question, influenced the way in which social policy has developed and what it has prioritized.

In the following section, I outline what I consider to be the central moral principles of a care ethic. Within the context of each precept I discuss specific intersections between care and justice. Not all theorists will accept a principled argument for care. I believe, however, that principles are important to an ethic of care, that they are necessary to the development of a publicly defensible ethic. I am not proposing that we simply fit the care ethic into pre-existing principles of justice; rather, I am suggesting that, if we take the care ethic seriously, then its values have the potential to transform our understanding and approach to principles. Principles do not necessarily have to be seen as impersonal, abstract, and rigid rules. And they are not necessarily synonymous with a justice orientation. Properly conceived, principles have the capacity to explicitly encompass the aims and objectives of a care ethic. Along the same line, Chris Crittenden has made a persuasive argument that care can include principles yet retain its distinctness.[26] Care principles, I argue, can inform a different, more flexible framework for social policy.

At the outset I acknowledge that this discussion is heavily focused on values and priorities pertaining to care. This is a way of countering the traditional dominance of liberal justice in the public realm of decision making. Indeed, the ethic of care has distinct presuppositions that reveal the missing dimensions of the ethic of justice paradigm. And it is through the *addition* of the ethic of care that transformation in public decision making can occur. In terms of social policy, its values and priorities can be construed as principles that challenge us to consider how we can accommodate the need for care in all stages of decision making. The principles outlined below, therefore, constitute a framework that provides the critical lens through which the case studies of this book are examined.

Contextual Sensitivity

An ethic of care explicitly prioritizes the principle of contextual sensitivity. This is a fundamentally different starting place from that of the justice perspective, which tends to overlook context in its formulation of a universal point of view. A care ethic begins with the assumption that it is morally relevant to acknowledge that all humans are specific, concrete individuals rather than abstract, generic beings. Not unlike a justice perspective, a care perspective acknowledges the importance of the individual. It differs, however, in its attentiveness to the complexity and relational qualities of individual lives. Congruence with contextual sensitivity insists that the basic knowledge of an individual requires full comprehension of that person's particularity.

To understand how someone comes to be who they are requires thoroughly analyzing all aspects of that person's life. This begins with focusing on the *whole* person. Benhabib maintains that such an approach "requires us to view each other and every rational being as an individual with a concrete history, identity and affective emotional constitution."[27] From the perspective of a care ethic, people are shaped by their contexts, including their social, economic, political, historical, and geographic circumstances. Contextual sensitivity therefore requires being attentive and sensitive to the influence of social determinants such as gender, race, class, nationality, religion, sexual orientation, and ability. The focus challenges liberal notions of uniformity and sameness by taking into account particular differences. Thus, in the process of decision making, contextual sensitivity requires that one consider a number of factors that cannot be captured by "impartial," "impersonal," and "repeatable" moral reasoning. If policy decision makers began with an active investigation of concrete particulars and unique differences in human lives, then they would better grasp the limitations of utilizing the standard of homogeneity. And the meaning and significance of human differences for making sound political decisions would become more apparent. The focus would shift to an enhanced understanding of "the difference difference makes."[28] This would also entail having the requisite information to determine what differences are relevant for approaching a wide range of social problems and issues.

It is true that this level of attention to individual particularities may not always be feasible within the realm of social policy. However, this should not deter us from attempting to apply the principle of contextual sensitivity to groups to which an individual belongs or with whom s/he identifies. Certainly, linking individuals to groups may risk essentializing the plurality of one's identity. However, in the realm of policy, identity and status are often connected directly with membership in a group based on any number of distinguishing social determinants and life experiences. Grace Clement has similarly argued that, although public policy decisions do not allow for attention to particular features of individuals, they do allow for attention to distinguishing features of groups.[29] Nancy Fraser has also suggested that we could shift our emphasis from the standpoint of a concrete individual to that of a collective made up of concrete "others."[30] Connecting individuals to groups, however, does not have to have a freezing effect. All individuals have life histories and experiences that may be linked with a group identity, but these do not deter these same individuals from departing from any one category of identification at any moment in time.[31] Sevenhuijsen correctly points out that "this counts especially in a post-modern era, where fluidity, multiplicity and flux considerably leave their mark on individual live histories."[32]

Alison Jaggar has argued that "attention to situations' specificity and particularity diverts attention away from their general features such as the social institutions and groupings that give them their structure and much of their meaning."[33] Jaggar's criticism is overstated. Because an ethic of care prioritizes a relational ontology, it also involves paying specific attention to how individual identities, social status, and needs are shaped and constructed through their intersection with a range of private and public social and institutional arrangements. Accordingly, contextual sensitivity includes assessing how individuals have been constructed through social institutions and the relations that develop in these environments. An integral part of this analysis is the recognition that human beings are part of interdependent relationships. We live our lives and develop our own particular identities in relation to one another. An ethic of care invites us to transcend the limitations of liberal conceptions of individuality to consider people in their dense contexts, where home, workplace, school, church, temple, neighbourhood – along with local, national, and international communities – are experienced primarily through the social relations built there.[34] As Sevenhuijsen points out, the ethic of care departs from the individualistic interpretation of human nature that often underpins liberal programs and policies and, instead, "starts from notions of relationality and interdependence: the basic idea that humans are engaged in each other's lives in a myriad of ways."[35]

As part our interdependent existence, we can also be thought of as being a part of a web of care upon which we all rely throughout our lives. When the human condition is understood in this way, then care becomes accepted as a normal aspect of all forms of social participation and citizenship. Contextual sensitivity reveals to us the social realities of care and situates care solidly within both the private and public spheres. As a result, this perspective allows us to interrogate the ways in which the state, through its policy choices, makes decisions about whether or not to invest in the care of its citizenry. Contextual sensitivity allows us to ask political questions about whose needs are taken care of, under what circumstances, and by whom. As part of this analysis, we can see how the continuity of care in our lives can be disrupted by the direct decisions made in the area of social policy.

In sum, contextual sensitivity facilitates a more comprehensive understanding of the human condition. It allows us to critically examine marginalization, disadvantage, and oppression. When informed by the critical standpoint of an ethic of care, the dynamics and reproduction of a range of human inequalities can be more realistically captured and therefore rendered much more difficult to ignore. This would also challenge the tendency, on the part of social policy developers, to look past the human interdependencies that form central human bonds and that give rise to varying care needs. The process of achieving contextual sensitivity reveals, as Benhabib has explained, "the traditionally *unthought,* the *unseen,* and the *unheard.*"[36] Such details are essential to being sympathetic to the full scope of any problem and to being able to deal effectively with complex social policy issues.

Responsiveness

Knowing the contextual details of any given situation also requires an element of responsiveness. Responsiveness goes beyond being sympathetic towards others, or even taking into account their needs, as *we* perceive them. It goes beyond determining what others need by generalizing from our own experiences. It differs from trying to imagine what it would be like to be in another person's situation. Responsiveness constitutes a unique way of listening to and observing those who are different from us. It is what Gilligan has explained as an "ability to perceive others on their own terms."[37] What is required for this form of engagement is a commitment to provide the opportunity and a safe space for others to express their "otherness." To be responsive requires a special form of mutual engagement in which participants are empowered to decide what aspects of their lives they want to include as part of the discussion. Some care theorists have described this unique approach to interacting with others as "dialogical" and "narrative." Sevenhuijsen, for instance, defines a narrative approach as refusing to separate needs from the people who claim them. She argues that this approach takes as its starting point the idea that people themselves are competent to express who they are and what they need.[38] Indeed, responsiveness requires attending to people's articulations of who they are, what their experiences have been, what their needs are, how these needs have arisen, and how they can best be met.

In emphasizing the importance of such interaction, not all care theorists have adequately addressed the potential dangers and problems of responsiveness. For example, it may be argued that narratives of experiences reinscribe assumptions about identities/differences in an essentializing manner.[39] And yet, if we do not allow that those who suffer harm are in the best position to articulate what they have experienced, then we deny them, as Stone-Mediatore argues, "the power to offer critical perspectives on their worlds by narrating their experience."[40] Thus, one can interpret the principle of responsiveness as explicitly recognizing that individuals' accounts of their experiences are socially constructed. At the same time, one can make the case that these accounts have the potential to illuminate the social arrangements that lead to experiences of marginality and, in so going, provide the basis for a critical dialogue on questions and concerns missing from liberal notions of social justice.

Accordingly, responsiveness is a key principle of care for a number of reasons. It provides an opening for those voices and perspectives that have not traditionally been heard in the political process. Aaron Wildavsky has written that those outside traditional politics "speak truth to power."[41] Responsiveness involves taking seriously the perspective of citizens who may be experiencing inequality, and it involves doing this by listening to their voices and being open to hearing how they articulate their discrimination. By taking into account how those who are "different" articulate their experiences of difference and disadvantage, an ethic of care can reveal that it is not necessarily human diversity that is the problem but, rather, social constructs that render differences problematic. Responsiveness is a way of overcoming negative associations with difference and of directing us towards new ways of responding to diversity. Writing in the realm of legal theory, Martha Minow has argued that "learning to take the perspective of another is an opening wedge for an alternative to traditional legal treatments of difference."[42]

Further, a process of responsiveness allows decision makers to effectively comprehend the range of human needs that is requisite for social justice. For instance, attention to citizens' expressed needs is central to the development of any conception of social welfare. In his now famous statement, Richard Titmuss explains: "all collectively provided services are deliberately designed to meet certain socially recognized needs; they are manifestations, first of society's will to survive as an organic whole and, secondly, of the expressed wish of all the people to assist the survival of some people. Needs may therefore be thought of as 'social' and 'individual,' as interdependent, mutually related essentials for the continued existence of the parts and the whole."[43] Recognizing experiences and concomitant needs of those who are most directly affected by policy decisions leads to a better understanding of the origins of caring needs in society. As Tronto explains, when we provide an opportunity for people to explain their individual lives from their own standpoint, "a shift occurs in what counts as 'knowledge' in making political judgments."[44]

When we include people who are affected by social policy in the decision-making process, important information is derived about the variety and nature of human needs, dependencies, and vulnerabilities. For instance, needs are often interpreted as physical and material. While required for basic subsistence, these particular needs are not exhaustive. Needs that reflect caring – our need to be cared for, the need to have social supports so that we can care adequately for others – are equally important to human flourishing. Indeed, there is a range of emotional, psychological, and spiritual needs that are not typically recognized but that are also necessary if one is to live the good life. Such needs are essential to human security. For policy decision makers, these needs could be more accurately identified if traditional social policy discourse were replaced with a discourse that respects and honours voices of experience.

Moreover, the process involved in being responsive to others allows us to broaden our understanding of *why* needs arise. We begin to recognize that needs do not simply arise because of "careless" or "irresponsible" personal choices but, often, because of social practices and human interactions. Using this lens reveals that needs are products of social relations rather than properties of individuals who demonstrate some sort of deficiencies in character.[45] Thus, the link between the experience of individuals and public priorities, arrangements, and institutions is revealed. Such information does not always reach policy decision makers. However, understanding how social and institutional structures and the relations that develop within these contribute to exclusion, oppression, and marginality is critical to developing a responsive social policy. It allows decision makers to recognize how people's needs arise from *both* distributive norms and from the relations of dominance and dependency that characterize our societal structures and institutions. In turn, this will allow those in positions of power to better react to the needs of all members of society, especially those who suffer disproportionately because of specific social policy decisions.

As part of this wider evaluation process, policy decision makers have a responsibility to re-evaluate their position of power as architects of social policy. As Tronto explains: "care demands that we constantly assess the position we occupy as we begin to make judgments. We must constantly evaluate whether we are being overly overprotective, too unresponsive, too reliant on our assumed 'expertise.'"[46] This type of reflection becomes especially important when policy decision makers are trying to be responsive to those who have difficulties communicating with us because of age, illness, or disability. Moreover, it is critical to being respectful towards those with whom we disagree. Responsiveness ensures that the process of gathering information required for policy decision making does not objectify or silence the voices of those affected by social policy. Concretely, this may entail using more qualitative research instruments to capture the multifaceted and complex nature of human experiences and caring requirements. When individuals are given an opportunity to be the "narrators of their own life story," the boundaries between where private and public responsibilities for care should be drawn may be redrawn.[47]

And finally, responsiveness can enhance autonomy because it enables people to determine, from their own perspectives, what should be part of policy deliberations. In particular, by providing a process for traditionally marginalized persons to articulate their experiences, needs, and goals (and, in turn, to ensure that these are respected and honoured), we empower them. By refraining from objectifying others or generalizing about them in the realm of social policy we confirm, as Benhabib explains, not only their *humanity* but also their human *individuality*.[48] More specific to the Canadian social policy context, responsiveness is congruent with citizens' expressed desire to be more closely involved in developing policy. Michael Prince and James Rice argue that "people with different orientations have different ways of knowing, seeing, understanding, and explaining the way the world operates and they want these differences reflected in the way that the state develops social policies."[49] Similarly, Frank Graves explains: "[a] citizen's desire for greater inclusion in decision-making is rooted in a sense of relative powerlessness and a growing conviction that citizens can operate as equals to elites and leaders, particularly in the realm of values."[50] Graves goes on to explain that such values include the desire for an active, humanist government. Simply put, responsiveness leads those in positions of power to engage ordinary citizens in social policy.

Consequences of Choice
Gilligan argued that the application of a morality of justice within decision making is susceptible to "indifference" and "unconcern" for others.[51] A traditional justice perspective does not consistently consider the effects of our judgments or actions. Consequently, this normative orientation does not always have the capacity to avert human harm or to eradicate inequality in its efforts to bring about social justice. Conversely, an ethic of care is concerned expressly with the actual outcomes and practical and material effects on people's lives of making certain choices and decisions. As many care theorists have argued, explicit in an ethic of care is a responsibility to make connections regarding how those around us are affected by our actions. It is about considering how decisions affect *real* people and their lived experiences.

From the perspective of care, no adequate social policy can ignore the health and safety of its citizens.[52] Social policy decisions that are in accordance with a care ethic would promote the well-being of others and focus on preventing harm and suffering. The true impact of social policy choices on society at all levels would be a priority. If the principles of contextual sensitivity and responsiveness are respected, then the best course of action should be more easily determined. Both the quantitative and qualitative information derived from these processes are essential to assessing the immediate and long-term consequences of policy choices. This knowledge can therefore inform a course of action or non-action regarding a given problem or set of problems.[53] For example, in some instances, this may entail following the precepts of an ethic of justice by upholding people's rights and using the same standards of treatment. It can also include, however, questioning the best way to interpret and uphold rights. With its emphasis on difference and disadvantage, an ethic of care broadens our understanding of what "equality," "fairness," and social justice require. It may also require being cognizant of responsibilities to others that have nothing to do with basic rights and freedoms. Policy decision makers would have the knowledge base to recognize that "not all goods of moral significance can be *claimed* by those who need or value them and not all those things we need or value make *sense* [my italics] in the context of a contractual ethics of rights."[54]

One should not assume that this requires governments and policy decision makers to attend to the needs of all. Certainly, this cannot be expected. Nevertheless, a fundamental shift in values and priorities could materialize. The shift would reflect an understanding that social justice requires taking into account a wider range of perspectives, which converge around the reality that all citizens have and will have needs that require caring responses. Because of its focus on consequences, an ethic of care brings to attention the possible harm that can be done and, alternatively, to the suffering that may be alleviated through responsible government action. In turn, this could renew our public commitment to honour and respect care. Without doubt, a better balance between public and private responsibilities for care could be established.

The positive implications would be numerous. Those who require public support and assistance would not automatically be stigmatized; instead, their needs would be understood as a normal development or occurrence in the course of human living. Their situation would be carefully assessed to determine how to best respond to them within the perimeter of available resources. An ethic of care may also avert decisions that appear to have short-term financial benefits and, instead, consider their long-term human costs and consequences. An ethic of care also creates the possibility of developing social policy that is flexible, creative, and responsive to the changing circumstance of people's lives.

Operationalizing the consequences of the principle of choice would entail a commitment to eradicating inequality and, in turn, to improving the social well-being and quality of life for Canadians. To this end, procedural and distributive considerations associated with a liberal ethic of justice would remain significant. These considerations would be enjoined with the realization that people's needs cannot always be so narrowly defined. The end result would be an approach that reflects an understanding of how oppression, domination, disadvantage, and suffering are shaped by "a series of collective social, political, and economic decisions *and* social economic relations [emphasis added]."[55] Such an approach would respond to a wide range of problems and needs that pertain to quality of life and priority of care. It would encourage the development of social policy that is efficient, effective, and caring.

In sum, the values of care articulated in the above principles are largely absent in social policy informed by a liberal justice ethic, even though these principles promote comprehensive approaches for examining people's lives and understanding their needs. The precepts of a care ethic encourage a contextual understanding of the social conditions that cause and/or contribute to marginalization, discrimination, and other harms. They promote the active participation of citizens (and their self-expressed needs) in social policy development. And, finally, they prioritize policy decisions that attend to the complexities of citizens who differ on the basis of gender, race, ethnicity, ability, and class but who are united in their need for care. Working within this morally adequate account of social justice, government and its policy makers would be inspired to consider how their decisions contribute to or impede the development of social policy that addresses inequalities and human sufferings.

However, such theorizing does not necessarily go far enough. As Joan Tronto has argued, "simply positing a moral ideal of caring will not suffice to make the world more caring; we need as well to be able to translate that moral ideal into practice. In this way, morality and politics must be interwoven to effect change."[56] What is required for real change in social policy is a distinct shift in the existing normative orientation of justice – a shift that will make a central place for the values of care. In other words, the status quo must be altered substantially both in theory and in practice. In the following chapters, I begin to investigate what social policy might look like if a care ethic and its principles are placed front and centre on the public agenda.

3
The Interpretation of Equality: A Study of Section 15 of the Canadian Charter of Rights and Freedoms

Case law is a critically important discursive field with respect to the ethic of care. It carries with it the authority of the state, and those who make claims for justice cannot avoid interacting with it. In addition, ethics have a role in both guiding and challenging the interpretation of law. Traditionally, case law has operated within a liberal framework and in accordance with a justice ethic that prioritizes abstract universality and obscures the meaning and significance of varied life situations. As this chapter demonstrates, there is a real need for an expanded set of values to deal with the diversity of persons making equality claims, the human traits we call differences,[1] and the social structures that reinforce our conceptualization of these differences. Arguably, judicial analysis would improve in significant ways if the traditional liberal approach to equality were modified by the inclusion of a care ethic.

Equality rights jurisprudence under the Canadian Charter of Rights and Freedoms is a particularly salient area of case law when it comes to the application of the care ethic. Since its inception in 1982, the Charter has provided a new forum in which Canadian citizens can make political demands for social justice. Under Section 15, the substantive model of equality, which is intended to accommodate differences and to consider the actual effects of the law on citizens, has been recognized. However, the dominance of a liberal ethic of justice has hampered equality rights jurisprudence. Claims for equality rights have been undermined by a lack of attention to contextual information, the self-reported experiences of discrimination, and how legislation actually causes or perpetuates inequality – the very precepts that a care ethic prioritizes. Consequently, legal reasoning and decisions often have little to do with understanding "human experiences, affect, suffering, and how people actually do live."[2] In fact, it may be asserted that liberal values underpinning legal approaches to equality rights tend to be antithetical to the realization of a substantive model of equality.

The argument that I make in this chapter is that an ethic of care and its principles can enrich and enhance the existing normative framework for substantive equality. By stressing previously overlooked elements in judicial decision-making, a care ethic has the potential to modify how equality claims are understood and adjudicated. Through the critical lens of a care ethic, it becomes clear for example, that to grasp inequality and be able to respond adequately to difference requires taking into account the context in which relations of human interdependence operate, how persons express their marginalization, and what kinds of needs arise from these experiences. If such criteria were systematically applied to equality rights interpretation, the ways in which government legislation contributes to systemic inequality and the complex processes by which disadvantage and discrimination are reproduced by the law would be more clearly revealed. The end result would be a more comprehensive understanding of substantive equality and its relationship to social justice.

To make my point, I focus on the historic development of sex equality rights cases in Canada. The equality rights of the Charter have been of significant interest to Canadian women's groups and feminists, who have been at the forefront of attempts to seek substantive sex equality in Charter litigation. Moreover, it was feminist political theorist Sandra Burt who first proposed the idea of investigating how an ethic of care and an ethic of justice could be connected in equality rights jurisprudence.[3] To demonstrate the difference care would make to rights jurisprudence, I draw upon judicial dissent in sex equality Charter cases (which, I contend, employ the logic of an ethic of care) and consider recent Section 15 cases in which traces of care principles can be observed. The argument of this chapter is part of a growing body of work that takes an ethic of care seriously as a starting point for the study of legal issues and the nature of justice. And, by exploring how rights, which are of primary importance to a liberal ethic of justice, can be altered and improved with the addition of care principles, I also demonstrate how justice and care can be combined successfully within equality jurisprudence.

Overview of Equality Rights Jurisprudence in Canada

The constitutional entrenchment of fundamental liberal democratic rights and freedoms for citizens of Canada has caused significant debate about the political implications of the Charter and rights-based litigation. Discussion around the Charter has focused on the "efficacy of reconstituting political discourse in terms of rights"[4] and, in particular, reconceptualizing struggles for social justice in terms of the equality provisions found under Section 15.[5] The question "Can we litigate our way to a more equal society?"[6] has divided political and legal thinkers. The debate over the Charter can perhaps be understood best in terms of a fundamental disagreement over the limits and possibilities[7] of rights-based liberalism with regard to the eradication of social, economic, and political inequality.

Typically, the liberal ethic of justice has two identifiable models of equality: formal and substantive. Historically, equality litigation in Canada has been dominated largely by variations of the formal approach to equality. Based on the Aristotelian concept of treating only likes alike, this model applies neutral rules to the interpretation of equality. It is now widely accepted that the formal model is inherently limited and, as a result, it has been displaced by a substantive model for measuring equality. The substantive model requires taking individual needs and positions into account when measuring equality claims under the law. It prioritizes the accommodation of differences and the weighing of how burdens and benefits of citizenship are shaped by the law. In general, this model is seen as more responsive to patterns of inequality and contextual realities of subordinate groups than is the formal model. As a result, many traditionally marginalized individuals and groups in Canadian society have come to see the Charter and Section 15 as important vehicles for protecting their equality rights.

The displacement of the formal model in favour of substantive equality, however, has not gone far enough in challenging the limitations of liberal equality rights interpretation. Judicial reasoning tends to screen out the social, political, and economic realities of people's lives, even though context is crucial to understanding the nature of equality claims. The abstraction and impartiality inherent in a liberal ethic of justice do no appear amenable to the kind of change that is required for any effective analysis of how diverse citizens experience injustice and oppression.[8] Others have made similar observations. Paul Green, for instance, maintains that the liberal dogma is unwilling and *unable* to take into account circumstances that create real differences between people.[9] Further, Joel Bakan maintains that Section 15 does not have the potential to affect social inequality in Canada because its interpretation is limited by the anti-statism and atomism characteristic of a liberal paradigm.[10] For Bakan, anti-statism is manifest in the tradition of limiting rights to protect individuals from state interference while not requiring positive state assistance. Atomism constructs social relations in terms of rights that deem power relations and social conditions beyond the rights/duty dyad to be irrelevant. According to Bakan, systemic inequality is beyond state power. For him, the causes and symptoms of social inequality are simply beyond the scope of the judiciary and, in particular, of the Supreme Court of Canada.

Indeed, one should in fact be clear that the entire objective of the Charter and Section 15 equality rights was not to eliminate all societal discrimination but only to challenge discriminatory government legislation. At the same time, the law and equality rights are important sites of struggle for social justice. In Naomi Sharp's words, "Charter litigation has become an important site in the struggle for the formulation and execution of social policy."[11] However, in order for rights to be effectual, the courts must properly interpret their scope and meaning.[12] To transcend the Charter's current limitations, we need to take into account the explicit and consistent recognition of context, attentiveness to the expressed experiences of the disadvantaged, and the weighing of actual consequences for those who are harmed by legislation. In what follows, I explore how applying these principles of care to the method of Section 15 equality rights interpretation can result in a legal framework that allows for complex analyses and that has the potential to be responsive to the experiences of subordinate groups in Canadian society.

An Ethic of Care and Law

The validity of investigating applying an ethic of care to Section 15 is bolstered by the fact that a number of legal theorists have turned to an ethic of care to suggest how the legal system may be transformed into a more desirable and responsive institution. Scholars have argued that care and relational theories have provided important methodological precepts for rethinking the law, and they have used the ethic of care to criticize rights theories and traditional legal doctrines.[13] Recent examinations that have specifically investigated the relationship between a care ethic and equality can be found, for example, in the works of Martha Minow,[14] Robin West,[15] and Colleen Sheppard.[16]

Minow, a US legal scholar, has attempted to examine how we can develop a "social relations" approach to understanding equality and difference in the language of rights. She argues that relational insights can be seen as imperatives to engage in the problem of difference as an observer (i.e., as a judge). These imperatives can be translated into a number of distinct steps: "*notice* the mutual dependence of people. *Investigate* the construction of difference in light of the norms and patterns of interpersonal and institutional relationships which make some traits matter. *Question* the relationship between the observer and the observed in order to situate judgments in the perspective of the actual judge. *Seek out* and *consider* competing perspectives, especially those of people defined as the problem. *Locate* theory within context; *criticize* practice in light of theoretical commitments; and *challenge* abstract theories in light of their practical effects."[17] For Minow, relational theories have much to offer legal thought and the legal treatment of "differences," which include but are not limited to gender differences.

In her work, Robin West has argued that, in order for jurisprudence to be adequate, judging must include an ethic of care as well as an ethic of justice. She explains that if judges "zealously pursue justice *to the exclusion* of ... care, they will fail: The results will be not only uncaring, but unjust as well."[18] West refers to the *Brown* v. *Board of Education*[19] case as an example of "caring justice" because she contends that it was premised on understanding and acknowledging the pain and hurt caused by societal racial relationships. In taking this approach to judicial decision making, West concludes that the court developed a new understanding of the constitutional protection of equality *as well as* a better understanding of the dynamics of racism and what is required for its eradication.

Discussions of care's utility have not been limited to American legal commentary. In elaborating a legal approach to equality, Colleen Sheppard, a Canadian legal scholar, has argued that the concept of caring may be helpful at two stages. First, it may contribute to the process of identifying inequality or discrimination. For Sheppard, the causes of inequality and its dynamics are the result of an absence of caring in human relations. Second, she argues that care may provide insights into the structuring of legal remedies.[20] Effective legal remedies would restructure relations of inequality and promote caring in personal, group, and institutional relations. Despite the fact that Sheppard and other legal scholars have explored an ethic of care, to date no one has considered its potential for informing the interpretation of Section 15. In general, very little attention has been given to considering how equality rights can better accommodate demands for social justice. After briefly reviewing a number of key gender equality rights cases in Canada, however, it is not difficult to demonstrate the deficiencies of liberalism that converge in such legal reasoning, and the need for an expanded normative framework informed by an ethic of care.

The Canadian Bill of Rights

To fully grasp the limitations associated with a liberal ethic of justice, it is useful to review some of the cases heard under the Canadian Bill of Rights – the precursor to the Charter. The content of these cases demonstrates the problems with early conceptions of formal equality and the protection of women's equality rights. The formal model draws on Aristotle's concept of justice, which posits that "persons who are equal should have assigned to them equal things."[21] Its only requirement is that, when measuring equality rights, only those who are alike should be compared. Assessing how to treat people equally requires a standard for making comparisons. The choice of standard determines the nature and outcome of equality comparisons. When women have argued for rights, the "standard" for equality comparisons has usually been a very specific, historically privileged group in society – white, able-bodied, middle-class males.[22] This group has been interpreted as reflecting the "norm" of society, against which all other equality claims are assessed. In some cases and with certain issues, using a uniform standard may be sufficient. Often, however, women and men are not similarly situated for the purposes of legal equality rights interpretation. Because women may differ from men in their capacity for childbearing and in their socio-economic status, there may be no basis in the male standard to prove the inequality they may be experiencing. When faced with issues such as pregnancy, childbirth, and sexual assault, to name a few, a formal approach to equality is confronted with a number of equality problems that "it cannot solve."[23]

Take, for example, the case of *A.G. Canada* v. *Lavell et al.*,[24] in which Jeanette Lavell and Yvonne Bedard challenged the discriminatory effects of Section 12(1)(b) of the Indian Act.[25] By classifying Indian women as a distinct group in the face of the law, the equality rights of Lavell and Bedard were bound up with questions of process and were approached in the abstract. Consequently, Indian women were subject to a different level of scrutiny than were Indian men. As long as all Indian women were subjected to the law equally, even if that equal treatment caused unfair burdens and disadvantages, the court argued that the law was not discriminatory. In reaching this conclusion, the court did not properly contextualize the socio-economic and cultural status of Indian women. It did not listen to the self-reported effects of Section 1(b) of the Indian Act. There was little consideration for the actual implications of the court's decision for Indian women.[26] From the perspective of a traditional liberal ethic of justice, the practical and legal consequences of intermarriage were not considered integral to determining the outcome in the case. Arguably, however, the losses and their concrete impact on Indian women's lives were real and were directly caused by government legislation. Such particularities and concrete information should have been considered integral to properly understanding and assessing Lavell's and Bedard's equality claims in response to the harm they experienced as a result of the Indian Act's "statutory ex-communication."[27]

Similar shortcomings characterize the other significant equality rights case decided under the Bill of Rights, *Bliss* v. *Attorney General of Canada*.[28] In this case Stella Bliss argued that the 1971 Canadian Unemployment Insurance Act's maternity benefits violated the equality provisions of the Bill of Rights. Although the Act specifically required pregnant women to work longer than others for the same benefits, the court did not recognize its disparaging effects. As in the case of Lavell, Bliss's disadvantage was created as a direct result of how the law constructed gender difference. By blindly classifying pregnant women as a group, the court failed to consider the way in which this caused pregnant women to bear material and financial burdens. It did not weigh the concrete details of the lives of pregnant women or acknowledge that the act caused real-life dilemmas. This contextually impoverished approach to assessing Bliss's claim precluded any reflective response to her experiences of disadvantage. The abstract method of considering her claim did not compel the court to look beyond the issue of pregnancy to recognize that Bliss's sexual discrimination and unfair material consequences were a direct result of government law – consequences that the legal decision in her case perpetuated. In both the Bliss and Lavell cases, the court distorted the meaning of difference in relation to equality by abstracting from the actual discrimination and inequality being experienced by those who were bringing forward their claims. Differences were either ignored or highlighted in ways that promoted unfavourable and prejudicial treatment, thus allowing the court to uphold offensive legislative distinctions based on sex.

The Charter of Rights and Freedoms
Not surprisingly, the equality provisions in the Charter of Rights and Freedoms were formulated specifically to attempt to avoid the outcomes of equality rights cases argued under the Bill of Rights. In both form and substance,[29] Section 15 appeared to promise a significantly new direction in equality rights interpretation under Canadian law.[30] However, the interpretation of equality under the Charter (especially before 1989) shared certain features with the interpretation of equality under the Bill of Rights.[31] The assumption of the courts was that all equality claims by women and men were being initiated from the same position of power and status. The resiliency and limitations of a formal model became apparent. One of the most problematic characteristics of this approach to equality rights issues is that it assumes that discrimination is rare. As a result, it also fails to recognize that the real world is characterized by various forms of systemic imbalance. Within equality rights interpretation, the thinking of the formal model can be observed when a similarity or difference is referred to without any understanding of what it means in terms of an individual's or group's access to equality – especially if they have been historically disadvantaged. What is needed, as Elizabeth Frazer has accurately explained, is a "critical conception of difference ... and ... criteria for judging what differences must be overcome (e.g., in what respects people ought to be the 'same') and which should be preserved."[32] In practice, this necessitates, at a minimum, moving beyond the confines of formal equality.

Many feminist lawyers have argued that, with the 1989 decision of *Andrews* v. *Law Society of British Columbia*,[33] the Supreme Court displaced the formal model of equality and introduced a progressive, substantive model of equality.[34] The case involved a male non-citizen of Canada who had been prevented from practising law in the Province of British Columbia because he was not a Canadian citizen. Having fulfilled all the requirements for admission to the British Columbia Bar Association, with the exception of being a Canadian citizen, Mark Andrews put forward the claim that Section 42 of the Barristers and Solicitors Act violated Section 15 of the Charter. While the challenge was successful, the reasoning in the case is arguably far more significant than the outcome. The Supreme Court argued that equality guarantees cannot be adequately protected by the formal approach to equality characterized by the "similarly situated" test. It asserted that this test was "seriously deficient" because it failed to capture fully and realistically the impact that legislative distinctions have on individuals and groups. The court concluded that "the accommodation of differences ... is the essence of true equality."[35] In other words, to effectively advance equality through Section 15, human diversities must be acknowledged, understood, and respected by the law.

The approach to equality stressed in *Andrews* seemed to promote a more complex and sophisticated examination of how such distinctions affect the distribution of burdens and benefits in society.[36] The Supreme Court appeared to be advocating an approach to equality rights interpretation that focused on how an individual's and/or group's status in society is affected by the law. As McIntyre stated, "to approach the ideal of full equality before and under the law ... the main consideration must be the impact of the law on the individual or group concerned."[37] The concern with actual outcomes is congruent with a substantive model of equality. The direction for approaching equality claims outlined in *Andrews* was therefore promising. And yet, the changes fell short of what was needed. The *Andrews* case did not establish a framework for interpreting Section 15 protection that would consistently avoid the limitations associated with the equality interpretation embedded within an ethic of justice framework.

Consequently, a range of deficiencies continued to characterize the reasoning and decisions in post-*Andrews* equality rights cases. For instance, in *Symes* v. *Canada*[38] Eliza Symes unsuccessfully argued that the non-deductibility of childcare expenses as business expenses under Section 18(1)(a) of the Income Tax Act violated her Section 15(1) equality rights. In rejecting Symes's argument, the court argued that, although women bear a disproportionate share of the social costs of childcare, they do not disproportionately pay childcare expenses. In making this determination, the court did not recognize the entire social, economic, and legal contexts that gave rise to Symes's claim. For example, the cost of childcare is a major barrier to women's participation in the labour force. As Lesley Harman explains: "many women find that having another person look after their children ends up costing them more than they earn. If they cannot afford to leave their jobs, they may then be heard to say, 'I can't afford to have children.'"[39] By disallowing Symes to include her childcare expenses as business expenses the court did not make the necessary links between the adverse economic implications of childcare responsibilities/expenses and women's access to and equal opportunities within the workplace. The

Supreme Court thus ignored the social reality of Symes and many other Canadian working women who were being unfairly discriminated against by the Income Tax Act.

Similar patterns can be found in the case of *Thibaudeau* v. *Canada*,[40] in which Suzanne Thibaudeau argued that the tax burden imposed upon her by the forced inclusion of child support payments in her personal income tax return directly violated her Section 15 equality rights. In this case, Justices Cory and Iacobucci concluded that "the group of single custodial parents receiving child support payments is not placed under a burden by the inclusion/deduction regime."[41] By simply considering how the inclusion/deduction system affects a divorced unit, the court screened out how the Income Tax Act actually affects the custodial parent. As Justice Gonthier put it: "the fact that the tax resulting form the inclusion/ deduction system does not benefit both parents in equal proportion does not infringe the equality right protected by the Charter."[42]

Focusing on the "couple" deflected the court from pursuing the kind of investigation that would have understood that, despite the fact that 2 percent of men belong to the group of separated custodial parents,[43] the majority of custodial parents in the country are women, and it is they who bear the most responsibility for caring. In particular, the court excluded weighing the vulnerability and economic burden of single custodial mothers. For example, 56 percent of single-parent families headed by women are poor, compared to 24 percent of those headed by men.[44] By not being responsive to these gendered differences, the court did not identify how government legislation was financially discriminating against Thibaudeau. Further, the majority was not concerned with how their final decision would contribute to Thibaudeau's continuing unfair hardships and discrimination.

In both *Symes* and *Thibaudeau,* the majority of the Supreme Court did not follow through on an approach conducive to substantive equality. In neither case did the majority decision address the ways in which provisions of the Income Tax Act contributed to women's systemic inequality. Distracted by impartial reasoning and legal technicalities typical of a liberal perspective, the Supreme Court failed to uncover and scrutinize how this piece of government legislation treated women prejudicially. Arguably, the majority did not pursue the kind of analysis that would have revealed how Sections 18(1)(a) and 56(1)(b) of the Income Tax Act perpetuate material disadvantage for working women with childcare responsibilities because that would have required moving beyond the values and foci prioritized by the liberal ethic of justice. Both cases show that positive changes to equality rights interpretation call for an approach that transcends the limitations of liberalism, thus allowing the causes and consequences of gender inequality, among other forms of inequality, to be properly identified and analyzed. This analytic capacity can be realized by applying the principles of care to Section 15. Not only can their inclusion lead to a different discourse around inequality, its dimensions, and patterns, but it can also precipitate changes requisite for the protection and promotion of substantive equality under Section 15.

A Care Ethic and Equality Rights Interpretation

What concrete difference would the inclusion of a care ethic make to equality rights case law? First, the principle of contextuality would direct judges towards the considerations necessary for a full and comprehensive analysis of the social place from which people are making their equality claims. This would involve taking into account the extent to which individuals and groups are marginalized, ignored, or devalued in relation to others, and the extent to which the law and other social structures either mitigate or perpetuate their social status. When attention is devoted to the context of equality claims, the necessity for equality rights protection can be seen not simply as a result of "individual deficiencies" but also as arising from the failures of society, its key institutions, and emergent relationships to provide requisite care for its citizens.

Care's commitment to responsiveness would ensure that judges would not presume to know what is best or desirable for those who have experienced inequalities without taking into account concrete human stories and their meaning to persons affected by inequality and discrimination. It would require systematically including and seriously listening to the ways in which persons describe their discrimination. When those who have been considered different become the source of information about a critical but previously suppressed perspective on the legal issues affecting them, the depth and complexity of inequalities is clarified. Responsiveness shows that equality claims cannot be resolved in a satisfactory manner without transforming traditionally abstract questions about equality into experientially based inquiries into discrimination and inequality. As Amy Bartholomew explains, "it is only by attending to the actual arguments of litigants, the social, economic, political and cultural assumptions ... that we can really begin to assess the possibilities ... of Charter litigation as part of a politics of rights."[45]

Finally, taking into account the consequences of choice would result in the court having to take explicit account of actual outcomes and the possible effects of decisions on people's lives. In determining whether or not government legislation causes disadvantage, the recognition of salient differences among the population (or, alternatively, the choice to exclude those differences from consideration) would not result in harm or further disadvantage. For example, there would be a careful weighing of whether or not the recognition of difference or demand for similar treatment would have a disadvantaging effect on women vis-à-vis the legislation. This would entail, as West has explained, taking into account the uniqueness of a litigant and the moral duty of relational recognition that the litigant imposes on the court and on the justices.[46] As such, gender difference would not preclude access to equality and women would be able to "reclaim equality across difference."[47] Accordingly, from care's perspective, the actual impact (potential for harm, suffering, or, alternatively, the possibilities of ameliorating inequality) of equality rights decisions on those who are bringing forward equality claims would be a priority.

It is also possible that responses to equality claims that are informed by a care ethic may involve the formulation of specific remedial approaches – an idea that is not altogether novel. For instance, Sheppard has proposed that remedial approaches would involve putting into place institutional mechanisms that would allow subordinated individuals/groups to transform institutional relations or free themselves from harmful relations of inequality.[48] Similarly, Sharp has put forward the idea of developing remedial jurisprudence as a method of implementing substantive equality. She has argued that, through section 24(1) of the Charter, the courts have at their disposal a remedial technique of structural injunction. These are "forward-looking plans created by the courts, which aim to affect structural change in institutions in order to alleviate the conditions which produce rights infringement."[49]

Moreover, a redefined approach to Section 15 may lead to the establishment of a more flexible approach to equality rights claims. This is not an implausible proposal. As Sheppard has noted: "though we tend to associate law with rules, we have recurrent examples of the need for flexibility."[50] In the same vein, Henderson has asserted that there are a number of legal precedents that demonstrate that flexibility is integral to determining justice.[51] Carol Lee Bacchi makes a parallel argument: "there is a need to remain theoretically flexible and to design policies to respond to immediate contingencies, instead of trying to fit them into some overarching abstract principles."[52]

Bakan maintains that even the existence of a new, non-liberal language of rights is no guarantee that it will be heard, listened to, or acted on by those who have social and political power.[53] It is true that there may be resistance to an approach to rights that embraces an ethic of care as it involves putting into legal practice a different kind of thinking. It may also seem incompatible with the jurisprudence goals of universality, impartiality, and consistency. In addition, as West notes, we do not associate the work of judges with the pursuit of care: "we do not typically demand of our judges that they be nurturant, or compassionate, or committed."[54] This does not mean, however, that judges should not strive to adopt this style of decision making. Former Supreme Court justice Bertha Wilson explains: "[it] is not an easy role for the judge – to enter into the skin of the litigant and make his or her experience part of your experience and only when you have done that, to judge. But I think we have to do it or at least make an earnest attempt to do it."[55] West furthers Wilson's line of reasoning by asserting that judges need to recognize that they are in relationship with particular litigants who come before them and who are seeking justice that only a judge can grant. For West, judges who decide issues before them "as though such [a] relationship did not exist" violate both justice and care.

So within the context of Section 15's equality rights interpretation, an ethic of justice and an ethic of care can interact effectively. Both can support the goal of rights and substantive equality. However, a care stance seems to provide the essential ingredients for developing a comprehensive approach to contextual, responsive, result-oriented equality rights jurisprudence in Canada. In the words of Clement, "while an ethic of justice is devoted to equal rights, care considerations seem necessary to develop a morally adequate account of rights."[56] One can gain deeper insights into biases, marginality, exclusion, and difference.[57] In the words of Narayan: "improvements along care dimensions, such as attentiveness to and concern for human needs and suffering, might provide the 'enabling conditions' for more adequate forms of justice.[58]

If one considers the judicial reasoning of Justices L'Heureux-Dubé and McLachlin in *Symes* and *Thibaudeau*, an alternative approach to equality rights interpretation is not only possible but can lead to very different judicial decisions and outcomes. In both cases, the opinions of these two justices dissented from that of the majority because their framework of analyses was distinct. Arguably, the content of their decisions can be interpreted as consistent with many of the values and priorities of an ethic of care. L'Heureux-Dubé and McLachlin utilized an approach to decision making that considered concrete circumstances, was responsive to the "stories" of women bringing forward their claims, and weighed the consequences of making a particular legal decision.

For instance, in *Symes,* Justice L'Heureux-Dubé strongly opposed the decision of the majority on a number of important grounds. She considered the context in which the legislation had been developed and argued that the whole notion of what might be considered an acceptable business expense under the Income Tax Act was determined predominately by men, that is, by people who do not face the same predicament of pregnancy and childcare as do women. Regarding Section 18(1)(a) L'Heureux-Dubé wrote that the definition of business expense:

> was shaped to reflect the experience of business men, and the ways in which they engaged in business ... [W]hen only one sex is involved in

defining the ideas, rules and values in a particular domain, that one-sided standpoint comes to be seen as natural, obvious and general ... the male standard now frames the backdrop of assumptions against which expenses are determined to be, or not to be, legitimate business expenses ... it is hardly surprising that child care was seen as irrelevant to the end of gaining or producing income from business but rather as a personal non-deductible expense.[59]

Justice L'Heureux-Dubé maintained that treating Section 63 as a limit to business deductions was wrong. She noted that when Section 63 was implemented in 1972 few women actively participated in the workplace and that, moreover, the ideals of equality had not been adequately developed. Indeed, it is reasonable to assume that legislation that is over twenty years old may not necessarily meet the contemporary needs of working women with childcare responsibilities and expenses.

Although L'Heureux-Dubé acknowledged that the changes in society since 1972 have resulted in more women entering the workplace and that men are "being called upon to bear a greater burden of childcare responsibilities and expenses," she nevertheless maintained that women remain the primary child-rearers. She argued that "at this time the reality is that it is primarily women who incur the cost both social and financial for child care and this decision cannot, as such, ignore the contextual truth when examining whether child care may be considered a business expense."[60] This is an important point. The distinction the court made when arguing that women bear disproportionate social but not economic costs of childcare expense ignores the social reality of many if not most Canadian women with children.[61]

Another reason the majority rejected Symes's argument was that allowing her claims would have placed her in a superior position to other women. The court essentially argued that it is preferable that all women be equally disadvantaged relative to men if the alternative is to improve the situation of some women. The idea that all women should be equally disadvantaged in relation to men seems to echo the arguments that had been made by the courts under the Bill of Rights.[62] Justice L'Heureux-Dubé argued, however, that as a matter of course Symes did not have to prove that all women experienced the kind of disadvantage she did in order for the court to accept her childcare costs as a business expense. If one considers the claim by *Andrews,* neither his status in relation to other immigrant professionals nor his occupation as a lawyer prevented the Supreme Court from recognizing his experiences of disadvantage. By making this requirement in *Symes* the court was able to divert the issue to Section 63, thereby ignoring Symes's reality of being unfairly discriminated against by the Income Tax Act.

In sum, unlike the majority, L'Heureux-Dubé recognized that, because women remain the primary child-rearers, and because it is primarily women who incur both the social and financial cost for childcare, the Supreme Court cannot ignore this truth when examining whether childcare may be considered as a business expense.[63] By honouring the context of working women's lives, and the self-reported discrimination reported by Symes (including the actual barriers and obstacles that women who enter the workplace experience due to childcare expenses), L'Heureux-Dubé recognized the disadvantaging effect of Section 18(1) (a) of the Income Tax Act. Her final decision in the case was therefore very different from that of the majority.

Similarly, in *Thibaudeau,* Justices McLachlin and L'Heureux-Dubé's analyses and conclusions differed significantly from that of the majority. At the outset of their submissions, both justices rejected the idea that separated or divorced custodial and non-custodial parents operate as a unit. In the words of Justice L'Heureux-Dubé, it is "unrealistic to assume that they continue to function as a single unit even after they have separated or divorced."[64] She also noted that, in most other respects, the Income Tax Act does not treat separated or divorced couples as single economic or taxation units. According to the dissenting justices, the court should not confuse the ongoing commitment and responsibility of both parents to support their children with their functioning as a single unit.[65]

In addition, these two justices argued that such a rationale prevents comparing the effects of the inclusion/deduction system on each of the custodial and non-custodial parents separately. While it may be true that in many cases the inclusion/deduction system may benefit the "couple" as a whole, one must note that the benefit often comes at the expense of the custodial parent. Custodial parents experience a dramatic increase in the direct and indirect economic burdens and earning limitations linked to child-rearing responsibilities.[66] Thus when considering the impact of the "system" on the custodial parents, who, for the most part, are women, the focus of analysis becomes very different. It becomes problematic to justify the disproportional negative impact of Section 56(1)(b) on the custodial parent. From this perspective, the kind of disadvantage that Thibaudeau claimed she was experiencing would not so easily escape or withstand Charter scrutiny. As Justice McLachlin stated, "the argument that the question of equality must be viewed from the perspective of the couple rather than the individual overlooks individuals' inequalities which Section 15 of the Charter is designed to redress."[67] Justice L'Heureux-Dubé also provided an effective example in order to undermine the majority reasoning. If their rationale had been applied to the Marital Property Acts of the nineteenth century, under which a woman's assets automatically became those of her husband upon marriage, she argued, "we would be precluded from looking to the effects of these provisions on each member of the couple, and we would have to conclude that they did not violate Section 15 of the Charter."[68]

In addition to challenging the use of the couple as a unit of analysis, Justices L'Heureux-Dubé and McLachlin also disputed Justice Gonthier's argument that most parents who are receiving alimony are subject to a marginal tax rate that is lower than that of the parents paying maintenance. McLachlin pointed out that this assumption "is less and less in accord with present reality and undermines the importance our society places on women attaining financial self-sufficiency."[69] The inclusion/deduction system of the Income Tax Act was introduced in 1942 to offset the financial burden of those who wanted to start a second family while still paying support towards the first. For its time, the inclusion/deduction system of the Income Tax Act provided some financial relief to non-custodial male breadwinners. At the same time, the system "contained the seeds of inequality."[70] Since 1942, the Justices argued, women and, more specifically, custodial mothers have become a permanent part of the workplace. At the time of the *Thibaudeau* case, approximately 60 percent of custodial and non-custodial parents were in the same tax bracket before child support payments.[71]

Both dissenting justices made essential observations about the contextual circumstances of the lives of custodial parents, which had not been properly weighed in the court's final decision. A dimension that was missing from the majority judgment was the explicit recognition that custodial parents are, for the most part, women and that custodial women are, "on the whole ... politically weak, economically vulnerable, and socially disempowered."[72] According to L'Heureux-Dubé, requiring Thibaudeau to include child support payments within her taxable income reflects a legislative regime that "materially increases the vulnerability of a particular group"[73] – one that is already marginalized. The two justices concluded that the inclusion/deduction system of the Income Tax Act contributed directly to Thibaudeau's gender inequality and that not recognizing this reality would exacerbate her experience.

In sum, the dissenting opinions in both *Symes* and *Thibaudeau* demonstrate how an approach to legal reasoning that is in keeping with an ethic of care can illuminate and further the understanding of important issues affecting equality demands. Such an alternative approach reflects a concern for others' well-being, is responsive to others' needs and hurts, and, most important, attends to the diversity of human contexts and consequences.[74] This framework of analysis promotes a complex examination of differences in relation to substantive equality and alters how one measures a claim for equality rights. Significantly, since the *Symes* and *Thibaudeau* decisions, the Supreme Court has increasingly highlighted elements of a care ethic by recognizing the importance of context and a more result-oriented approach to evaluating equality claims.

Recent Developments

A number of recent decisions made under Section 15, in which aspects of judicial reasoning can be considered congruent with some aspects of the ethic of care, are worth mentioning. In highlighting these cases, I present a qualified defence of the direction that the Canadian court is taking. Realizing the potential of a normative framework for substantive equality that is fully informed by an ethic of care requires a far more systematic and thorough transformation of judicial reasoning than is provided by these cases. The first case worth highlighting is that of *Eldridge* v. *British Columbia (Attorney General)*.[75] It involved the question of whether the decision of the medicare system in British Columbia not to provide sign language interpreters for the deaf was an infringement of Section 15(1). The appellants in the case – Robin Eldridge and John and Linda Warren – argued that, because of the communication barrier that resulted between deaf persons and health care providers, they received a lesser quality of medical services than did hearing persons. They were successful in claiming that their right to equality benefit of the law without discrimination based on physical disability had been violated.

In explaining the majority opinion, Justice LaForest touched upon critical contextual information about the exclusion and marginality of disabled persons in Canada that is worth highlighting in some detail. He wrote that persons with disabilities "have often been excluded from the labour force, denied access to opportunities for social interaction and advancement, subjected to invidious stereotyping and relegated to institutions. This historic disadvantage has to a great extent been shaped and perpetuated by the notion that disability is an abnormality or flaw. As a result, disabled persons have not generally been afforded the 'equal concern, respect and consideration' that s. 15 (1) of the Charter demands. Instead, they have been subjected to paternalistic attitudes of pity and charity, and their entrance into the social mainstream has been conditional upon their emulation of able-bodied norms."[76] The acknowledgment and detailed analysis of disabled persons' lives is consistent with an ethic of care. The court also went so far as too address remedy, which touches on care's attention to the consequences of choice in decision making. The court acknowledged that it is not its role to dictate how the government should rectify the unconstitutionality of the current system. It did, however, offer "guidance" as to how to accommodate the needs of disabled persons, and this could be interpreted as setting out the kinds of remedies, in the form of positive action, that might ensure reasonable accommodation for those affected by a superficially neutral policy or rule.

References were offered to the US experience with the Rehabilitation Act, 1999, and the Americans with Disabilities Act, 1997. These acts require health care providers to supply appropriate auxiliary aids and services to ensure "effective communication" with deaf persons.[81] In raising the issue of remedy, however, the court did not make explicit the need to include the voices and needs of those affected by the lack of effective communication in the design and delivery of medical services.

The reasoning in the case of *Vriend* v. *Alberta*[77] also demonstrates that an approach to Section 15 consistent with aspects of an ethic of care is possible. This case involved Delwin Vriend, a laboratory coordinator, who had been terminated from King's College in Edmonton, Alberta, because of his homosexuality. Finding that he could not file a complaint with the Alberta Human Rights Commission on the grounds that his employer discriminated against him because of his sexual orientation, Vriend took his case to the Court of Queen's Bench of Alberta. He argued that Alberta's Individual's Rights Protection Act (IRPA) contravened Section 15 of the Charter by not including sexual orientation as a prohibited ground of discrimination. The case was eventually appealed by the Alberta government and heard before the Supreme Court. In this instance, the Supreme Court recognized the context in which the claim was made and, in particular, the wider societal discrimination that gays and lesbians continually experience in their lives. Justice Cory, representing the majority opinion, wrote: "the reality of society's discrimination against lesbians and gay men demonstrates that there is a distinction drawn in the IRPA which denies these groups equal protection of the law by excluding lesbians and gay men from its protection, the very protection they so urgently need because of the existence of discrimination against them in society."[78]

The Court also acknowledged the psychological harm (interpreted as entailing harm to dignity and perceived worth of gay and lesbian individuals), and the dire and demeaning consequences for gays and lesbians of having no protection from discrimination on the basis of their sexual orientation under the Individual's Rights Protection Act.[79] The court elaborated: "the exclusion [from the IRPA] sends a message to all Albertans that it is permissible, and perhaps even acceptable, to discriminate against individuals on the basis of their sexual orientation. The effect of that message on gays and lesbians is one whose significance cannot be underestimated. As a practical matter, it tells them that they have no protection from discrimination on the basis of their sexual orientation. Deprived of any legal redress they must accept and live in constant fear of discrimination."[80] According to the court, the results of this discrimination are harmful to personal confidence and self-esteem. This treatment demeans the individual and strengthens and perpetuates the view that gays and lesbians are less worthy of protection than are other individuals in Canadian society. The court stated that, in excluding sexual orientation from IRPA protection, the government had, in effect, stated that "all persons are equal in dignity and rights" except gay men and lesbians.[81] In sum, the court did recognize the extent to which government legislation has harmful consequences for the diversity of citizens in Canadian society. A liberal ethic of justice may in fact accommodate the extension of rights to gays and lesbians. What is unique to this case is that, in extending these rights, the courts acknowledged issues of psychological harm, stereotyping, and stigma – experiences of oppression not typically recognized by traditional judicial reasoning but certainly prioritized by a care ethic.

In March 1999 the Supreme Court further elaborated on the framework for substantive equality set out in the *Andrews* case. The case of *Law* v. *Canada (Minister of Employment and Immigration)* involved an appeal of a ruling against a claim of age-based discrimination arising because Canada Pension Plan survivor benefits are denied to able-bodied surviving spouses under age thirty-five who are without dependent children. While the court dismissed the appeal it consolidated and refined previously stated principles concerning the purpose of and approach to Section 15. The discussion of the purpose of Section 15, the importance of protecting human dignity, and the significance of attending to context can be seen as generally consistent with the aims and objectives of a care ethic. According to the court, "in general terms, the purpose of s. 15 (1) is to prevent the violation of essential human dignity and freedom through the imposition of disadvantage, stereotyping, or political or social prejudice, and to promote a society in which all persons enjoy equal recognition at law as human beings or as members of Canadian society, equally capable and equally deserving of concern, respect, and consideration."[82] The court's understanding of human dignity is especially noteworthy: "human dignity is harmed by unfair treatment premised upon personal traits or circumstances which do not relate to individual needs, capacities, or merits. It is enhanced by laws which are sensitive to the needs, capacities, and merits of different individuals, taking into account the context underlying their differences. Human dignity is harmed when individuals and groups are marginalized, ignored, or devalued, and is enhanced when laws recognize the full place of all individuals and groups within Canadian society."[83]

According to the court, human dignity necessitates that an individual or group feels self-respect and self-worth. It is concerned with physical and psychological integrity and empowerment. All of these goals are congruent with an ethic of care. The court also stated that to be able to perform a complete analysis of an equality claim, the "nature and situation of the individual or group at issue, and the social, political, and legal history of Canadian society's treatment of the group"[84] must be taken into account.

To this end, the court listed some important factors that are consistent with care's emphasis on contextual sensitivity when making equality rights decisions – namely, pre-existing disadvantage, vulnerability, stereotyping, or prejudice experienced by the individual or group at issue. The court also stated that there are a variety of factors that may be referred to and that, therefore, the list of factors is not closed. Last, the court's discussion of the importance of involving a claimant in reaching contextual knowledge to identify discrimination can be seen as overlapping with care's principle of responsiveness. The Supreme Court stated that "contextual factors which determine whether legislation has the effect of demeaning a claimant's dignity must be construed and examined *from the perspective of the claimant*. The focus of the inquiry is *both subjective and objective* [emphasis added]."[85] Indeed, if one takes the components of analysis central to *Law,* along with the other cases highlighted above, these provide further justification for why an ethic of care should be, and indeed can be, incorporated into equality rights decision making.

Conclusion

An ethic of care holds significant promise for modifying and elaborating the interpretation of substantive equality rights under the Canadian Charter of Rights and Freedoms. Unlike the traditional liberal framework, which lacks the capacity to sufficiently critique the status quo or to do much to ameliorate the lives of those who are already experiencing unfair burdens or disadvantages, an ethic of care raises important questions and establishes different criteria for equality rights interpretation. It requires, consistently and in a comprehensive manner, attention to issues and factors that may otherwise go unnoticed. Unlike the liberal-impartial view of persons, care focuses on the wider social, economic, and political contexts in which equality claims arise. Because a care ethic requires responsiveness, it redirects us to alternative conceptions of differences and concomitant needs that arise from experiencing unfair burdens because of one's status in society. Taking this broader perspective can reveal new and more realistic ways of determining how government legislation affects people. It can, for example, inspire equality analysis that considers the substance of differences in a way that does not harm women and that is concerned explicitly with the consequences of legal decisions and whether these improve or perpetuate disadvantage. Accordingly, such a creative and counter-hegemonic analysis could better name and scrutinize discriminatory government legislation.

By acknowledging the often neglected importance of contextual details and particularities, a paradigm shift can occur in equality rights jurisprudence. Here I am in full agreement with Manning, who has argued "there is no reason that we couldn't adopt the language of rights to further the commitments of care."[86] The analysis of equality claims under Section 15 can be transformed to raise concrete rather than merely abstract questions about justice. Most important, widening the inquiry into what counts as relevant would undoubtedly allow the courts to better understand what is necessary for substantive equality and, in turn, for social justice. A serious consideration of the values of an ethic of care could therefore contribute to a more humane, responsive, and caring approach to claims of discrimination and disadvantage. Countering the liberal ethic of justice framework with the values and priorities of an ethic of care can help to protect against unfair and unjust outcomes in equality rights interpretation. As such, the inclusion of care principles can greatly affect what kind of decision is reached by the courts.

4
Therapeutic Jurisprudence: A Care-Informed Approach for Compensating Victims of Institutional Abuse

In this chapter I move on to examine how the principles of care, when applied to redress and compensation, can enhance a therapeutic outcome. Increasingly, in the pursuit of social justice and healing, persons who experienced abuse at various institutional settings in Canada are seeking some form of redress and compensation. For the most part remedies have been sought outside the traditional criminal justice system. Victims have turned to criminal injuries compensation packages and a range of unique compensation mechanisms developed by governments and other organizations responsible for running institutions in which children and youth have been abused. These remedies have been developed without an adequate conceptual framework – one that would ensure not only a suitable response but one that resonates with the needs of survivors. Not surprisingly, the Law Commission of Canada has concluded that finding an appropriate and effective response to past institutional child abuse is a current and urgent social policy concern.[1]

The development of a redress mechanism has the potential to "heal" and is congruent with the interdisciplinary approach to law reform known as therapeutic jurisprudence. What is therapeutic is linked to the health (including mental health) and well-being of people engaged with various aspects of the law. Therapeutic jurisprudence cannot be adequately operationalized within a paradigm of liberal justice. Within the rigid contours of traditional jurisprudence there is little concern for the unique particularities of any one situation or of any one person. The system is adversarial and impersonal. There is little priority given to attending to real human predicaments. Appropriate redress for harms is often reduced to monetary compensation synonymous with tort law. Ameliorating the experiences of those who engage with the law, or improving their overall situation, is not considered as a matter of course in liberal justice. To be realized, therapeutic jurisprudence must be informed by a care ethic. Both have similar goals: therapeutic jurisprudence and an ethic of care are committed to the promotion of well-being and to the prevention or elimination of harm and suffering. It is, however, an ethic of care that can direct us to an enhanced understanding of what exactly *is* therapeutic for survivors and their families in the processes and outcomes of redress and compensation schemes. It is only with the addition of this ethical stance that victims' therapeutic needs can be addressed adequately.

Throughout this chapter, I argue specifically that care's emphasis on being responsive would prioritize the voices of those who have been wronged and who are the subjects of restitution processes. The information these persons provide is essential to the development of a framework that would adhere to legal requirements while simultaneously attending to the emotional well-being and complex healing needs of survivors and their respective communities. The application of an ethic of care can lead policy makers to an appropriate social policy response that would make it possible for "victims" of abuse to move towards becoming "survivors."

In developing my argument, I provide a brief overview of therapeutic jurisprudence and the development of redress options for victims of crime and wrongdoing in Canada. To illustrate the relevance of ethic of care principles to the further development of therapeutic redress and compensation, I draw upon preliminary research findings in the Canadian context and, where relevant, emerging literature in the international arena. In particular, I draw upon research that evaluates the Agreement between the Grandview Survivors Support Group and the Government of Ontario, as well as the compensation options available through the Criminal Injuries Compensation Board of Ontario.[2] Here I consider the themes and patterns inherent in the retrospective accounts of those who have gone through both of these processes. In addition, I consider the results of the review of the needs of victims of institutional abuse published by the Law Commission of Canada.[3] I argue that the self-expressed therapeutic needs and expectations of survivors can be more effectively identified, understood, and accommodated in the process and substance of redress and compensation schemes if principles of care are included in their design and implementation.

Background to Therapeutic Jurisprudence
The concept of therapeutic jurisprudence (TJ) began appearing in legal literature in the early 1990s.[4] TJ is a framework for analyzing whether the law and extra-judicial processes can be more humane, beneficial, humanistic, healing, restorative, and curative than is now the case.[5] The founders of TJ, David Wexler and Bruce Winick, describe it in the following way: "therapeutic jurisprudence is the study of the role of the law as a therapeutic agent. It looks at the law as a social force that, like it or not, may produce therapeutic or anti-therapeutic consequences. Such consequences

may flow from substantive rules, legal procedures, or from the behaviour of legal actors (lawyers and judges). The task of therapeutic jurisprudence is to identify – and ultimately to examine empirically – relationships between legal arrangement and therapeutic outcomes."[6] This definition has been expanded by Christopher Slobogin to include "the extent to which a legal rule or practice promotes the psychological or physical well being of the people it affects."[7] TJ's focus on the human side of law, including its emotional and psychological dimensions, can be understood as a response to the perimeters under which law has traditionally operated.

Entrenched in the operationalization of the law has been an ethic of justice. The justice paradigm prioritizes abstraction, consistency, universality, and predictability over any therapeutic considerations. Charles Barton and Karen van den Broek explain: "a central feature of the ethic of justice is that its judgements and decisions are purported to be somehow universally right and applicable, at least within certain categories or domains. These judgements and decisions are deemed to be best arrived at in practice by means of pre-established, universally applicable rules and principles. Moreover, where discretion is to be applied, such judgements and decisions are believed to be best made by dispassionate third parties in the interests of eliminating bias and emotion. The implicit assumption is that fairness and justice are best secured through total detachment and disinterestedness in the decision making process."[8]

While respecting values such as justice, due process, and other normative values, TJ understands law as a social force that can produce behaviours and consequences that are more or less therapeutic. In recognizing this, TJ transcends the bounds of traditional analysis. As David Wexler notes, "it is simply a way of looking at the law in a richer way, and then bringing to the table some of these areas and issues that previously have gone unnoticed."[9] It provides us with a critical lens through which to analyze the extent to which legal rules, procedures, and roles of legal actors can be reshaped so as to enhance their therapeutic potential. It is about making the law more responsive and holistic without subordinating due process principles. TJ is therefore an ideal concept to apply to the task of integrating the ethic of justice and the ethic of care.

In the literature on TJ, the definition of "therapeutic" has been left intentionally vague to allow scholars to debate and discuss its contours.[10] Indeed, much work remains to be done in regard to conceptualizing a comprehensive understanding of what is meant by the term "therapeutic." Ken Kress has suggested that this term should draw on the insights of moral theorists and adapt them in order to account for features that are peculiar to TJ.[11] Accordingly, while the potential relevance of an ethic of care to therapeutic jurisprudence has been noted,[12] the relationship has not been thoroughly analyzed. In particular, the systematic application of an ethic of care to compensation and redress packages has not been investigated. A care ethic's principles can assist in developing the necessary criteria and framework for the realization of the goals of therapeutic redress.

Redress: A Brief Background

Traditionally, reparation in the form of redress has been understood as an attempt to make victims whole again and to return them, to the extent possible, to the way they were before they experienced their harm, injury, injustice, or wrongdoing.[13] It is not possible, however, to restore people to how they were before they experienced a harm such as abuse. It is perhaps more realistic to see reparations as providing them with *some degree* of restoration and an ability to better situate the experience within their lives. Martha Minow expresses this best when she states that reparations are invitations for victims and survivors to walk between vengeance and forgiveness.[14]

Forms of redress, according to Roy Brooks, can be divided into a number of categories. Reparations are responses that seek atonement for the commission of an injustice. Responses that do not involve any expression of atonement are settlements. They can be directed towards individuals (compensatory) or groups (rehabilitative in nature). To be compensated, survivors must demonstrate, according to the standards set up by extra-judicial processes, that they were injured by the wrongs committed against them.[15] Both forms of redress can be further divided into monetary or non-monetary responses. In terms of process and outcome, there is a need to ensure justice for both victims and governments or other responsible organizations. Key to the balancing of such interests is allowing only legitimate claims to come forward and handling them with sensitivity and fairness.[16]

In Canada, the need to find proper avenues for redress for past human injustices or wrongdoings is growing. Especially acute is the demand for recognizing and addressing systemic institutional abuse. Historically, within Canada there have been numerous institutions that were run by or on behalf of federal, provincial, and territorial governments. At many of these, children and youth experienced varying degrees of abuse. In total there have been twenty-three non-Aboriginal institutions in the provinces of Newfoundland, Nova Scotia, New Brunswick, Quebec, Ontario, Alberta, and British Columbia at which residents were physically, sexually, and psychologically abused.[17] In addition, at one time or another, over 100 Aboriginal residential schools operated nationally, leaving over 100,000 survivors.[18] Record numbers of victims of these institutions, as well as child sexual abuse victims in the general population, are coming forward and searching for redress mechanisms that will address their need to be acknowledged and responded to with compassion and justice.

The increasing popularity of redress options stems largely from the shortcomings of the traditional legal remedies that are available to survivors in both criminal and civil court processes. Research has demonstrated that such remedies can take an enormous physical and emotional toll on the survivor.[19] Moreover, because criminal and civil remedies are focused on legal liability, they do not always attend to the broader needs of survivors or to the diversity of their communities. Being responsive to diversity is especially important given the number of First Nations survivors of institutional abuse. Survivors often report seeking justice in alternative legal processes – justice that had been denied them in traditional civil and criminal proceedings. They often turn to provincially administered criminal injuries compensation boards. In the Canadian context, nine such programs exist nationally, providing compensation to victims of crime (including sexual assault).[20] In addition, many unique redress and compensation packages have been developed to process claims directly against governments and responsible organizations. These packages address a group of claimants and propose processes of redress for its members.

Until recently, almost no research had been undertaken in regard to the therapeutic and, conversely, anti-therapeutic outcome of redress packages. With preliminary results now available, it is possible to begin the process of assessing the components of a therapeutic redress mechanism. The interview data that I draw upon involve the experiences of survivors who filed claims with the Criminal Injuries Compensation Board (CICB) in Ontario or who were claimants under the Agreement between the Grandview Survivors Group and the Government of Ontario (Grandview Agreement).[21] These data support the need to methodically instill principles of care into redress processes and compensation packages.

The Ontario CICB is a statutory body[22] that provides government compensation to victims of crimes of violence to pay for therapeutic expenses and pecuniary loss arising from injury, pain, and suffering. The applicant, with the assistance of the staff, is responsible for compiling and submitting documentation demonstrating that a crime has occurred, that the victim has been injured or has died, and that there have been financial losses as a result of this. It is not necessary to prove a prior criminal conviction. The decision of whether or not to award compensation is made by a quasi-judicial administrative tribunal. Claimants may elect to make their claim through a documentary hearing. Otherwise, an oral hearing is held and evidence is taken under oath. There are limited rights of internal appeal as well as court appeal (on a question of law), and there is also the right to re-open the hearing to seek compensation for increased expenses.

The Grandview Training School was a custodial institution for girls between the ages of twelve and eighteen. It operated between 1933 and

1976. Often the girls who were sent to the school were deemed "unmanageable," and their parents or guardians could not or would not provide for their social, emotional, and educational needs. Upon entering Grandview, these girls became wards of the Province of Ontario.[23] Many experienced physical, sexual, and psychological abuse while in custody. In 1991 former residents of Grandview formed the Grandview Survivors Support Group. In 1994 the group negotiated a redress package referred to as an "Agreement between the Grandview Survivors Group and the Government of Ontario." The agreement is commonly referred to by government officials and claimants alike as the Grandview "healing package." The Grandview process was consensual and was negotiated by a victim support group.

The focus of the Grandview Agreement was explicitly therapeutic. It permitted all former Grandview residents to apply for specific medical and other benefits. Additional financial and other benefits, such as vocational and educational training and therapy, tattoo removal,[24] scar reduction programs, and access to a crisis line, were also made available. The adjudicators were women with expertise in and sensitivity to female sexual abuse (one was an Aboriginal woman who specialized in adjudicating claims made by Aboriginal survivors). The adjudicators were chosen with the approval of the support group. Hearings were private and were held in public buildings or, occasionally, in hotel rooms. It was not the purpose of the process to allocate blame to individual perpetrators. An award for direct financial support to a maximum of $60,000 was available upon validation.

In addition to the focused analysis of the data from the CICB and the Grandview claimants, I consider research that was funded by the Law Commission on institutional child abuse in Canada and the needs and expectation for redress explored in this work.[25] This review included a detailed examination of survivors from five primary institutions and six secondary institutions. The five primary institutions included Mount Cashel (Newfoundland), the Nova Scotia School for Boys, the Nova Scotia School for Girls, the Nova Scotia Youth Training Centre, Grandview (Ontario), the Duplessis Orphans (Quebec), and the Michener Centre (Alberta). Secondary institutions were Jericho Hill School (British Columbia), St. Joan's/St. Joseph's (Ontario), Kingsclear (New Brunswick), Batshaw Centre (Quebec), Sir James Whitney Centre (Ontario), and foster care institutions. Although the redress mechanisms varied across the institutions examined, the results of the Law Commission's investigation resonate with the findings from the Grandview and CICB respondents. Combined, they provide preliminary insights into a range of redress and compensation approaches and the impact that these have had on survivors of child sexual abuse. They also provide supporting data to explain why an ethic of care is crucial if redress packages are to meet their therapeutic goals. I outline this in detail below.

Contextual Sensitivity

Interviews with survivors have made it clear that contextual information is crucial to reaching an understanding of the full dimensions of a survivor's life. Survivors have consistently emphasized that those who are involved in compensation schemes need to have a better understanding of what it means to be a survivor of abuse and, in particular, of child sexual abuse. They argue that all legal or administrative "actors" should be sensitive and knowledgeable about sexual assault. Some Grandview and CICB survivors commented: "They should really know what it is like," "More empathy and understanding and personable skills were needed to deal with a public that has gone through devastation."[26] Taking child sexual abuse as an example, an ethic of care's principle of contextual sensitivity would require in-depth, multidimensional knowledge of a survivor. This knowledge would include an understanding of the incidence of child sexual abuse, the impact of the abuse on the survivor, and an appreciation of the intergenerational consequences of such abuse. Certainly, the proliferation of research on the problem of child sexual abuse over the last thirty years has raised awareness about these issues. Data have substantiated that child sexual abuse is a social problem of enormous proportions and devastating effects. However, despite the advances made to date, few people recognize the *full* extent to which child sexual abuse affects survivors and society as a whole. Such information is critical for developing an appropriate redress package as well as for knowing how to respond in a respectful and sensitive manner to the injustices that survivors have experienced.

Incidence and Prevalence

Although international and national statistics on child sexual abuse show variance, research to date underscores the frequency with which this form of abuse occurs. In Canada the earliest national survey – the 1984 Bagley report – found that approximately one in two females and one in three males have been victims of unwanted sexual acts. Four out of five such acts were committed against the person as a child or youth.[27] More recent contributions include the *Ontario Mental Health Supplement*.[28] Released in 1997, the study ($n = 10,000$) found that a history of child sexual abuse was reported by 12.8 percent of females and 4.3 percent of males in Ontario residences. In 2001 the *Canadian Incidence Study of Reported Child Abuse and Neglect* (CIS) reported national estimates of child abuse and neglect reported to, and investigated by, child welfare services in Canada between October and December 1998. Out of an estimated 135,573 child maltreatment investigations that were carried out, a total of 15,614 (12 percent) child investigations involved sexual abuse as the primary or secondary reason for the investigation.

In Canada only those incidents that come to the attention of child welfare agencies and the police are documented officially. These include cases of child sexual abuse reported to Child and Family Services[29] in the provinces and territories, and to the police (as reflected in the Revised Uniform Crime Report Survey coordinated by the Canadian Centre for Justice Statistics). It is important to note that most abused children, and, in particular, sexually abused children, never come to the attention of authorities.[30] It has been estimated that only 2 percent of cases of intra-familial and 6 percent of cases of extrafamilial child sexual abuse are ever reported to the police.[31] Children often fail to report because of the fear that disclosure will bring even worse consequences than being victimized further. Not surprisingly, it was during police investigations of institutional abuse in Canada (many years after the events had transpired) that adult survivors first disclosed publicly their abuse. There is also emerging evidence that as many as one in two incidents of child sexual abuse are not remembered by the adult who experienced them.[32]

Institutional Abuse
Residential institutions in Canada were run by governments as well as by religious organizations and their lay orders. Disability, special needs, Aboriginal origin, poverty, illegitimacy, and "ungovernability" were often grounds for taking children from their homes and placing them in residential facilities.[33] There were four types of institutional facilities: special needs schools, child welfare facilities, youth detention centres, and residential schools for Aboriginal children.[34] Within these institutions, vulnerable and marginalized children experienced disconnection, degradation, and powerlessness.[35] Their experiences of physical, sexual, emotional, spiritual, racial, and cultural abuse were typically discounted and dismissed. Their lives were shaped and permanently altered by the experience of being placed in settings that were established specifically to nurture, protect, and care for children. The harms sustained can be understood as a by-product of institutions that overwhelmingly served the interests of powerful individuals and groups at the expense of children and youth.[36]

Of particular importance is the unique character of residential schools for Aboriginal children. The purpose of residential schools was to provide Aboriginal children with a specific education – one that deprived them of their mother tongue and their culture and that severed their ties with their families and extended communities. So, although many experienced abuses similar to those foisted upon their non-Aboriginal institutional counterparts, their experiences were distinct. The abuse experienced in residential schools was embedded within the official government policy of assimilation. The cultural devastation as a consequence of this policy has been effectively described by Agnes Grant: "every child experienced the devaluing of parents and culture. Psychological and spiritual abuse were institutionalized, no child could escape the debilitating consequences of being victimized and brainwashed ... since the children were taught to abhor how their parents lived, no more diabolical plot could have been conceived to destroy the harmony ... and effectiveness of the culture."[37]

Moreover, children with disabilities can also be considered a distinct group. As the Law Commission puts it: "They are more vulnerable to abuse in the first instance, may find it more difficult to disclose that abuse, are less likely to have criminal charges laid in respect to their abuse, less likely to have their offenders be convicted of a crime, and less likely to advocate successfully for compensation."[38]

Impact

Approximately one-third of victims of child sexual abuse may have no overt symptoms.[39] For others, however, the effects can be life-altering. The degree of impact is determined by a number of factors, including the victim's age at the onset of abuse, the duration and frequency of the abuse, the type of abuse, the relationship between the abuser and victim, and the response to the abuse once it is made public.[40] While definitive causal relations are difficult to establish, there is general agreement that child sexual abuse is a major risk factor for a variety of problems, both in the short term and in later life functioning.[41] The short-term or delayed long-term consequences of abuse often include increased risk for physical and psychological problems. These include, but are not limited to, self-harming behaviours, post-traumatic stress, depression, greater risk for psychiatric hospitalization, eating disorders, addictions (substance-abuse problems), indiscriminate sexual behaviour leading to a higher propensity for STDs and HIV/AIDS, and suicide. In addition, survivors are prone to lower educational and employment attainment, difficulty functioning in the workplace, prostitution, criminal activity, and homelessness.[42] They can also experience shame, isolation, and poor self-esteem. In the case of Aboriginal people, the impact of childhood sexual abuse includes dependency on non-Aboriginal society; feelings of shame towards their culture, language, and value systems; and spiritual crisis and psychological deterioration.[43]

Contextual sensitivity leads us to recognize that childhood sexual abuse has a ripple effect on family and friends. It reveals the extent to which we are all "particularized by historical connections and relationships."[44] Parents, partners, and children of survivors are often described as *secondary victims*.[45] Parents can feel guilty about the abuse their children experienced. Survivors find it difficult to establish healthy relations with others and to parent effectively. As one survivor has explained, "My kids are being hurt by my recycling all this stuff now. I had it blocked out of my mind for 29-30 years. I take it out on my wife."[46] Often, survivors are vulnerable to re-victimization (increased chance of woman abuse, sexual assault, rape)[47] and have a high propensity to themselves become perpetrators of child abuse/child sexual abuse.[48] In the case of Aboriginal victims, the damage of the policy of assimilation extended to families, communities, and Aboriginal peoples in general. The framework of assimilation under which the residential schools operated "was used to denigrate and erase all aspects of Aboriginal heritage and justify a number of harmful practices that were undertaken in the name of instilling non-Aboriginal values in Aboriginal children."[49] Because their experiences are embedded within the context of family and community, survivors are not the only victims of abuse: many have reported loss of "connection, community, family."

Child sexual abuse also has an enormous financial cost, exceeding $3.6 billion dollars annually.[50] This includes both public and private costs across four policy areas: health, social/public services, justice, and education/research and employment. Contextual sensitivity would entail understanding that it takes time for many survivors to come to grips with their abuse and the impact that it has had on their lives. Often, a significant period of time may have passed before survivors come forward to make a claim for compensation. And, once they do, there should be a better understanding of these disclosures, of their negative impact on the functioning and well-being of survivors. In sum, the ability to identify the circumstances of a claimant's life is crucial to understanding what is required for a realistic and useful therapeutic process and outcome.

Responsiveness

Often, those in positions of power vis-à-vis redress or compensation schemes engage in a paternalistic role by assuming that they know what is in a survivor's best interest. Paternalistic attitudes, Winick argues, undermine the participatory value and dignity of compensation procedures.[51] They can silence, marginalize, and disempower victims of abuse. Accordingly, it is inappropriate for legal and administrative actors to make comments such as "I know what you are going though" and "I know how you feel." The assumptions inherent in such comments are a direct violation of the ethic of care and its principle of responsiveness. As Toronto points out, responsiveness requires that we consider the other's position as she/he expresses it.[52] The harms that are suffered are best articulated by those who have experienced them. Minow reaches similar conclusions in her examination of genocide and mass violence victims. She argues that the voices of individuals express concrete experiences of pain and despair.[53] The Law Commission of Canada has also acknowledged the need to include the perspectives of survivors in redress processes: "After all, it is they who have suffered the harm and they who are best able to articulate the harm."[54]

In tandem with the principle of contextual sensitivity, the principle of responsiveness provides us with accuracy and depth of knowledge regarding the life of an abuse survivor. To come to appreciate people's human essence it is necessary to make a compassionate attempt to understand his or her lived dilemma.[55] This information is key to fully grasping what kind of responses to lived experiences are appropriate and will cause the least amount of harm. We get a better sense of what is therapeutic and what is anti-therapeutic. Kate Paradine, in her research on domestic violence, points out that "legal actors need to listen to survivors and understand their stories so that legal responses to domestic violence maximize safety, condemn violence and do not have negative or 'anti-therapeutic' effects on survivors' emotional and psychological well-being."[56]

And while it is important to recognize that each survivor's experience is unique and that needs and expectations vary, a number of overlapping themes and patterns are emerging in the research to date. From the perspective of survivors, the need to participate, to be heard and respected in all stages of the compensation or redress processes, is seen as essential to empowerment and a therapeutic outcome. Tom Tyler explains that "people's evaluations of the fairness of judicial hearings are affected by the opportunities which those procedures provide for people to participate, by the degree to which people judge that they are treated with dignity and respect, and by judgements about the trustworthiness of authorities."[57]

In terms of participation, survivors repeatedly state that they need an opportunity to tell their story in a respectful and dignified manner: "I am seeking to be heard ... to be able to speak about what had happened to me," "I had unresolved issues which I wanted resolved. I thought it was time to come forward to tell my truth," and "I think that it's cathartic to talk to someone who will listen and not judge you."[58] Victims need to be accorded a sense of "voice" (the ability to tell their side of the story) and validation (the sense that what they have to say is taken seriously).[59] This is akin to the need to empty a wound of its old infection before expecting any healing to start.[60] South Africa's Truth and Reconciliation Commission hearings also acknowledged the importance of telling one's story. A South African black survivor of apartheid, who had been blinded in a political conflict, explained, "I feel that what has been making me sick all the time is the fact that I couldn't tell my story. But now – it feels like I got my sight back by coming here and telling you the story."[61]

Being able to tell one's story in a safe and non-threatening environment is essential. Survivors express the need for hearing to take place in "settings that are informal and safe." The lack of a relaxed and non-threatening environment can cause participants to experience stress, trauma, and feelings of re-victimization. As one respondent explained: "The setting, the atmosphere ... the adjudicators were sitting on a bench a lot higher than me. My whole life adults have always been standing above me and hurting me. I have no power/control."[62]

Claimants may require considerable time if they are to tell their stories in their own way. They need to feel that they are not being rushed and that they are retaining control over the process of articulating their experience. Often, as is illustrated by the following, survivors often feel a lack of control: "I said, 'This is my hearing,' and the adjudicator ... she said, "This is not your hearing, it's my hearing," "I took a break and when I came back the adjudicator said 'I have a plane to catch.' That made me feel unimportant. I didn't feel I could say what I needed to."[63] Those who had time to respond had a positive experience, and the therapeutic outcome of adjudication was achieved. One Grandview survivor describes her adjudication process as follows: "She [the adjudicator] was respectful and considerate. There was nothing but total support and empathy."[64] "She made me feel very comfortable and I could take as many breaks as I wanted. She was very, very caring and I never felt any pressure."[65] The telling of one's suffering does not necessarily have to be achieved orally. Some survivors prefer writing the story of their abuse, or they may wish to contribute to a historic record or archival collection. Some may communicate through a creative form, such as artwork, poetry, a film, or a video. Policy decision makers should be cognizant that, ideally, there should be a range of choices and forums from which survivors may choose in the process of recounting their stories of abuse.

One of the most important needs identified by survivors is the need to be included in the negotiation, design, and implementation of compensation packages. The Law Commission has also noted that "it is important to offer survivors an individualized opportunity to be involved in the design of programs and processes designed to assist them."[66] Some survivors have proposed that they should be appointed as adjudicators in redress processes and that this would ensure more just outcomes. By deriving information from survivors about their needs, policy decision makers become more informed and garner insights into the kinds of choices that are most appropriate. Engaging survivors in this way allows for the design of more effective compensation packages. Alternatively, imposing "solutions" without survivors' input or consultation, and without considering their needs, can be just as offensive as not offering redress at all.[67] So, while telling the story is important, providing opportunities for survivors to share their needs and wishes is just as important.

Consequences of Choice

Contextual sensitivity and responsiveness are the principles that form the foundation for assessing the therapeutic consequences of redress packages.

The combined knowledge derived from these principles allows policy decision makers to understand better what approaches will best attend to the needs and wishes of survivors, and to avoid those that have the potential to further traumatize them. Here an ethic of care would necessitate that all actors – from policy decision makers to adjudicators – consistently take into account the actual impact of redress processes, including their content and substance, on survivors. If one carefully considers research to date, one sees that survivors have provided numerous suggestions about how processes and outcomes might be improved in order to minimize negative consequences and to increase therapeutic benefits.

Process

In terms of process, an important theme that has emerged concerns the need for accurate information about the legal options available to survivors. This includes comprehensive and accurate information about each step of the procedure, such as time lines, emotional risks, the roles and responsibilities of the different actors (including staff, lawyers, and adjudicators), and the remedy that can reasonably be expected at the end of the proceedings. Some have also asked that the information include a list of experienced lawyers, therapists, and a volunteer roster of women who have gone through similar processes: "If we are going to create a system, have a roster of women on call who are experienced and who have been there"; "If you could have the choice of someone to talk to even over the phone ... someone who had gone through this."[68] This level of information would empower survivors by giving them the knowledge that would enable them to make informed choices about their options. In addition, survivors often ask for assurance that they will have adequate counselling before entering into any redress process.

Once a process is initiated, claimants often refer to the importance of a "support person" who will help them through the process. They wanted "someone who is qualified helping with the application and helping to get information." And they suggested that the government should "assign a person to support each step and give more preparation on how much time, how long the process may be."[69] In addition, claimants emphasized the significance of survivor support groups/networks, crisis lines, and "healing centres." As is illustrated by the following quotes, many survivors see these supports as essential components of the process: "Very important, played an important role for many survivors with practical support, validation, and friendship."[70] "Helped people get it out ... we had a common goal ... strong voices that really helped each other ... made demands and asked questions."[71] Indeed, research has demonstrated that groups are invaluable for survivors of child abuse. As Herman has explained, traumatized people feel alienated by their experience, and the group provides them with an opportunity to connect with others that have undergone similar experiences. This experience of "universality" has the potential to dissolve feelings of isolation, shame, and stigma.[72]

In terms of the process itself, survivors asked for a reduction in the length of time each process takes: "It has to be swift. It costs everyone so much money. The emotional stuff is draining and taxing health-wise. It's not necessary to drag it out." They disliked "the waiting and not knowing the real physical and psychological side effects of the procedure." Research has demonstrated that delays are a serious problem for claimants. Lawyers, judges, government staff, and adjudicators should be made aware of this concern so they can do whatever is possible to alleviate unnecessary delays. Finally, in terms of process, claimants asked for a fair appeal mechanism: "Give women an alternative forum to appeal their awards – only allowing Divisional Court appeal is problematic – Who has the money?"[73]

Content and Substance of Redress Packages

Attempts to restore injured parties have given priority to a dollar compensation that is based on a valuation of injury. A significant number of survivors do identify money as one of their reasons for making a compensation claim. For a small number of respondents, money seems to be their sole motivating factor in seeking redress. For these individuals, financial compensation is therapeutic in so far as it allows them to purchase certain items, support, and services that otherwise they would not be able to afford. This may include counselling, education, and family care costs. In comparison, those who do not receive awards or, alternatively, are given awards that seem inappropriate, are often devastated. For example, Grandview and CICB claimants who did not receive compensation stated that they were "angry," "outraged," "disappointed," and "heartbroken."

Survivors have also provided substantial feedback about the monetary awards themselves. First, many question how the award amounts are established: "I am still confused about how they put a dollar amount to what happened to people."[74] Second, they critique the sliding scale/matrix that allows for individual variation in award amounts. Indeed, compensation grids have been critiqued by many survivors and researchers.[75] Survivors commented: "Everyone should be treated the same ... how can you put a figure on such crimes?"; "Have set amounts no matter what 'kind' of rape you experienced. Take out the qualifications"; "Getting graded on a scale is not fair – it's degrading."[76] The unique emotional and psychological impact of child sexual abuse and sexual assault, including pain and suffering and lost quality of life, make it difficult to place a value on such damage.[77] And not everyone believes that an individualized damage award is therapeutic. Many survivors have asked for financial support/planning: "'Here's your package; here's your award. Now go away.' You are like, 'Huh?'

I know for someone who has been ... sexually abused, it's like, 'What now?'"; "Give more advice to women on how to use their money – advice not control, give them their options."[78]

Some respondents referred to their financial awards as "dirty money," "hush money," and "blood money." Generally, financial awards present their own difficulties for survivors, who report problems with using the money. As evidenced by the description of one Grandview survivor, the money becomes synonymous with the price placed on their experiences of trauma and abuse: "With some of the money I did get awarded, I ended up buying this couch and it's totally different from my other furniture. This couch is what I suffered for. The couch has to make up for the childhood I missed, the pain and suffering, and the family I lost. And it doesn't. It never will."[79]

For most survivors money is not of primary importance. Retrospective accounts of survivors underscore the limitations of monetary compensation with regard to therapeutic healing. According to their feedback, compensation awards do not necessarily improve survivors' sense of hopelessness, loss, violation, and exploitation. The majority of respondents stress that money could never compensate for their experiences: "Money helps but it does not heal"; "For some stupid reason, I thought the money would heal the wound. It hasn't"; "They dangled justice in front of us and then gave us money and this was supposed to make everything go away."[80] Central to this finding is understanding that certain traumas and experiences can never be adequately addressed solely through financial compensation. In his analysis of the situation in South Africa, Joseph Singer has similarly concluded that "compensation can never compensate."[81]

Conceptualizing compensation solely in financial terms may therefore tend to trivialize the survivor trauma and distract from more important therapeutic options. As one Grandview woman said, "Money is not what it is all about – I know an addict that killed herself with her compensation money."[82] Similar observations have been made by those examining restorative justice conferencing. Barton and van den Broek argue that "conferencing which focuses merely on material outcomes and agreements between the parties, but fails to address issues of emotional disruption, disconnectedness, and social isolation, is not of a restorative nature."[83] From the perspective of survivors themselves, their needs and expectations cannot be met with compensation that is limited to a monetary award. Policy makers need to listen to this and be more creative in terms of how to respond to people in non-monetary ways. Indeed, as Daniel Shuman has effectively argued, "the suggestion that as a responsible, caring people the payment of money is all that we can do to address the harm we cause belies our experiences of the way in which many people deal with a lifetime of hurts.[84]

In addition to, or instead of, monetary compensation, survivors stress how important it is to have their abuse acknowledged, their experience validated, and an apology received. For instance, most Grandview and CICB respondents stated that they were seeking public affirmation that a wrong had been committed against them. They emphasized that they wanted to be heard, believed, and acknowledged: "I needed someone to say that they know all the hurt I'd been through, all the wrong"; "I wanted someone to acknowledge that I was there and went through hell and that it's responsible for who I am today"; and "I never realized how much I needed to be affirmed." Many of the victims/survivors also emphasized a need to receive affirmation that they had been wronged from a person in a position of power, someone they perceived to be "important" or a "legal authority."[85]

Not surprisingly, several respondents linked whatever monetary award they received to their self-reported therapeutic priorities. They explained that the financial award was gratifying because it symbolized an acknowledgment and understanding of the impact of their experiences of assault and abuse: "To me it wasn't the award. I was more glad that someone had believed what happened to me"; "It wasn't the amount ... it was the fact that someone acknowledged that my life is screwed up because of what happened"; "The adjudicator heard me, believed me. It gave me something I thought I would never have. It gave me 'Someone believed me.'"[86] As Bawdon has noted elsewhere, "A substantial sum of money can be seen as an important recognition that the woman has been through a terrible ordeal and can give back power to someone who may have felt totally powerless during the rape."[87]

Typically, a substantial majority of survivors expressed the need for an apology either from the perpetrator of their abuse or from a responsible third party. "An apology – that more than anything else is what I wanted and it was the thing I didn't get"; "I won't feel relieved until I get a letter of apology and public apology. Only then will I feel complete closure"; "I want from the government, not just, 'Oh yeah, we're sorry for what our predecessors did,' but, 'We acknowledge that government can err in this way and this is what we are going to do about it to ensure that it won't happen again.'"[88] Responsible individuals or institutions must fully appreciate the significance of their moral obligation to apologize when requested to do so.[89] Failure to apologize can result in the most anti-therapeutic outcomes. For example, the Helpline Reconciliation Agreement to compensate victims of St. John's and St. Joseph's in Ontario almost fell apart after some parties refused to issue apologies.[90]

The overall objective of an apology is to restore dignity and social harmony.[91] An apology has the potential to help people who have suffered serious emotional harm in ways that monetary damages alone cannot.[92] It has been theorized that an apology helps with recovery because it is a vehicle for adjusting the imbalance of power in a relationship that occurs when a wrong is committed by one party against another. As Daniel Shuman explains it, an apology attributes responsibility for harm. It tells the victim, "It wasn't your fault," thus deflecting self-blame or self-criticism.[93] After this, the recipient of an apology is in the position of choosing whether or not to accept it and to forgive the wrongdoer.[94] As Martha Minow has noted, "The ability to dispense, but also to withhold, forgiveness is an ennobling capacity and part of the dignity to be reclaimed by those who survive the wrongdoing."[95] Finally, an apology has the potential to reduce anger and, therefore, to allow victims to forgive and move on with their lives.[96]

The Law Commission has argued that for an apology to be meaningful it must contain the following elements: "acknowledgment of the wrong done, the acceptance of responsibility for the wrong that was done, the expression of sincere regret or remorse, assurance that the wrong will not recur, and reparation through concrete measures."[97] It should also be timely, sincere, and culturally appropriate.[98] As illustrated by the delay in the Grandview process, a substantial delay in apology coloured the entire therapeutic impact of the healing package. The reconciliation agreement stated that individual apologies would be forthcoming once all criminal matters were settled. As some Grandview claimants reported: "I wanted an apology which I still haven't received"; "Several letters you receive say you will get an apology. When? When we all die?"; "I don't feel validated because I got a few bucks. I haven't got a real letter of apology." For those who responded favourably to an apology, the benefits were clearly therapeutic. As a Shelbourne survivor noted, "I got an apology and you can't put a price on that"; "I expected an apology and got one. This was the most important part."[99] As Daniel Shuman has explained, "words can often help with intangible pains."[100]

It is also important to acknowledge that not all survivors want an apology. Whenever possible, the choice should be left to each survivor as to whether or not she/he needs or desires an apology. This choice may not always be available if a public apology is made;[101] however, in the case of private apologies, it is a viable option. Having a mechanism of choice in place is empowering. Clearly, apologies should not be used to replace other forms of compensation, including financial compensation and other rehabilitative supports. Minow effectively documents the strengths and limitations of apologies: "official apologies can correct a public record, afford public acknowledgement of a violation, assign responsibility, and reassert the moral baseline to define violations of basic norms. They are less good at warranting any promise about the future, given the shifts in officeholders. Unless accompanied by direct and immediate actions (such as payment of compensation) that manifest responsibility for the violation, the official apology may seem superficial, insincere, or meaningless."[102]

In addition to apologies, policy makers can develop other non-monetary supports and benefits by listening directly to what survivors say they are seeking therapeutically. For example, respondents noted the significance of the articulation of an award. One respondent explained, "The wording was just as important as the money." For another it was the importance of "letters explicitly validating my abuse/experience."[103] Similarly, respondents stated that it was significant to have the awarding body acknowledge that the compensation amount was symbolic rather than an attempt to compensate for the gravity of the experience: "it was nice that they mentioned that no monetary value can replace what you lost."[104] There is, after all, no appropriate amount of money that can compensate for the experience of a lost childhood or youth. As Herman says, "the childhood that is stolen from [child sexual abuse victims] is irreplaceable."[105] This kind of loss does not have a commensurable monetary value.

Numerous victims also asked for education and training since, as one Grandview respondent said, "Educational benefit was most valuable because that was what Grandview took from me."[106] Related to this were requests for support and training to start new business ventures. For a significant number of survivors, it was important to have a longer-term follow-up to the impact of redress and compensation packages. They asked for "research into the positive results women experienced as a result of receiving the package – what they have accomplished."[107] It would seem that many survivors would find it of therapeutic benefit to hear the success stories of survivors who have had the opportunity to rebuild their lives.

Moreover, survivors felt strongly that they require more counselling for themselves and for their families in order to deal with their past abuse as well as the potential trauma of having to relive that abuse by going through a process of redress or compensation. As one Grandview survivor explained, what survivors need is "more counselling – and counselling for families." Counselling for survivors was seen as key both during the process and beyond the conclusion of any settlement: "It was the only thing government did right in this entire matter"; "It saved my life."[108] According to the Law Commission, emerging knowledge of the therapeutic needs of survivors of institutional child abuse suggests that, in some instances, long-term counselling is required to assist survivors to stabilize their lives and to function effectively. A time-limited span of one to three years may not always be sufficient in addressing the abuse.[109] Some require appropriate substance abuse counselling. Survivors also express much concern for their families. Despite the fact that support and counselling for family members is frequently recommended,[110] packages to date have not provided compensation or counselling for secondary victims such as parents, spouses, children, and siblings, all of whom often suffer indirectly.

Of great importance to survivors was the need for "commitments from those in power to put every effort into stopping institutional abuse."[111] Survivors themselves strongly believe that critical information can come directly from their own experiences. Those interviewed for the Law Commission review suggested numerous prevention measures to stop institutional child abuse. These included keeping children in the community, screening staff at institutions, independent monitoring by a non-government entity, better training, higher staff-resident ratios, informing residents about rights, educating children about abuse, using cameras to monitor facilities, and helping staff to prevent burn-out.[112] Such recommendations can lead to the restructuring of institutions that have caused much harm and suffering.

On a more general level, suggestions were made about raising public awareness and improving prevention. Survivors consistently requested "research into abuse," including public education. Many survivors wish to see the creation of a memorial such as a monument, plaque, museum, historic site, film, or the establishment of a historic record/archive so that their experiences will not be forgotten.[113] For example, a number of Grandview survivors participated in the development of a video entitled *Until Someone Listens*. The accompanying handbook states: "The Grandview survivors themselves hoped that their experiences can be [sic] instrumental in the prevention of hurt and abuse to other children."[114] Indeed, one of the central reasons that survivors come forward is to protect further generations of vulnerable children from abuse. According to Herman, this is an essential element of healing: "survivors may focus their energies on helping others who have been similarly victimized, on education, legal or political efforts to prevent others from being victimized in the future ... Common to all these efforts is a dedication to raising public awareness. Survivors understand full well that the natural human response to horrible events is to put them out of mind ... Survivors also understand that those who forget the past are condemned to repeat it. It is for this reason that public truth-telling is the common denominator for all social action."[115] For survivors, public awareness is linked to societal accountability. The way in which government responds to its past failures is critical. Its action, or lack of action, has the potential to harm or, alternatively, to better the lives of aggrieved citizens. Amnesia and inertia are not appropriate government responses. Victims do not, and in many cases cannot, forget the harms they have suffered.[116] Governments and other responsible organizations must be cognizant of their responsibility to respond to historic abuses. Satisfying the social justice needs of survivors of abuse would give society the opportunity to come to terms with the past and to make assessments for the future. As Neil Kritz says, "publicly condemning the abuse draws a line between the past and the present and renews public confidence in the new order."[117] In this way a care ethic's focus on the consequences of choice involves reviewing the public commitment to care as it relates to those who have been wronged. Adhering to the consequences of choice contributes to ensuring social justice for victims of abuse.

Conclusion

It is important to point out that no restitution mechanism can be expected to provide complete closure or healing. As Judith Herman puts it, "resolution of the trauma is never final; recovery is never complete."[118] Some benefits are simply beyond the scope of any response. Nevertheless, it is important to strive for redress processes and outcomes that provide as much benefit in terms of therapeutic healing as is possible. This cannot be realized within the ethic of justice model. The therapeutic needs of victims can only be realized through a careful application of an ethic of care to the design, implementation, and evaluation of compensation schemes. Care's principles – contextual sensitivity, responsiveness, and consequences of choice – are, literally, irrelevant to a liberal ethic of justice. And yet, as has been shown, they capture the experiences, needs, and expectations of survivors of abuse and organize them within an effective framework.

By following the principles of an ethic of care we come to understand, in the survivors' own words, that therapeutic healing is dependent upon more than financial compensation. It is dependent on a process that empowers victims, allows them to participate in the development of redress programs, and provides them with an opportunity to tell their stories and to express their experiences with dignity. The self-identified therapeutic needs of survivors demonstrate that monetary compensation and other supports need to be balanced. The role of acknowledgments and apologies is also clarified. Arguably, by considering the retrospective accounts of survivors we can see how principles of care can ensure that redress packages can be designed to better capture therapeutic needs and expectations.

Following the precepts of an ethic of care can also direct policy decision makers to be more flexible in responding to the distinct needs of different groups of survivors. Although in many instances survivors have overlapping needs and expectations, it is critical to be able to respond to significant variances. What decision makers need to keep in mind is that, while one agreement may be appropriate for a particular group, that same agreement may not be appropriate for the next group. Each group should decide for itself what is right for its unique situation. In doing so, it should not be constrained by preconceptions of a universally right outcome.[119] Perhaps the most important conclusion that should be drawn from the application of care in this context is that society ought to provide a number of legal options to victims of abuse – options that are driven by the needs of survivors.

5
Economic Costing in Social Policy: The Ethics of Quantifying Intangible Losses

Policy analysts are constantly faced with making decisions about scarce resources. Cost containment has become critical to social policy decisions, and economic evaluations of policies and programs are proliferating. Nowhere can this be more widely observed than in the field of health policy. Health economists maintain that the positive contributions of the tools and techniques of economics to health policy decisions are only starting to be realized. Concurrently, several philosophers, lawyers, and economists have started to challenge the interpretation of economics as a "box of tools that can be used for whatever purpose if only applied in a proper and correct manner."[1] Serious questions are being raised about the proper boundaries of economic evaluations. Discussion has focused on examining whether there are aspects of our personhood and lives to which market norms should not apply for the purposes of determining social policy.[2]

The argument that I develop in this chapter furthers this line of interrogation by investigating how an ethic of care illuminates the limitations of economic theories of value priorititized by liberalism. Using cost of illness studies as an example, I consider economic evaluation methodologies, including the commodification of human life and intangible experiences of pain and suffering. Without doubt, these are of great importance in any society that is concerned with the quality and value of life. I argue, however, that, from the perspective of a care ethic, valuing these intangibles may not be congruent with simply assigning a dollar figure to them. Without doubt, there are many ways in which we understand and give meaning to human interactions, relationships, and experiences that have nothing to do with economic measurements. Some of these ways, according to the directives of a care ethic, may undermine their true value for the purposes of making critical policy decisions.

Essentially, an ethic of care is not an ethic of commodification. It prioritizes how we can best meet our caring obligations in society and shows that, more often than not, such obligations transcend economics. Accordingly, the care ethic provides us with principles from which we can develop alternative, multifaceted approaches to decision making, which is currently dominated by considerations of efficiency in the delivery of public goods. Principles of care challenge us to *widen* our perspective on how we value certain "goods." A care ethic enhances our capacity to understand that the concept of value can have many meanings other than just those associated with a quantifiable measure. At the same time, the principles of care *narrow* our view of what may be appropriate for economic quantification. As Virginia Held writes: "where the boundaries of an economy should be, what should be in the market and what should not be, will look very different depending on whether we recognize care as a central consideration."[3]

The argument of this chapter builds upon the work of Margaret Jane Radin, who has argued that "there can be a coexistent commodified and non-commodified understanding of various aspects of social life."[4] Radin's argument is particularly significant for appreciating the relevance of a care ethic for social policy. Economic evaluations are important and should be utilized. However, their limits and perimeters need to be interrogated. There are limits, for example, to how far we should quantify human costs and experiences for the purposes of policy judgments. The care ethic and its principles can advance this understanding. Significantly, it has the potential to counter the expanding dominance of economic evaluations by presenting them with non-commodified perspectives. It moves us to consider "economics as if people mattered." As such, an ethic of care also prompts us to look beyond economics to consider what additional values we want to embrace in setting our social policy objectives and goals.

The Liberal Paradigm and Commodification

An effective starting place for investigating care's potential is to first identify the shortcomings of the current liberal theoretical paradigm, within which economic evaluations are operationalized. Liberal theory and economics go hand in hand. Underpinning a liberal understanding of society and politics is social contract theory. It is built upon the premise that individuals are rational economic actors who are also selfish profit maximizers. They agree to create civil society because the benefits of so doing outweigh the costs. Once civil society is established, individuals continue to pursue choices that maximize their welfare largely in terms of material possessions and gains. Interactions are focused on an ideal market in which prices form the only necessary form of communication.[5] Thus, the relationship between buyer and seller is assumed to be the model of all human interactions.[6]

This model's underlying assumptions about individuals' behaviour and choices reflect a particular view of human nature – one that is found within the justice ethic. Generally, this view does not allow for moral values such as altruism, cooperation, or commitment to care to enter into individuals' intentions or motivations when acting in the public sphere and making decisions about their own and other people's lives. Rational actors are conceptualized as independent, unemotional, and having no sense of community or society. The net result is that human behaviour and political and social interactions tend to be linked to the rational pursuit of self-interest and an optimal economic result. Consumer preferences are considered the norm for democratic politics.[7] The social ideal reduces to efficiency.[8] Even Rawls's theory, often seen as a progressive articulation of social justice, appears to be premised upon the "advantages of efficiency." Efficiency, according to Thomas Kuhn, is perhaps the most common meaning of liberal justice.[9] The justice ethic employed in political decision making can therefore be interpreted as one of wealth or welfare maximization.[10] In sum, liberal views of citizenship, politics, and social policy are couched in the discourse of commodification.

One should therefore not be surprised that there has been a steady growth of economic evaluations within social policy. The foundation for the "discourse of commodification" is inherent within the liberal paradigm. The logical endpoint is the prioritization of economic valuations in social policy. When analysts measure, define, and aggregate "costs" and "benefits," they are producing results that are both politically and morally relevant in liberal societies and complying with relevant norms and values. As Joseph Heath notes: "Efficiency is a value. And whether we like it or not, it is the central value in Canadian society."[11] Within the context of health policy, as evidenced from economic costing studies, the focus on economic measurements and efficiency has meant that economic measurements are encroaching on areas of our lives that, previously, have been valued according to non-market methods.

Because economic evaluations are derived from the normative values of a liberal paradigm, the latter is unable to provide direction with regard to the appropriate scope of economics in our lives, to separate between what aspects of our lives should and should not be commodified. As Held writes: "Among the issues that liberal theory does not handle well are those concerning what should be out of the market and what should be in it."[12] She concludes that liberalism does not provide us with any clear indication of what aspects of social policy decision making should be left outside the reach of the market. In a similar vein, Anderson has argued that liberal theorists have not examined what it means to let markets govern the production of particular goods, and more important, what we make of ourselves when we do.[13] This lack is reflected in the illustration of cost of illness studies and their approach to the value of life and the measure of intangible losses such as pain and suffering.

Cost of Illness Studies

Cost of illness (COI) studies are considered to be partial economic evaluations because they focus only on costs associated with a particular illness or disease. No alternative costs and consequences are considered in these cost description exercises. However, in their attempts to demonstrate the magnitude and scope of particular phenomena, these studies have become popular with policy analysts, researchers, organizations, and interest groups. In recent years there has been a substantial amount of research conducted on the economic costs of various health-related issues and social problems. For example, studies have been conducted on the economic costs of illness,[14] substance abuse,[15] smoking,[16] AIDS,[17] schizophrenia,[18] crime,[19] and child poverty,[20] and the economic toll of family violence.[21] Methodologically, all these investigations are based on COI studies first developed by American economist Dorothy Rice.[22]

COI studies often combine health data and financial data to generate a monetary cost to individuals and governments concerning a particular disease, illness, or experience. In its simplest forms, the COI method calculates the dollar cost of disease as the sum of medical resources used to diagnose and treat the disorder and the value of lost productivity due to morbidity and mortality. A given disease may produce more than one kind of health damage, and a given disability may arise from more than one cause. COI studies are intended to provide policy decision makers with an understanding of the enormity and reach of costs associated with various illnesses and diseases.

COI studies are considered to be precursors to fuller cost-benefit,[23] cost-effectiveness,[24] and cost-utility economic evaluations, where both costs and benefits of particular health programs and policies are measured for their efficiency and efficacy. In addition, COI results are used by a wide range of constituents to set priorities and to make policy decisions. As Alan Shiell explains: "such work is of value in indicating the burden of disease and in setting priorities in research, prevention and treatment."[25] At the same time, because the objective is to demonstrate the financial toll of a particular disease, economists and policy decision makers are increasingly expanding into new areas for cost calculation. Any changes in assumptions about how costs should be calculated, therefore, can lead to major changes in total overall costs. In turn, this can have an impact on whether a particular problem is recognized and prioritized in the government policy cycle. So, in the pursuit of demonstrating high costs, many economists have challenged the boundaries of traditional cost categories. More and more they are quantifying aspects of human lives that have not traditionally been measured and valued within an economic paradigm. To illuminate the more controversial aspects of economic evaluations, it is useful to briefly review the methodology and cost categories utilized in COI studies.

Tangible Costs

In most economic costing projects, a distinction is made between tangible and intangible costs. Tangible costs can be differentiated as direct and indirect costs. Both direct and indirect costs reduce the total sum of goods and services that any given society can devote to other social policy priorities. Direct costs represent the value of resources used to prevent, detect, and treat health impairments or their effects. They typically include goods and services used for the diagnosis, treatment, continuing care, rehabilitation, and terminal care of people experiencing a major illness or impairment, usually categorized according to major diagnosis or diagnosis groupings. For example, these cost categories include expenditures for hospitalization, outpatient care, services of physicians and other health care professionals (e.g., counsellors, psychologists, social workers), and pharmaceuticals. Also included are costs to third parties. These may include insurance companies, government agencies, or even family or friends. This category of costs may also extend to patients who incur direct expenses. Direct costs can therefore include the financial outlays connected with services directly required as a result of a particular illness, disease, condition, or experience. This applies not only to the state (government) but also to the individual, her/his family, and third parties.

Indirect costs include morbidity and mortality costs. Morbidity costs represent the value of lost output through reduced productivity or lost productivity (absenteeism) due to short- and long-term disability caused by illness or disease. Mortality costs are those associated with premature death. According to Rice, "morbidity and mortality destroy labour, a valuable economic resource, by causing people to lose time from work and other productive activities or by bringing about premature death."[26] These cost categories are high. Based on a literature review of studies that consider the indirect costs of disease, Leona VanRoijen et al. reported that "on average indirect costs represent 52% of the total disease costs."[27]

There is no single value of life that is universally recognized in public-sector decision making. However, the most widely used measure is referred to as the human capital approach. It is by far the most commonly used approach to valuing forgone productivity/output in COI studies. In the standard human capital approach it is assumed that the value to society of an individual's life is measured by future production potential, which is usually calculated as the present discounted value of expected earnings. The use of market measures to value a person can be found as far back as Thomas Hobbes, who wrote, "Value or WORTH of a man, is as of all other things, his Price; that is to say, so much as would be given for the use of his Power."[28]

Calculating morbidity costs involves applying average earnings by age and gender to work-loss days for those currently employed, attaching a dollar value for unpaid work and applying labour force participation rates and earnings to persons who are unable or too sick to be employed. This approach is not without its shortcomings. Because the value of human life is based on market earnings, it yields very low values for children/ adolescence (pre-work years) and the retired elderly (value of retirement). The human capital approach may undervalue or overvalue life if labour market imperfections exist and wages do not reflect true abilities, as may be the case with many women.[29] For example, it sets results in an unavoidable bias towards those diseases that affect the employment of white, middle-class males.[30] In sum, Steven Grover et al. argue: "The human capital approach ... is often criticized because it tends to discriminate against economically disadvantaged people and groups with lower participation in the labour force, such as women, young people, those with disabilities and the elderly people."[31] Nevertheless, in COI studies this remains the standard approach for valuing life.

Intangible Costs

As a result of certain illnesses there can be a variety of psychological, emotional, and social losses. Unlike tangible losses such as medical expenses or lost wages, there are certain "commodities" that have no obvious market price or value. These include, for example, anxiety, loss of self-esteem, grief, resentment, isolation, heightened anxiety, loss of companionship/ friendship, pain and suffering, and reduced quality of life. Intangibles have also been identified as functions of government, a healthful environment, wisdom, religious/philosophical commitments, and the right to bear children.[32] Intangible costs do not directly involve a loss of output and are not readily measurable.

Nevertheless, several economists have developed techniques to quantify intangible losses.[33] They have developed specific methodologies for quantifying psychological and emotional losses such as pain and suffering and reduced quality of life. Economists who have attempted to calculate intangible losses use two basic methods. First, they rely on surveys in which people place a value on different dimensions of their ability to function (mobility, cognitive, bending and grasping, pain, sensory, cosmetic). Capacity losses are then combined into a single quality-adjusted life year lost per injury, using survey data on the relative value loss associated with each dimension and level of functional loss. This is what is often referred to as a *willingness to pay* approach. For example, based on what people state they are willing to pay, or what they actually pay for small gains in their survival probability, Miller and Galbraith have calculated as $2.4 million per workplace fatality.[34] A similar willingness-to-pay approach to calculating the quality of life costs of alcohol-involved automobile crashes yielded an amount of $1,803,423.[35]

The second method that has emerged is a court-awards approach to valuing the loss of quality of life, using compensation awarded by juries for pain and suffering. For some economists, these awards demonstrate a society's willingness to attach a dollar figure to elements such as pain, anguish, grief, and suffering. McLurg explains this approach by referring to the American legal system: "the standard method for computing pain and suffering damages is the *per diem* approach by which a plaintiff's counsel asks a jury to multiply the period of time during which a plaintiff can be expected to experience the pain and suffering (broken down into seconds, minutes, hours, days, months or years) by an economic value assigned for each unit of time. The product is the suggested pain and suffering award."[36] As part of investigating the cost of crime to victims, Miller and Cohen[37] have estimated pain, suffering, and lost quality of life based on jury award data from jury verdict research in the United States, which lists compensatory damage awards and medical care and productivity losses. This approach predicated that between 70 percent and 80 percent of jury compensation amounts could be equated to reduced quality of life, pain, and suffering.

In full economic evaluation studies – namely, cost-effectiveness and cost-utility analyses – there has been some movement to measure intangibles using non-economic measures.[38] However, the quantification of human losses – the loss of life and psychological and emotional losses such as pain, suffering, grief, and deterioration in the quality of life – continue. This practice is an issue for social policy debate. While the great majority of economists agree that intangible costs are substantial, whether or not they should be quantified is a point of contention. At the heart of the debate is whether or not putting a dollar figure on intangible human costs, or even on the value of life, should be part of any policy evaluation process. This is part of a larger discussion that involves questioning the extent that market rhetoric, which is central to the liberal policy paradigm, should be relied upon to measure all that we value.

On the one hand, there are those economists and policy decision makers who support universal commodification. They believe that all that we value can be quantified, including the value of life and pain and suffering. Moreover, proponents of this position maintain that these *should* be quantified. Economists often point out that it is a moot point to debate the quantification of the value of life. They correctly point out that the practice is well entrenched in policy decision making. For instance, Single et al. argue that, "when it comes to policy advice, an economist cannot always avoid putting some value on life ... In practice, we incorporate some value for lives saved when we make policy decisions, even if a dollar value is not stated. All economists are doing explicitly is what other policy advisers and policy makers do implicitly."[39] Moreover, to refrain from such calculations can have undesired consequences. For some the refusal to compare lives and money is not to treat life as infinitely precious, it is to treat life as worthless.[40] Economists like Robert Evans believe that to leave the value of life and intangible costs out of an evaluation process is bad economics as well as bad policy.[41]

Others, however, have questioned the proper limits of commodification. Radin provides one of the most compelling critiques of universal commodification. She maintains that the archetype, universal commodification, is oversimplified – a caricature, a one-dimensional world of value.[42] Her argument is persuasive because she makes it explicit that there are certain things that monetary evaluations cannot capture; in fact, they may debase what humans value in regard to their personhood. To this end, Radin examines the appropriate scope of the market for *contested commodities,* which, she explains, are instances in which we experience personal and social conflict about the process and results of placing a market value on a particular aspect of human life. These include, for example, prostitution, the selling of babies, and tort compensation for pain and suffering. Radin does not entirely reject the commodification of such goods close to personhood; rather, she argues for a compromise to which she refers as *incomplete commodification.* Incomplete commodification can be interpreted as "a recognition that some form of purchase and sale are called for but with restrictions of one kind or another."[43]

Similarly, in her critique of market-determined valuations, Anderson asks, "why not put everything up for sale?"[44] In answering this question, she argues that there are a number of reasons we should not utilize market norms to govern decisions in areas such as safety and the environment. She proposes an effective framework for determining the proper limits of the market for valuing certain goods, and she poses two questions: "do market norms do a better job of embodying the ways we properly value a particular good than norms of other spheres? If not, then we shouldn't treat them as commodities but rather locate them in non-market spheres. Second, do market norms, when they govern the circulation of a particular good, undermine important ideals such as freedom, autonomy, and equality, or important interests legitimately protected by the state? If so, the state may act to remove the good from control by market norms."[45] Similarly, Joshua Cohen argues that universal commodification conflicts with appropriate ways of valuing goods. Treating something as a commodity is tantamount to asserting that its value can be expressed in a price. He argues that this is not always the case.[46]

The argument that there may be serious problems with quantifying certain human "goods" – properties of persons and their human interactions – is directly relevant to health economics. Some economists have argued that the value of human life should not, and indeed cannot, be expressed in monetary terms. They argue that any cash representation for the value of human life should be resisted.[47] As Rothchild explains, "life is not a marketable good and there are no obvious alternative market signals which could serve as indicators for evaluation."[48] A similar argument has been made regarding the quantification of pain and suffering. Reynolds, for example, argues that "it is beyond the competence of the economist to assign objective values to the losses suffered under [pain, fear, and suffering]."[49] This argument is premised on the assumption that such experiences are *incommensurable,* or, in other words, that they cannot be measured by the same monetary standards as, say, a visit to the doctor. Here Deborah Stone's analysis of quantitative measures is instructive: "once a phenomenon has been converted into a quantitative measure, it can be added, multiplied, divided, or subtracted, even though these operations have no meaning in reality. Numbers provide the comforting illusion that incommensurables can be weighed against each other because arithmetic always 'works' ... Numbers force a common denominator where there is none."[50] For a variety of reasons linked to incommensurability, several economists maintain that it is beyond the competence of the economist to assign objective values to the losses of pain, fear, and suffering.[51] Placing a dollar figure on certain human losses limits our perception of the scope and magnitude of their impact. Without doubt, there is a story of human life and suffering that is not always captured by numbers (e.g., restrictions in activities of daily living, functional health status, pain and suffering).[52]

Outside the realm of health policy, a similarly contentious debate is ongoing in the field of environmental policy. On the one side of the debate there are economists who maintain that economic evaluations must be applied to environmental issues – especially with regard to assessing pollution and the destruction of natural resources. Larry Ruff points out that, "as important as ethics are to the pollution question, all such approaches are bound to have disappointing results for they ignore the primary fact that pollution is an economic problem."[53] This position is also taken by V. Kerry Smith, who argues that "what was a small little noticed area of environmental economics has been a front burner preoccupation of many economists and lawyers."[54]

Certainly, there are real difficulties in assessing a monetary price for the environment (e.g., the value of clean air, water, and animal life). For instance, Anderson points out that there are no satisfactory cash equivalents for unique and irreplaceable goods such as those related to environmental quality and safety.[55] Marilyn Waring argues that it is ironic that the need to establish adequate environmental indicators is market-driven rather than emanating from a concern for the well-being of the community.[56] Their respective discussions open the way to seeing how many aspects of the environment are intrinsically valuable and, therefore, defy monetary quantification.

Ethics and Economics

The question of how far we should apply market norms to certain human goods, and even non-human goods (e.g., the environment), raises what Amartya Sen refers to as the "ethics" question in economics.[57] Arguably, ethics have the potential to inform methodological issues within economics and can be invaluable for directing economic costing studies. And yet, within the discipline of economics, there are conflicting views on whether there is, or should be, any relationship between ethics and economics. The question of the commensurability of the two disciplines has also been raised.[58] Often economists believe that their role is to provide value-free information to policy decision makers.[59] They view economics as a scientific, objective, value-free, positive discipline whose main (if not only) proper concern and criterion of valuation is economic efficiency – in terms of the allocation of scarce resources. And yet, many other economists remind us that the dissociation of economics from ethics is a relatively new phenomenon[60] and that, as a result of this disconnection, economics has become "substantially impoverished." Several economists are therefore attempting to reconnect economics and ethics.[61] They argue that economics does not exist in a vacuum, that economics and ethics naturally come into intimate relations with each other since both deal with the problem of value.[62]

There are a number of specific reasons why ethics matter in economics. First, ethical concerns inform what economists choose to investigate and what questions are asked. Themes, methods, and principles regarding research are all embedded in ethical considerations. As Rothschild explains: "valuation enters quite unavoidably at the start of every research project even though the scientist may not be aware of it."[63] Thus economists have ethical values that help shape the way they do economics. Second, economic actors – citizens from all walks of life – have ethical values that help shape their behaviour. Economists need to take this reality into account when hypothesizing about human nature and human motivations. Third, the public at large and policy decision makers expect advice from economists – advice that is often put into operation. In sum, economics operates in a social context that affects what kinds of investigations are conducted. Moreover, the decisions and advice of economists have practical and material consequences.

It is therefore impossible for economists to avoid making value judgments when they act as policy advisors. Thus, as Weston argues, "one thing that economists could do is to divert more resources to the study of ethics, in an effort to become as proficient at philosophical ethics as they now are at mathematics."[64] Arguably, drawing upon ethics can improve economic analyses and, in particular, the moral dimension of policy problems. In 1977 Cook and Graham noted that, within the discipline of economics, very little theoretical work had been undertaken on the "large class of commodities that are essentially unique or irreplaceable (commodities for which there are no perfect market substitutes)."[65] The paucity of research in this area of economics remains. More recently, Radin has argued that the matter of universal commodification in areas linked to personal identity needs further working out.[66] I contend that an ethic of care provides important direction for the further "working out" of why the propensity to monetize various aspects of our lives, experiences, and interactions may need to be seriously rethought. As Anderson argues: "we can question the application of market norms ... by appealing to ethical ideals which support arguments that goods should be valued in some other way."[67] Radin maintains that it is precisely because the liberal paradigm separates the realm of the market from other areas of our lives that it is unable to effectively respond to the need for the co-existence of both commodified and non-commodified valuations: "for a [liberal] compartmentalizer, the crucial question is how to conceive of the permissible scope of the market. An acceptable answer would solve problems of contested commodification ... I argue that traditional liberal compartmentalization is at best oversimplified and cannot lead to the kind of answer envisioned. Worse, it may tempt us to overlook the ways in which market and non-market compartmentalization of social interactions can and do coexist, and it fails to give us a theoretical handle on how to evaluate these cultural crossroads."[68] In looking at each of the principles of care, I now show how adding an ethic of care to the policy paradigm, which is now solely dominated by liberal values, allows us to begin the process of resolving the issue of contested commodification.

Contextual Sensitivity

The transformative potential of care begins with an examination of the principle of contextual sensitivity, which reveals the distortions inherent in the one-dimensional projection of human nature reflected in liberal theory and mainstream neo-classical economics. Harstock describes the interactions between "rational economic men" within this model: "the paradigmatic connections between people are instrumental or extrinsic and conflictual, and in a world populated by these isolated individuals, relations of competition and dominance come to be substitutes for a more substantial and encompassing community."[69]

Without doubt, because the widely accepted model of rational choice is void of expressive norms and contexts, it sets a standard that is inextricable from the marketplace.[70] From the perspective of a care ethic, this is an incomplete model of human nature and behaviour because it is the product of a context-free analysis. As such, it leads to faulty conclusions regarding human nature, motivations, and standards for human life. To interpret human behaviour without considering an individual's context is to treat a human being as a "social moron."[71] Far from being precise, scientific, and objective, the liberal standard does not adequately represent the diversity of values required for social policy decision making. A contextual understanding of human beings reveals that we are not simply autonomous, rational individuals whose relations with others are competitive and adversarial. An ethic of care reveals that care and human connectedness are key aspects of the human condition and, at the same time, that traditional economics renders them invisible. The principle of contextual sensitivity challenges numerous assumptions that are integral to the neo-classical model.

To begin with, seeing human beings in their full contexts leads us to see that human actions are not always motivated by calculated self-interest; rather, people value reciprocity, altruism, and responsibility towards others. We prioritize choices and outcomes that preserve and protect human and social relationships. Love, obligation, and reciprocity are essential to human lives.[72] We have a psychological need to create something special in our lives and to experience non-instrumental and non-fungible relationships with things and people.[73] As Henry Aaron explains, "People care about others as 'ends' not solely as means to their own egoistic pleasure ... and humans normally derive enormous satisfaction from interpersonal relationships."[74] Likewise, Scott Altman has noted that we have a strong motivation to avoid thinking of others only in terms of their dollar value.[75] Observations of this kind can have a profound impact on how we conceptualize human nature and motivations. They are essential for seeing that there are many valued and cherished aspects of human life that are in no way connected to economics.

For most, human relationships and attachments and the quality of life that we create are just as important, if not more important, than are economic considerations. Mark Sagoff persuasively makes this point: "Not all of us think of ourselves simply as *consumers*. Many of us regard ourselves as *citizens* as well. We act as consumers to get what we want for ourselves. We act as citizens to achieve what we think is right for the community."[76] However, this critical distinction is not made in economic evaluations. This leads us to more readily accept that all that we value can be captured by some monetary calculation. When we accept that everything about our lives can be reduced to a monetary evaluation, we lose sight of the fact that what people value does not always coincide with a monetary sum.[77] Commodification emphasizes a separation between ourselves and what we value, and between ourselves and other people. And yet, what we value and what contributes to our sense of well-being are often directly connected to our ability to "engage in various forms of familial and social interactions," and to our ability to "live life in one's very own surroundings and context."[78]

By applying an ethic of care's principle of contextual sensitivity to mainstream economic models, we uncover the latter's neglect of numerous important dimensions of our human lives, experiences, and behaviours. We begin to see the need for transforming discourse about aspects of our lives and experiences. We begin to see more clearly that there are many ways in which we value things. Economic evaluations that rely upon market norms represent only one dimension of valuation. There are many other ways of expressing and justifying value judgments pertaining to human goods. As Anderson explains, we need to see that goods are plural and that "they can differ in kind or quality: they differ not only in *how much* we should value them, but in *how* we should value them."[79] Indeed, this manner of thinking allows us to seriously reconsider what should fall within the realm of market evaluations. It allows us to think critically about what aspects of our lives should and should not be open to commodification.

To say that something is properly regarded as a commodity is to claim that the norms of the market are appropriate for regulating its production, exchange, and enjoyments. To the extent that moral principles or ethical ideals preclude the application of market norms to a good, we may say that the good is not a proper commodity.[80] To be sure, consensus on these matters does not exist, especially when it comes to questions of infants and children, human reproduction, sperm, eggs, embryos, blood, human organs, and human pain.[81] In these and other cases there are reasons for our refraining from commodification. As Held explains, with regard to such phenomena as education, childcare, health care, culture, and the environment, there is a very good reason for not only or primarily locating them in the market: the market is ill-equipped to pursue many values, including those pertaining to mutually shared, caring concern.[82]

An ethic of care and its principle of contextuality can assist in providing a framework for demarcating which goods can be appropriately commodified. From a care perspective any notion of universal commodification would be rejected as antithetical to a contextual understanding of personhood. There is growing support for this position among economists, legal scholars, and political theorists. For instance, Radin argues that it seems to be intuitively clear that monetizing all aspects of a person, including relations with others, undermines personal identity and fails to capture what is important to human beings: "It appears to facilitate assimilating aspects of personhood to the realm of commodities, which in turn threatens to make personhood as we know it disappear."[83] Similarly, Martha

Nussbaum argues that treating elements of self-constitution in terms of universal commodification is repellent: "to treat the functions themselves as commodities that have a cash value is to treat them as fungible, as alienable from the self for a price; this implicitly denies what the Aristotelian asserts: 'that we define ourselves in terms of them and that there is no self without them.' To treat deep parts of our identity as alienable is to do violence to the conception of the self that we actually have and to the texture of the world of human practice and interaction revealed through this conception."[84] Anderson also maintains that "goods" such as love, admiration, honour, and appreciation constitute distinct modes of valuation.[85] The proper way to value these goods is incompatible with assigning them a price. Finally, Cohen argues that to assign such goods a price is to attribute to them a kind of worth that is incompatible with their true value.[86]

However, an ethic of care demonstrates that human beings see themselves as inherently valuable rather than just in terms of their economic contribution to society. This is a profound challenge to the human capital approach to valuing life. It reveals that life should also be understood in ways that defy commodification. A human capital approach systematically undervalues life by failing to take into account variables such as the pleasure of living and the desire to live. It measures only the economic importance of an individual to society, excluding their significance to their family and friends. People live for reasons other than economic production and material gain. Here the Kantian argument regarding the commodification of slaves is informative. We do not simply value persons because of their utility or their economic contribution to society: we value them because they are worthy in themselves – worthy of dignity and respect. And for Kant, human beings do not have a price because "whatever has a price can be replaced by something else as its equivalent."[87] For him, no exchange value can be placed upon the value of life.

Contextual sensitivity allows us to transcend traditional economic conceptualizations of persons. It necessitates treating all persons as ends in themselves and not as a means to a particular end or consequence. It entails making a distinction between (1) persons who have dignity beyond price and who are owed respect and (2) things which have a price and are valued solely for their use.[88] Just as human lives have more than one form of valuation, so we may infer that the absence of pain, suffering, and discrimination can also be valuable and valued independently of their economic consequences. Contextual sensitivity makes more explicit the realization that, for human beings, value is not unitary. It is not synonymous with a monetary price. It is not reducible to that for which we can determine a market price. Moreover, the worth of a particular good does not necessarily increase with its price. To overlook this fact inevitably leads to a narrow understanding of human nature and an inferior understanding of human beings, what they value, and how they value it.

Responsiveness

When economists and policy decision makers assume that everything that we value can be reduced to a monetary evaluation, the result is the objectification of people. Radin puts it best: "by assuming that all human attributes are possessions bearing a value characterizable in money terms ... we lapse into extreme objectification."[89] From a care perspective, the objectification of persons needs to be countered by responsiveness. Instead of objectifying people, responsiveness empowers them. It provides them with the opportunity to be actively involved as collaborators in a shared inquiry process that seeks to determine what values and needs should be reflected in policy making. Indeed, as Anderson explains: "democratic respect for citizen values is expressed by taking their reasons and principles seriously, not by blindly satisfying their unexamined wants as these are interpreted by economic technocrats."[90]

Responsiveness prioritizes listening to the voices of those who may be affected by policy decisions, "to the voices that are often silent."[91] Martha Nussbaum also emphasizes the importance of narratives: "any social theory that recommends or uses a quantitative measure of value without first exercising imagination along these lines seems to me to be thoroughly irresponsible."[92] Responsiveness widens the inquiry to include an interpretation of value that comes directly from those who may be affected by policy decisions. It derives a very specific form of knowledge that Sen has described as "knowledge based on positional observation."[93] Responsiveness also requires effective mechanisms for participation in social policy decision making. Appropriate institutions and structures are needed to allow people to ensure that their values are responded to and reflected in public policy.

For the most part, however, policy decisions that are informed by economic evaluations tend to ignore "information about individuals' valuations discoverable only through voice and provide no integrated mechanism for enabling people to express valuations of goods that essentially require voice."[94] As a result, the self-expressed, particular needs and desires of citizens cannot be known. What policy makers think of as being responsive to citizens' values may actually be antithetical to what people prioritize. It cannot, however, be assumed automatically that citizens will be satisfied by having all aspects of their lives monetized. Policy makers often fail to capture the ways people value goods outside of market contexts, which in principle cannot be measured by a cash value.[95] By listening to those who are articulating their experiences, needs, and desires, we comprehend more fully the extent to which humans have values that defy economic worth.

For instance, many people consider health to be important in its own right, whereas from the perspective of the market economy, health is only important insofar as it affects the efficient production of commodities.[96] In her recent book, Janice Stein makes similar arguments regarding priorities and the public agenda of Canadians. She contends that "quality of life" issues are at the forefront: public goods such as health care and education are the most important concern for almost 50 percent of all Canadians.[97] Moreover, in its final report, the Romanow Commission on the Future of Health Care in Canada concluded that, in considering whether health care should be a business, the consensus view of Canadians is: "No! Not now, not ever. Canadians view medicare as a moral enterprise, not a business venture."[98] The commission emphasized that Canadians are clear in their support for the core values upon which the health care system is premised – equity, fairness, and solidarity.[99] And, as one presenter to the commission noted, "I think if we could have a health care system that would listen more to the people that it's providing care to, that we would probably be doing a whole lot better."[100]

West has similarly noted how, inappropriately, market commodification dominates legal decision making in contract cases. Simply commodifying damages and losses is, in her view, a failure of the relational ethic of care.[101] For West, commodification conveniently takes the place of treating litigants as *particular* litigants, with the result that the court sees litigants as having the interests of a general class of "contracting parties." According to West, what judges have to do instead is to "listen to the injured patient, the ruined farmer, or the despondent mother to understand the *particularizing details of their predicament*, not simply universalize each case, each injury, and each contract so as to fit it within a more general rule" (emphasis added).[102]

There are other examples that illustrate the reluctance to conceive of everything in economic terms. When economists Robert Rowe and Lauraine Chestnut[103] asked people how much money they would demand in compensation for power plant pollution that would damage the visibility of the scenic Southwest, more than half the respondents had a very strong negative reaction. They either rejected the terms of the question outright or demanded infinite amounts of compensation. The people surveyed perceived the question as an interrogation of their value system, and they responded by stating that this could not be adequately represented by a monetary measurement. Another example can be found in a recent Canadian study of child sexual abuse,[104] in which survivors were asked to document the economic costs of their childhood trauma. While not denying the economic repercussion of their experiences, most survivors emphasized the human costs, for which there is no price or compensation. Respondents explained: "We know that the cost to this country is staggering not only financially but with lost humans never reaching their rightful potential. No amount of money would ever compensate any victim of child sexual abuse so we do ourselves a disservice thinking it will." And, "In reflecting about the cost of the abuse to me my first thoughts are of financial costs. Financial cost to me, oh, that seems too minimal compared to the other things I have lost. Irreplaceable things to which value cannot be attached." And, "How do you restore a whole person? What is the price of a whole person? A whole lifetime?"

Giving voice to persons requires a different methodological approach to policy decision making than the one offered by classical liberal economics. It requires us to go beyond quantitative measurements – even those that attempt to measure outcomes in non-monetary ways.[105] This necessitates a significant shift in traditional methodological approaches to economic evaluations. As Henry Aaron contends: "profound changes in theoretical orientation and research methods are necessary if we are to make significant progress in analyzing major social issues."[106] To this end, social policy decision makers and economists engaged in economic evaluations need to prioritize qualitative methods.[107] Interdisciplinarity in research methods is also required. Jacobson and Newman point out, however, that, "rather than reinventing the wheel when it comes to research methodology, economists can learn from empirical paradigms in related social science disciplines, as well as from interacting with those researchers with inter-disciplinary training."[108] Günseli Berik suggests that economists "should enrich [their] analyses by using data generated in other disciplines on the basis of qualitative methods, which include unstructured interviews, participant observation and fieldwork."[109] Without doubt, qualitative methods help us to better understand why some things cannot be measured using quantitative methods. But they also reveal to us non-economic considerations that we, as citizens, value and want taken into account in social policy decisions.

According to the care principle of responsiveness, policies can no longer be assessed by a group of experts who apply a narrow economic evaluation to determine appropriate policy decisions; rather, those whose lives are affected should be included in all aspects of the evaluation process. We need institutional mechanisms for allowing these persons to articulate their needs and wants in the policy agenda. Responsiveness in the decision-making process is essential to enabling people to describe their situation and to take costs and benefits into account.[110] And, if we ensure that this happens, then there is a good probability that the market norms associated with a liberal paradigm will be shown to produce frameworks that are simply not adequate to enabling people to express how they value their lives, their experiences, their relationships, their communities, and their policy priorities.

Consequences of Choice

By applying an ethic of care focus on the consequences of choice we are able to see how the very existence of a commodification discourse affects social policy decision making. This is because, as Daniel Engster notes, "care ethics ... starts out from the practices and values necessary for individual development, social reproduction and human well-being."[111] The implications of having policy makers accept economic measures for quantifying all aspects of human life should never be underestimated.[112] Such a shift has a direct effect on how we conceive our priorities, values, and society in general. As Stein points out: "values are the bedrock of political and social life; they are our conceptions of the good, of what is desirable, of how social and political life should be configured, and they inform our judgements about public issues."[113] When commodification encroaches upon our lives, alternative forms of evaluation are difficult to champion: after all, there is a trend towards finding better and more comprehensive ways of quantifying our lives. Non-monetary considerations become more difficult to assert and sustain in policy arguments. With Waring, we need to ask: "Do we want all of life to be commodified in an economic model? Must there be only one model, and must economics be at the center?"[114] She warns us that continuing along such a perverse path will lead us into a vicious vortex where we are no longer able to determine the value or worth of anything. This will result in us all "counting for nothing." Indeed, the myopic view of economic primacy leads to misvaluing and undervaluing many aspects of human life. In such a process, we lose the gentler and more humane side of our lives. Indeed, the range of potential harms is substantial and worthy of careful consideration.

When policy makers fixate upon economic costs, they should be criticized for not taking into account the full implications of their decisions. When they reduce everything to numbers, their decisions may well be erroneous. Surely some decisions are morally sound even if they are not cost beneficial or cost-effective. For example, many of the recent decisions concerning deinstitutionalization in the Canadian health care system were justified as cost-saving measures. Increasingly, however, we are beginning to see that communities and families are neither prepared nor able to provide the care and services needed to respond to this shift. In many instances, this policy change is increasing rates of morbidity and mortality among patients as well as among their caregivers. A recent economic cost study on cigarette smoking, undertaken by Phillip Morris for the Czech government, also reveals the dangers of relying exclusively on economic evaluations when making policy decisions. The study concluded that smoking is not costing the Czech government money because government costs in treating smoking-related illnesses are offset by the early death of smokers. In fact, the company reported that, in 1999, smoking produced a net gain of approximately $150 million dollars for the government.[115] The results of this study show that it is not necessarily cost-effective to discourage smoking. However, these results are, without doubt, morally objectionable.

When we are fixated on economic costs, the risk of harm or error in policy decision making is high. Anything that does not fit neatly into the framework of cost calculations can be improperly valued or overlooked and not considered to be of real policy significance. And yet, the personal, community, and societal dimensions of any policy decision are real and significant. Radin provides us with a compelling example when she looks at the impact of rape on its victim. Bodily integrity is non-monetizable. She argues that "we feel discomfort or even insult, and we fear degradation or even loss of the value involved, when bodily integrity is conceived of as a fungible object."[116] The same position is taken by Nussbaum, who argues that "to treat deep parts of our identity as alienable commodities is to do violence to the conception of the self that we actually have and to the texture of the world of human practice and interaction revealed through this conception."[117] Overlooking the significance of human costs and losses that are not easily commodified has serious consequences for persons who may be directly or indirectly affected by a policy decision. The potential for alienation, threat to personhood, and harm is antithetical to an ethic of care.

To avoid harming people and, indeed, degrading their worth, we must be aware that there are different ways of prescribing value. Without doubt, economic calculations provide us with important financial knowledge about the breadth and scope of social problems and health-related illnesses and disease. They can provide information to policy decision makers regarding the monetary consequences of various policy alternatives. Economic evaluations cannot, however, be the definitive means by which we make social policy choices. Economics can never replace morals or ethics. A care ethic helps us to understand that "we value things not just 'more' or 'less' but in qualitatively higher and lower ways."[118] And this leads to a different approach to economic evaluations in health and social policy in general.

The key is to see how economic evaluations fit into a wider decision-making frame, where other values and priorities have equal or sometimes more importance. This is especially true for health policy. Indeed, the commodification of health has been widely criticized. And, as Victor Fuchs reminds us, "major health problems are *value choices:* What kind of people are we? What kind of life do we want to lead? What kind of a society do we want to build for our children and our grandchildren?" He further argues that "the answers we give to these questions, *as well as the guidance we get from economics* [emphasis added], will and should shape health care policy."[119] The approach to value choices resonates with Adam Smith's definition of a "necessary": "by necessities I understand not only the commodities which are indispensably necessary for the support of life but whatever the custom of the country renders it indecent for creditable people, even of the lowest order, to be without."[120] As one participant in the Romanow Commission explained: "For my husband, the war against cancer ended on February 11, 2000. When he and I were married, we had made vows that each of us would stand by the other in sickness and in health, until death did us part. We also held the belief that the health care system in this country had a similar obligation to the people who paid taxes and spent their lives making this a better place."[121]

Further, this line of thinking leads one to reconsider which aspects of human life, experience, and choice should be shielded from universal commodification. The United Nations Human Development Report of 1996 provides some direction in this regard. The report claimed that "many elements of choice defy monetary measurement: the enjoyment of an unspoiled wilderness, the satisfaction from our daily work, the sense of community that grows out of engagement and social activities, and the freedom, peace and sense of security that are common in a good society – all these are impossible to quantify yet they form part of the essence of human development."[122] The process of rethinking the limits of economic evaluations also leads us to critique aggressively the trend of reducing all that we value into an economic calculus. Rather than leading to a progressive development, this trend constricts our understanding of social values and leads us to distort how and why we value those things that have meaning for us. Not everything about our lives can be bought, sold, or quantified in economic terms. E.F. Shumacher's observations concerning the limitations of taking into account all costs – especially those that are difficult to quantify and may therefore be otherwise disregarded – are especially informative for my argument: "[the] procedure by which the higher is reduced to the level of the lower and the priceless is given a price ... can ... never serve to clarify the situation and lead to an enlightened decision. All it can do is lead to self-deception or to the deception of others; for to undertake to measure the immeasurable is absurd. The logical absurdity, however, is not the greatest fault of the undertaking; what is worse and destructive of civilization is the pretence that everything has a price or, in other words, that money is the highest of all values."[123]

If economists and policy makers take seriously the care ethic's principle of the consequences of choice, then they can understand better how important it is to keep certain aspects of human lives, relationships, and even communities separate from market evaluations. Michael Sandel contends that the over-reliance on the market is perhaps the most corrosive threat to social values and civic virtues of communities.[124] The solution is to be clear about what can and should be measured using market reasoning and what should not. As Stein puts it, "we need to pay attention not only to what we can measure, but even more important, to what we cannot."[125] An ethic of care clearly reveals that such distinctions are essential to the well-being of humans. There are aspects of our lives that are too sacred to be bought and sold.

Understanding that there are aspects of our lives and identities that transcend quantification in economic terms can profoundly alter our approach to determining the value of life and pain and suffering. In terms of the value of life, we have reached the point in policy decision making where arguments calling for the elimination of monetary quantifications would be rejected. In the matter of how we value life, the ethic of care makes explicit both the benefits and limits of economic calculations. It helps us to conceptualize a distinction between what Michael Bayles has referred to as "social price" and "personal price."[126] Social price can be understood as the value that one's life has to social policy decision makers. Being able to determine social price is important with regard to making decisions about social policy. However, an ethic of care emphasizes the need to also consider personal price – the value of life to an individual, his/her family, friends, and community. Love, companionship, and caring relations are relevant to how we conceptualize personal price. From the care perspective, "calculations" made in aid of government decisions need to consider personal price. Personal price is reflective of the non-monetary aspect of human life. Because persons should be treated as ends rather than simply as means, both economic and non-economic methods should be employed in making judgments regarding people's worth. Anderson makes a parallel argument with respect to the market in aesthetic goods (such as art): "the fact that there are markets in aesthetic goods does not show that market prices comprehensively measure their value."[127]

So in terms of valuing human life, we can come to a kind of *caring commodification,* which, on the one hand, recognizes the need for some monetary evaluation but, on the other hand, promotes an understanding that human life is worth more than any economic calculation can express. Here Radin's proposal of "coexistence" is informative. She explains that, where different meanings coexist, it is simplistic to think of our social policy choice as binary – as either complete commodification or complete non-commodification. Instead, she argues that it becomes important to recognize the division over how we view commodification and the many non-market aspects of our lives.[128]

In the case of intangibles such as pain and suffering and lost quality of life, a compelling argument can be made about why no monetary quantification should be attempted. Simply put, economic evaluations are sufficiently narrow to make them irrelevant for the broader discussion of certain dimensions of our lives and experiences. Not quantifying intangibles, however, is not the same as denying their existence; rather, non-economic means of illustrating the value of these losses avoids undervaluing and misvaluing these experiences in a way that is harmful to those who undergo them. Thus, there are arguments that hold that some objects should not be applied to market evaluation because this may fail to value them in a proper way.

Important insights in this regard can also be found in tort law. Courts routinely award compensation for pain and suffering. However, Radin correctly argues that any notion that recovery of non-economic losses such as pain and suffering and loss of enjoyment of life "rests on a legal fiction that money damages can compensate for a victim's injury."[129] Compensation for pain and suffering and other intangible losses cannot bring about restitution because the value to the victims of freedom from pain and suffering cannot be reduced to money.[130] Any form of compensation for intangible losses should therefore be considered to be, at best, a symbolic recognition of the harm experienced. To summarize, intangible losses should always be included when considering the overall impact of any health issue. At the same time, it is extremely difficult, if not completely impossible, to put a figure on emotional suffering or deterioration of the quality of life.

To accept a particular choice is to find its consequences acceptable. An ethic of care shows us the harmful consequences of determining social policies through utilizing economic evaluations not bound by considerations of human well-being. It moves us towards an increased appreciation of the significance of non-monetizable aspects of our lives and experiences. Human life and its many dimensions are not merely commodities, and this must be reflected in the policy decisions that we make. Finally, an ethic of care shows us that any economic evaluation of policies and programs needs to be considered for the impact it has on the people it affects, their families, and their communities. After all, in the end, a care ethic "posits meeting needs for care, rather than the pursuit of profit, as the highest social goal."[131]

Conclusion

In applying an ethic of care to our analysis of economic evaluations, we can see how the existence of a commodification discourse affects not only social policy but also society in general. The net result of this discourse has been that market forces are increasingly shaping our values and our lives. Following the principles of care does not necessitate a rejection of economic evaluations. It does, however, require recognizing the limits of such analyses, especially when considering the value and quality of our lives. It leads us to confront that what we count really does matter.

From the standpoint of a care ethic, it is not difficult to see that we are not solely "rational contractors" shaped and motivated by wealth maximization and other related economic considerations. While material production and wealth can be seen as fundamental components of our quality of life and well-being, there is much more to it.[132] In fact, our lives and activities are often embedded in social relations characterized by trust, loyalty, and family commitments. The love, admiration, and affection that we may experience as part of our human relations are often completely distinct from our economic transactions. Care is central to these relations, and it is not exclusively motivated by wealth maximization; rather, it involves "taking the concerns and needs of others as a basis for action."[133]

A care ethic reveals that human lives and human losses are much more than commerce, that they cannot always be forced into an economic evaluation mould. It is therefore critical for us to question and challenge "the commodification of our unique experiences."[134] The ethic of care raises vital questions about policies and programs that use a one-dimensional economics measure. It reveals that there are many different ways of determining the value of something or someone. To value something, Anderson reminds us, "is to have a complex of positive attitudes toward it, governed by distinct standards for perception, emotion, deliberation, desire and conduct."[135] An ethic of care encourages a more humanistic view of economic evaluations and, in turn, of social policy decisions.

While economic evaluations provide important data and insights, they are only one of several inputs in a complex decision-making process. The policy decision framework is not monolithic. However, as long as we continue to allow commodification to squeeze out all other considerations, we will not see what other decision-making values are essential to sound social policy. In the final analysis, it is not that we need to refrain from economic evaluations; rather, we need to broaden what we consider to be *effective* evaluation. As David Seedhouse argues, "it is easiest to measure those things that can be measured most easily. But it is not always true that the most measurable things are the most valuable."[136] An ethic of care focuses our view to this reality. Social policy and, in particular, health policy have both economic and ethical dimensions. The former, however, cannot be overlooked in favour of the latter.

6
Caregiving: Reconceptualizing the Public/Private Divide

Caregiving provides a logical conclusion to an examination of care and social policy because the ethic of care is inextricably linked to this activity. Caregiving also demonstrates the extent to which human beings are interdependent and in need of others for their growth and survival. At the same time, care work has traditionally been synonymous with women's work. In fulfilling their socially prescribed roles as "caring" wives and mothers, women are expected to engage in activities that are often self-sacrificing and that lead to "gender-specific harms"[1] in terms of their status and equality as citizens. There is, therefore, a complex relationship between caregiving and a care ethic. According to Friedman: "on the one hand, care is essential for the survival and development of both individuals and their communities, and care giving is a noble endeavour as well as being often morally requisite. On the other hand, care is simultaneously a perilous project for women, requiring the sacrifice of other important values, its very nobility part of its sometimes dangerously seductive allure. An ethic of care, to be fully liberatory for women, must not fail to explore and reflect this deep complexity."[2] The association of care with women and the unfair burdens that it has placed on them are issues that feminist theorists have had to confront in demonstrating the public relevance of a care ethic. In exploring this tension many feminist care theorists have distanced the care ethic from the gendered activity of caregiving. The task, as described by Tronto, is "disentangling feminine and feminist aspects of caring."[3] As a result, many theoretical conceptions of the care ethic are failing to glean adequate epistemological insights from the actual practices of care. My aim in this chapter is to explore the social practices of caregiving within the context of home care. In so doing I hope to show the relationship between care as an activity and care as an essential moral and political disposition.[4]

Throughout this chapter I draw upon the theoretical principles of a care ethic in order to rescue[5] caregiving from how it has traditionally been conceived within theory and social policy. I intend to demonstrate that the principles of an ethic of care allow us to see more clearly the level of indifference towards care work in general and, in particular, the contributions of informal caregivers. First, by applying the principle of contextual sensitivity, I reveal the gendered effects of current home care policies. Contextual sensitivity uncovers important information about caregiving and nurturing activities. We get a better sense of who is caring and how care work fits into and is complicated by the wider circumstances of these people's lives. Second, the focus on responsiveness reveals the actual effects that policies are having on informal caregivers, including associated caregiving burdens that perpetuate inequality and ill health. Attending to the consequence of choice provides invaluable information, based on the experiences and narratives of caregivers themselves, regarding what concrete policy reforms are needed to mitigate the negative, and to promote the positive, aspects and outcomes of informal caregiving.

An ethic of care thus provides us with the theoretical basis from which to challenge the status quo and, in particular, the current trend towards deinstitutionalization, which is further off-loading a range of caregiving responsibilities onto the private realm. If the principles of care were institutionalized in home care policies, we would take seriously the idea that care, being an essential human need, must be seen as a collective social responsibility to be shared fairly between the government, the community, and the family. It would lead to an approach that deprivatizes care and renders it no longer predominantly a women's responsibility or a matter of morality.[6] It would lead to the proper recognition of and support for those who engage in care work. Drawing on the care ethic, this chapter offers an interpretation of caregiving that recognizes, legitimizes, and values the importance of care but, at the same time, situates itself in "resistance."[7] In the process, we begin to see precisely why a more equitable distribution of care is both a requirement of the care ethic and an issue of justice.[8]

Caregiving and Home Care Policies

"Caregiving" has no unitary definition. It can involve a range of activities, including but not limited to physical and emotional activities associated with looking after, responding to, and supporting others.[9] Care recipients are those with a range of health needs that arise from acute health conditions and chronic or terminal diseases. They are the vulnerable in society – persons belonging to a policy-defined dependency group.[10] The activity of caregiving can take place in a variety of settings in both the public and private spheres, and there are two principal forms of care – informal and formal. Informal care is typically unpaid care provided by family and "significant others," while formal care complements the former and is provided by paid workers.

Currently, and increasingly, the most important source of all forms of care is informal care. Informal care responds to care deficiencies that develop as a result of government policies. The most common form of informal care is home care, which, generally speaking, covers both short- and long-term care. It allows individuals of all ages and with a variety of health conditions to receive medical and social services in the comfort of their own home environment.[11] The specific functions of home care have been defined as: substituting services provided by hospitals and long-term care facilities, allowing patients to remain in their current living environment and thus to maintain a certain level of independence, and providing services and monitoring that lead to lower care costs.[12] Home care allows us to see how essential, yet challenging, care work is to human life. Caregivers must communicate, respond, and relate to those for whom they care.[13] The skills required of a caregiver demand what Hilary Rose describes as a combination of "hand, brain, and heart."[14]

Home care is not under the jurisdiction of the Canada Health Act, and there are significant variations across the provinces in terms of supports available to informal caregivers and recipients.[15] What is consistent across jurisdictions is that the downloading of health care to communities and families is an attractive policy option. It is seen as a way to alleviate demands on the health care system while improving "quality of care" for patients. Perhaps most important, it is considered key to controlling health care costs for governments. In 1995, with the introduction of the Canada Health and Social Transfer (CHST),[16] the federal government embarked on a process of decentralization that has resulted in major reductions in funds for social spending, including health care. Efforts to control public spending on health care have included the shifting of services previously provided in hospitals and other institutional settings to community-based and home care. There has been a marked shift from care provided by skilled health professionals to caregiving provided by less skilled family and home care workers.[17]

Policies pertaining to deinstitutionalization, however, are premised on a number of faulty assumptions, and these require unpacking. First, policy makers assume that there exists, and will always exist, a pool of private labour to provide home care that is "subject to the pressures of affect, kinship obligation and duty, reciprocity, biography, altruism and habit."[18] There is a widespread belief that care provided by families, friends, and communities is more effective because it is thought to be more loving and compassionate than care provided within an institutional settings. Moreover, policy makers *expect* that family and voluntary community organizations will take over "costly public care" work and that, indeed, they have a moral responsibility to do so. As Sheila Neysmith puts it, "caring for others is seen by Canadian policy makers as a private responsibility."[19]

Policy makers assume that the private sphere, centred around a "familialist model," will automatically take over full responsibility for care. As a result of this, governments are not redirecting enough of the resources realized from hospital closures to the families and communities who provide and receive care.[20]

Not surprisingly, home care does result in substantial cost savings to governments. A growing body of literature substantiates the fact that home care is less costly than is institutional care.[21] Nationally, between 1993 and 1996 hospital care expenditures fell by $1,205 million while home care expenditures rose by $452.8 million.[22] Other examples include a 1996 study in Manitoba that demonstrated that providing care in a home yielded a cost saving of 40 percent.[23] Further, a 1998 Saskatchewan study found that government saves $830 per patient when non-acute care is provided in the home rather than in the hospital.[24] Governments work on the premise that, for an equivalent patient and equivalent treatment, care will always be less expensive at home because some kind of personal infrastructure and family support are already there.[25] In the final analysis, governments expect that families should be largely responsible for their own members' dependency. Resorting to public care and collective resources is often considered a failure on the part of families – a failure deserving of condemnation and stigma.[26]

It is not difficult to see that cost savings and cost-effectiveness are premised on the availability of free caring in the home and community. Built into such an assumption is that there is a home and some form of family to care for those who are dependent. Just because informal care is not reflected in any public expenditure equation does not mean, however, that it has no value, associated cost, or negative policy consequence. In a recent study by Fast and Frederick, the estimated replacement value of the work performed by informal caregivers in Canada exceeds $5 billion annually.[27] And there are numerous other economic and human consequences, including those associated with social and psychological well-being. Preoccupied with the financial benefits of home care, governments do not take into account the true costs of deinstitutionalization. Government cost savings calculations gloss over the real costs of off-loading services onto the community and families.[28] In the process, care gets reframed in purely economic terms: it is seen as a problem of "bottom lines" and "cost containment"[29] rather than as an activity that is imperative for social preservation and growth.

Within home care literature, caregivers consistently report feeling a sense of accomplishment and satisfaction thanks to being able to care for loved ones in a setting that is familiar to them. At the same time, their accounts reveal the unfair burdens and disadvantages that home care policies, and the lack of appropriate policies, create for caregivers. Empirical insights from everyday caregiving experiences reveal the extent to which the activity of caring is rendered invisible and politically irrelevant when it is provided in the private realm. The responsibility for care is often off-loaded to the private sphere without adequate public supports and services. For many who partake in care work the system is untenable. The demand for their labour in the home is increasing exponentially as traditional public support systems continue to erode, the populations of seniors increase,[30] and the incidence of diseases such as Alzheimer's, Parkinson's, diabetes, cancer, and HIV/AIDS continues to rise.

The social policy milieu in which home care is operationalized has started to shift. The need for reform in home care has been recently acknowledged by the Romanow Commission's final report, in which it was noted that "caregiving is becoming an increasing burden on many in our society, especially women."[31] Romanow proposed expanding the principle of comprehensiveness, as it appears in the Canada Health Act, to include targeted home care services (e.g., home mental health case management and intervention services, post-acute home care and rehabilitative care, and palliative care). With its 2003 budget, the federal government introduced a $16 billion health reform fund for provinces and territories to target primary health care, home care, and catastrophic drug coverage. Specifically, short-term acute home care, including acute community mental health and end-of-life care, has been identified as an area of priority. In addition, under employment insurance (EI) the government has introduced a six-week compassionate care leave benefit to enable people to care for a gravely ill or dying parent, child, or spouse.[32]

While these policy initiatives provide important improvements to the current situation, they do not attend to the full scope of health needs that give rise to home care. And they do not provide adequate mechanisms to support caregiving in Canadian society. For example, according to a 2002 Decima poll, the majority of caregivers provide care for longer than six months. Over 20 percent report providing care for more than ten years.[33] In addition, the compassionate care leave under the EI program does not attend to women caregivers who do not work or who, because of their specific work situations (e.g., part-time, contract work), do not qualify for EI. So although we are seeing more attention being paid to home care, care work is still relatively marginalized within social policy and its normative underpinnings. And we are far from having a comprehensive home care program in Canada.

The current situation gives rise to the question posed by Hochshild: "If the state refuses to provide a public solution to the care gap by funding service programs, *can* the private realm now really serve as the main source of care?" (emphasis added).[34] I would add to this the following questions – "What are the implications for those who are most affected by policy changes, namely, the givers and receivers of home care?" and "What is the range of policy options and institutional practices available to respond to the demands for care work and the societal norms that currently marginalize and stigmatize care as both a need and a practice?" I approach these questions by applying the principles of care to an examination of how home care policies relate to informal caregivers – the backbone of all societal care work – many of whom are afforded no choice about their roles and responsibilities within the current policy environment. Home care policies informed by a liberal framework do not adequately illuminate or document the realities of deinstitutionalization; they fail to adequately capture the experiences and needs of unpaid caregivers, and they fail to provide adequate solutions to the unfair burden on unpaid caregivers.

The Ethic of Care and Home Care Policy

To understand the difference that the institutionalization of a care ethic could make, one must first examine the inadequacies in the normative assumptions underpinning current home care policy. According to the liberal paradigm, citizens are independent and self-reliant. Our interactions with others assume an equality of social relations that does not recognize the inherent dependencies within which we are all immersed.[35] As mentioned earlier, according to Kymlicka, "justice reasoning not only presupposes that we are autonomous adults, it seems to presuppose that we are adults *who are not care-givers for dependants.*"[36] The caring needed to sustain our lives is segregated into the private sphere, and care work has not been recognized as an integral part of citizenship; rather, it has been recognized as the responsibility of "second-class citizens" – women, slaves, or members of the lower classes.[37] It has not been prioritized as part of "normal" social participation or the "good life," even though it permeates our existence.[38] Illness, disease, and/or disability are thus perceived as rare deviations from our normal functionings rather than as an inherent part of any human life.[39]

The liberal assumption that human beings are self-sufficient is "political solipsism."[40] This "ideal" standard for citizenship does not reflect reality. Much of our lives is devoted to developing and sustaining relationships and communities.[41] It is through our relationships with others that we develop a sense of self and a sense of our place in the world around us. Much of our lives is also spent receiving or providing some form of care. Indeed, illness, disease, incapacitation, and other forms of dependency are regular occurrences throughout the lifecycle. Any conception of society as being something that is composed of autonomous equals blinds us to the inevitability of interdependencies and the provision of care as essential to human life. As Kittay powerfully argues, "we may even say that the long maturation process of humans, combined with the decidedly human capacities for moral feeling and attachment, make caring for dependants a mark of our humanity."[42] Care work is therefore an essential public good. As Fineman reminds us, "every society and every institution in society is dependent upon care taking labour in order to perpetuate and reproduce itself."[43]

And yet, the human need to give or receive care is in no way prioritized by the liberal paradigm. The concept of "citizen as carer" is not as firmly entrenched as that of "citizen as wage worker."[44] The "real worker" of society is someone who engages in paid public work and who is seen as self-sufficient. This, however, is an illusion. The traditional wage worker, like all human beings, has care needs. Inevitably, she/he will also engage in care work. But the caring dimension of these people's lives is rendered invisible because care work is relegated to the private sphere. Moreover, within the current social policy paradigm, individuals are rewarded more for their "selfish" pursuits of economic and material wealth than they are for the care they may provide to others. In fact, the two activities of wage worker and caregiver are often incompatible. The repercussions of this impasse are numerous. From the standpoint of society, the time (often years) that we commit to care work and the lives that we may affect do not seem to matter. Indeed, by undertaking work that is not considered productive, and that does not come with adequate social entitlements, informal caregivers frequently jeopardize their economic futures. As Arnlaug Leira explains, "what matters is the formal work contract and the wage. Access to the full range of societal entitlements, and to the better income when pensioned, is accorded only to those who are attached full-time to the formal labour market in adult years."[45]

In order to shift our thinking about the significance of care, the prevailing values and priorities arising out of a liberal paradigm require serious interrogation. The conceptualization of the self as free, independent, and involved in freely chosen relationships should be challenged on the grounds that it does not realistically depict the human condition. Tronto argues that "the most pressing political discussions for us to have require us to toss away forever this model of man as a robust autonomous, self-contained actor."[46] What is needed is a shift in the moral language that underpins social policy. Johnson, for example, calls for a language that establishes "human solidarity and reciprocity as central features of our social order."[47] Ultimately, what is required is a framework that explicitly recognizes the fact of our social interdependencies and the significance of caregiving work. The ethic of care can provide this alternative moral language precisely because it "elevates care to a central value in human life."[48] From the perspective of a care ethic, caregiving is a typical experience. An ethic of care allows us to recognize that, at different points in their lives and in different contexts, most citizens alternate between the roles of care-providers and caregivers.[49] In fact, an ethic of care raises the possibility that every citizen will be a caregiver at some point in their lives.[50]

According to the Canadian Institute for Health Information, there is little information currently available on the experiences and, specifically, the burden of care being reported by informal service providers.[51] While more research may be needed, there is enough data to understand the current problems, burdens, and needs of informal caregivers. And one can derive enough of a knowledge base from the self-reported experiences of informal caregivers to inform policy changes in home care and beyond. Therefore, I draw upon a number of Canadian studies that report qualitative findings about the experiences of informal caregivers[52] and analyze these in accordance with a care ethic.

Contextual Sensitivity

Typically, social policy analyses do not adequately take into account the social contexts within which caregiving takes place. Because care has typically been viewed as an integral part of the private domain, caring work tends to be invisible. Yet caring for others doesn't just happen. As Lappalainen and Motevasel remind us, care demands time and work as well as someone to carry it out.[53] Contextual sensitivity reveals to us where the majority of care work takes place, who carries it out, and under what conditions. Perhaps most important, contextual sensitivity allows us to grasp the grave social imbalance between formal support and services and informal caregiving.

The overwhelming amount of caregiving in Canada and elsewhere is provided in private households by informal caregivers.[54] In fact, between 85 percent and 90 percent of all care is provided informally.[55] Informal caregivers are predominantly family members, although friends, neighbours, and volunteers also do a considerable amount of caring work.[56] More often than not, informal caregivers – regardless of class, race, culture, age, marital status, or sexual orientation – are women. All caring work falls disproportionately on the shoulders of women, and often disproportionately on the shoulders of immigrant women and women of colour.[57] Research has demonstrated that, in all industrialized Western countries, caring work – ranging from attending to the needs of children, the elderly, the sick, and the disabled – is largely provided by unpaid women and takes place in the private realm. In comparison, little care is provided by the state, through the market, and/or by voluntary non-profit organizations.[58]

According to Statistics Canada, 66 percent of informal caregivers are women. This translates into approximately 14 percent of all Canadian women over the age of fifteen.[59] By way of particular examples, research has demonstrated that 75.4 percent of dementia patients living in the community have a female caregiver.[60] Further to this, 96 percent of the primary caregivers of children with disabilities are women,[61] as are 61 percent of the caregivers of seniors with functional disabilities.[62] In some cases, men are becoming increasingly engaged in caregiving work. According to the 1996 General Social Survey,[63] 10 percent of the men compared to 14 percent of the women provided help to a person with a long-term health issue.[64] Nevertheless, the overall responsibility still falls disproportionately on women even though *both* men and women are equally vulnerable to dependency needs. There continues to be little recognition of this gender disparity and of how current social policies reinforce this imbalance in caring responsibilities. Because it is assumed that women are available to undertake caring work, they shoulder the burden of this work, which offers little recognition, compensation, training, or protection in case of injury. Annette Baier correctly refers to women caregivers as "the long ... unnoticed proletariate."[65]

Although only one family member may be experiencing an illness, disease, or disability, in many cases the entire family is affected.[66] And it is important to point out that many caregivers provide care to more than one person. For example, almost 9 percent of female caregivers of seniors with functional limitations were caring for five or more persons at one time, compared with 5.5 percent of male caregivers.[67] In addition to their family responsibilities the majority of informal caregivers are employed outside the home. According to Keating, this pertains to three-quarters of the men and half of the women who do care work.[68] These dual responsibilities often lead to work and caregiving conflicts. Research has shown that caregiving interferes with the work environment in terms of absenteeism, increase in sick days, increase in irregular hours, and use of work time for caregiving activities.[69] These may be exacerbated for women, who are less likely than men to have any flexibility in their work situation.[70] It has been demonstrated that women are at higher risk of choosing part-time employment or quitting their jobs.[71] Fast et al. have estimated that women caregivers who relinquish their paid employment for unpaid labour may give up between $15,000 and $26,000 annually in income.[72]

For informal caregivers there are high economic costs associated with caregiving. They report substantial out-of-pocket expenses and little financial remuneration through the tax system. At present, there is a medical expenses tax credit. Beginning in 1998, the federal government started offering a caregiver tax credit for those who live with and care for dependent relatives. The relative has to be a Canadian resident, eighteen years of age or older, and a child, grandchild, brother, sister, niece, nephew, parent, grandparent, aunt, or uncle. The credit available cannot exceed $400 and is available only to those whose annual income falls below $13,853.[73] For many caregivers, the amount is insignificant in terms of overall economic status and in fact does not offset many out-of-pocket expenditures.[74] As Rice and Prince point out, financial relief is "selective." Numerous caregivers are ineligible because the person for whom they care receives the federal elderly income benefits, which put them above the threshold for relief.[75]

The physical effects of caregiving are profound. Acute, chronic, or terminally ill patients have different needs. Home care is unique in that it both encompasses and transcends traditional medical services. Caregivers provide what are referred to as the instrumental activities of daily living (IADL). These range from housework (including cooking, laundry, and cleaning) to errands, shopping, banking, transportation to appointments and home maintenance (including yard work). In addition, tasks can involve the more personal and medical aspects of care, which are referred to as activities of daily living (ADL). These include dressing, bathing, eating, toilet use, brushing teeth, washing hair, and the administration of various forms of medication.[76] Then, of course, there is emotional care, which, by many accounts, is what is of primary importance to gravely ill or dying patients.

In terms of tasks performed, gender differences have also been identified. Women tend to provide intimate, hands-on care, including bathing and grooming, while men provide care such as transfer and transportation.[77] Female caregivers often provide the most personal and stressful kinds of caring.[78] In all instances tasks are becoming more challenging because caring work is becoming medically complex and technologically advanced. Despite those who contend that the shift from institutions to hospitals to the home is simply "care being sent home," there are growing expectations that informal caregivers should be capable of such sophisticated medical interventions as tracheotomy care, supervising the use of ventilators and oxygen administration, and tube feeding.[79] Challenging the assertion that this is simply returning care work to its rightful place, Armstrong and Kits point out that "our grandmothers never cleaned catheters or checked IV tubes, they did not examine incisions or do much wound care."[80]

Caregiving is also affected by the province/territory in which one resides. The standards for home care eligibility requirements are different in different areas, and costs to the caregiver and patient vary. Home care can be publicly funded, privately delivered, publicly funded and publicly delivered, or privately funded and privately delivered. In many jurisdictions user fees are part of support services for home care. Service limits mean that only those with the financial wherewithal are able to purchase needed services and respite. Not surprisingly, it is those with material resources who are best able to cope with the burden and costs of caring. They are able, for example, to purchase private help.[81] Those who may need to move to another province to receive care from a family member may, due to residency requirements, not be eligible for home care services there. As a result, many informal caregivers leave their homes, families, and jobs to move to another province to provide care.

Informal caregiving is further complicated by geography, depending on whether one resides in a rural or urban setting. In general, rural caregivers provide more hours of unpaid work than do urban caregivers. In addition, those for whom they care are typically older and experience higher rates of disability and chronic illness than do those cared for by their urban counterparts.[82] Rural caregivers often lack income security in the face of longer-term illnesses and disabilities.[83] They also provide care in relatively poor-quality housing conditions with fewer social services and supports than are available to urban caregivers.[84] For example, rural settings often impede access to a range of social services, transportation, and respite facilities. Family supports may also not be readily available. As a result, the ability of rural caregivers to do their job is adversely affected.[85] This has been reported as particularly acute in Aboriginal communities. For example, Aboriginal women are often charged with caring for children who have chronic chest ailments. They are expected to provide chest care, pummelling, and suction in cold, damp, substandard housing conditions and often with no running water.[86]

Finally, caregiving is affected by changing demographics and social trends. Decreased family size, increased geographic mobility, rising numbers of women entering the workforce, and elevated divorce rates are affecting the availability or willingness of family members to provide care.[87] And we must consider the pressures of globalization. International trade agreements have and will continue to have implications for government services, including health care. In fact, home care has been identified as one of the health care service areas that is most affected by the General Agreement on Trade in Services (GATS) and the North American Free Trade Agreement (NAFTA).[88] The gendered effects of this dynamic have also been identified.[89] These agreements may undermine public supports for home care and informal caregivers. Specifically, they may affect the ability of the federal government, provinces, and territories to reform home care and to increase public funding and delivery of health care services.

Responsiveness

Often, governments discuss care in terms of partnerships, but as many studies have concluded, informal caregivers do not feel that they are being listened to in any meaningful way.[90] Policy makers often assume that they are in the best position to frame social problems and to develop appropriate social policy responses. In the case of home care, they assume that they have the knowledge to be able to judge what is in the best interest of the patient and care provider. There is real danger that those in positions of power shape decisions in a way that does not correspond to the real-life situations, ideas, and priorities of people affected by policy.[91] What an ethic of care's principle of responsiveness underscores is the need to challenge this hegemony and to allow traditionally absent perspectives to be reflected in social policy deliberations and decision making. This entails listening to voices that may be silent and/or marginalized. It entails recognizing those perspectives, even if they challenge the status quo. Clement has similarly noted what is required is a discourse that is available to the average citizen so that each person has the power to participate and to effect political and social change.[92] People and communities need to be able to determine their own needs and the most appropriate ways to meet them.[93] This enables them to experience a greater sense of control, empowerment, and self-determination.

Within the context of home care, responsiveness necessitates listening to the voices of both patients and caregivers. From a care ethic perspective, policy problems would be framed differently and policy responses would not be limited by what the "system" or policy makers think is necessary; instead, they would expressly reflect the insights and self-identified needs of those who receive care in what Fraser refers to as a "politics of needs-interpretation"[94] and within what Sevenhuijsen has described as "on the ground knowledge of actual needs for care."[95] Without doubt, home care policies can be substantially improved if the perspectives of patients and caregivers are enjoined with those of "expert" policy makers. Discursive space for providers and receivers of care is necessary if we are to better grasp the dynamics of caregiving. In this regard, informal providers of care, as the majority group of all caregivers, have particularly unique insights to offer. They make care publicly visible in a way that makes it difficult for policy makers to discount it. Listening to their collective experiences we see why care is needed, what it means to be dependent and vulnerable, and what is required if effective caregiving is to take place.[96] Hooyman and Gonyea explain that attending to caregivers in this way "is the first step in breaking the silence that surrounds the issue of caregiving and is a basis for changing the prevailing pattern of care."[97]

Canadian research has also shown that caregivers want their expertise and insights to be recognized and to inform home care policy. As one Nova Scotia study concluded, informal caregivers express a "need to be involved in shaping policies, programs, and treatment choices that affect them and those that they care for."[98] A care ethic's principle of responsiveness not only makes this possible but also considers attentiveness to others' particular needs as a fundamental prerequisite to sound social policy. Here it is also important to emphasize that every caregiving situation is different and that every caregiver has unique concerns and difficulties.

The narratives of caregivers substantiate this diversity. Their experiences and concomitant needs are as diverse as the range of care that is provided in the home. At the same time, there are a number of common themes that underscore their experiences and illuminate the impact of care work. While the narratives of informal caregivers reveal that burdens are often great, and that in many instances the system contributes to these, they also divulge benefits associated with the experience of caring. In the final analysis, responsiveness leads us to understand that both burdens and benefits need to be considered and evaluated.[99]

At times, informal caregivers report that they willingly undertake their roles and responsibilities. As a caregiver in Quebec explains: "When you love someone you want to do what you can and as much as you can for them. They need love, companionship, and understanding."[100] Informal caregivers also emphasize their desire to reciprocate the care they received as children: "It was only fitting because as a child she was the one who took care of me when my parents died. It is she who paid for my university studies. So for me, it felt like it was my turn to take care of her."[101] And "I'll do what I can to keep my mother away from institutional care. She has been a good parent and I like to respond in kind."[102] Not all caregivers choose their roles voluntarily: informal care does not always occur within the context of a loving relationship. Sometimes caregivers undertake and continue their work out of a sense of forced obligation or even fear. As Hilary Graham argues, "caring ... is experienced as a labour of love in which the labour must continue even when the love falters."[103] Regardless of why they become informal caregivers, many informal caregivers share experiences – a number of which have real implications in terms of their health, social life, relationships, and economic status. Caregivers experience a range of consequences within a societal context in which governments and institutions are not always responsive to the unfair burden of care work. As Fineman notes, the caregiver is often "caught within social configurations and institutional arrangements that are unjust."[104]

For example, all informal caregivers consistently report health disturbances. Statistics Canada has reported that 20 percent of Canadian caregivers report deterioration in health.[105] Women report impacts on their health twice as often as do men. Keating has found that almost one-third of women (27.5 percent) versus just over one-tenth of men (10.6 percent) report impacts on their health as a result of caregiving.[106] Health disturbances and impacts can be in the form of physical side effects, including muscle strain, spasms, knee injuries, back pains, and sleep disturbances.[107] They also include a range of emotional stresses and frustrations. One Saskatchewan caregiver explains: "My disabled son was born 35 years ago ... Today I am 75 years old and a widow. I'm finding caregiving for my child to be more stressful than it used to be. The most difficult part of taking care of my son is his mood swings. Sometimes he can be really stubborn, while at other times he just outrightly refuses to talk to me."[108] Another describes the frustration and monotony of caregiving: "I don't find the physical activities, such as lifting him, demanding. Instead the repetitiveness of the tasks is what I find frustrating. Having to do the same tasks over and over again and always at a specific time and place is almost maddening."[109]

Many say that their stress comes from not having enough support to assist with their care work. For example, studies by the Roeher Institute in 2000 found that stress was caused not by having a child with disabilities but, rather, by the lack of community care and support for helping to care for that child.[110] Most worry about the cumulative physical and emotional effect on their health. As one Nova Scotia caregiver explains: "If we don't take care of ourselves physically, mentally, and spiritually, we then become invalids ourselves."[111] And another talks about the effects not only on one's health but also on one's sense of self and on family life: "If caregiving becomes all-consuming one can lose their identity. Emotions can build causing anger and frustration; family breakdown can even occur."[112]

Caregivers also report on the economic consequences related to their work. Informal caregivers experience economic costs as a result of interruptions to their employment and/or out-of-pocket expenses. In the 1996 General Social Survey, 55 percent of women and 45 percent of men stated that their employment had been affected. In a 2002 study of palliative caregivers in Nova Scotia, Quebec, and British Columbia, roughly 25 percent of caregivers reported working fewer hours as a result of their role and concomitant responsibilities. Their experiences, as well as those of other caregivers, are reflected in the following quotes: "I'm in debt now and I have to work when I could have been retired now. I used all my RSPs to pay for her. I spent around $200,000 in total for rent, food, medications, [and] therapy, including my own expenses."[113] And "It's hard to keep on top of work and caregiving responsibilities. Working less would make things easier but that's impossible because we really need the money right now."[114]

It is interesting to note that caregivers often do not report economic losses, even when their caregiving interferes with promotions and employment status.[115] Indeed, economic hardship results from more than work disturbances: it also results from lost opportunities for career development. In the words of one unpaid caregiver in Newfoundland, "I missed opportunities for professional development, such as conferences. My career advancement was put on hold. I know a woman who gave up working to care for a husband with Alzheimer's disease."[116] Personal and out-of-pocket expenses are also often part of caregiving. National studies have reported that between 44 percent and 63 percent of caregivers incur extra expenses, which include anything from medical items, social service costs, gifts, entertainment items, and travel to food expenditures.[117]

Beyond health and economic consequences, informal caregivers claim disruptions to their day-to-day lives. For example, in the General Social Survey of 1996, 45 percent of caregivers reported modifying their social activities (25 percent changed vacation plans).[118] In a 1999 provincial survey in Alberta, 44 percent of caregivers reported that their work and responsibilities were a minor inconvenience and 12 percent reported that they involved a major disruption of their normal activities.[119] It is also reported that a sense of isolation is consequent upon informal caregiving. This seems to be greatest among immigrants whose first language is neither French nor English and who face difficulties gaining access to culturally appropriate services and programs.[120] Those who provide care often have to move. According to the same General Social Survey noted above, 12 percent of caregivers surveyed reported that they had moved to be close to the person for whom they were caring. Indeed, in 1996 nearly half a million Canadians moved in order to receive or to give care. What is even more significant is that the majority of these people were married, and more than one-third had children of a young age (fifteen years or younger) and were employed.[121]

Another consistent theme among informal caretakers involves their sense that they cannot, despite their best intentions and efforts, care enough to satisfy all the needs of their patients. For example, palliative caretakers[122] frequently report that, in retrospect, they should have been more patient, attentive, and kind: "I would have controlled myself better," "I wouldn't have screamed at him," and "Because of my exhaustion, I felt impatient and tried not to show it but I did." Informal caregivers also talk about the difficulties they experience in making the transition to a caregiving role with someone with whom they have shared friendships and other intimate relationships. This often requires caregivers to take on dual and sometimes conflicting roles. This conflict is perhaps best illustrated in the recollection of a BC informal AIDS caregiver: "we were friends to begin with and I cared for him. To get into it, I had to become two people. One, his friend, and second, his caregiver ... The two can't meet – the friend and caregiver can't mix because a caregiver requires the ability to do the job but, at the same time, in order to accomplish something like feeding or bathing him or changing his diaper for example, a friend can't do that. A friend can't push him to eat, a friend can't change his diaper." Care theorists have grappled with the potential harm of "caring too much." While the principle of responsiveness does require the caregiver to be attentive to the care receiver, it does not require self-sacrifice. It does not require caregivers to maintain their relationship with a care recipient without any regard to the quality and health of that relationship. Caregivers need to see how caregiving activities, including the emotional investment involved, can undermine their integrity as caregivers. Being responsive to others should not be confused with being absorbed into others.[123] Here it is crucial to acknowledge that an ethic of care does prioritize the autonomy of the caregiver. However, unlike autonomy as conceptualized in the justice tradition, we are talking about an autonomy that prioritizes relationships, integrity, and self-respect. Applied within the context of the caregiver-care receiver relationship, it is the skills associated with relational autonomy that allow a caregiver to critically reflect on the kind of care she or he is providing.[124] In sum, it protects against any system that places unjust burdens or expectations on care providers.

Aside from the considerable negative impacts and burdensome costs and consequences, informal caregivers do report positive aspects of their roles and responsibilities. For example, in the national study of palliative caregivers, over 90 percent of all informal caregivers reported that their experience gave meaning to their lives because they were able to help another person in a profound manner.[125] Many reported that they felt it was a "privilege" and a "gift" to be part of the palliative care process. As one cancer informal caregiver in British Columbia explained: "I had something to do. I was helping her and it was a good feeling. I felt important." Said another: "It was the most incredible experience other than giving birth." Among GSS respondents, the majority of caregivers (64 percent) responded that caring for others strengthened their relationship with them.[126] Keating's[127] numbers were higher, with 90 percent of female and 86 percent of male caregivers of seniors reporting that their relationships with their patients had improved throughout the process of caregiving. Some examples include the following report by a male Nova Scotia AIDS caregiver: "It brought us closer together. It is a privilege to be with someone at the end of their life. I would have hated to miss the opportunity."[128] In sum, those who engage in caring work understand the value of the work and its contributions to society. According to Tronto, "that care-givers value care is neither false consciousness nor romantic but a proper reflection of value in human life."[129]

Consequences of Choice

Within the current Canadian policy context more attention is being given to home care. And, while some important changes have recently been introduced through targeted federal monies and a compassionate caregiver leave, these initiatives do not go far enough in challenging the extent to which "families supplement public care."[130] Translated into home care policies and programs, the "family supplement" is, for the most part, the unpaid work of women. As the narratives of informal caregivers show, the effects of caregiving coupled with oft-lacking public support seriously undermine caretakers' abilities to provide effective care.

Informal caregivers are incurring substantial economic and human costs that are undermining their equality. For many, the demands of caregiving are exceeding their capacities to cope. Short-term cost savings due to the retrenchment of government-supported services will be subsumed by a variety of medium- and long-term consequences.[131] By not providing adequate resources to informal caregivers, policy makers are risking, for instance, increases in health care costs due to related injuries and illnesses.[132] This can further strain the health care system and even spill over into other sectors, including social services and social assistance. As one caregiver succinctly states: "As a caregiver, you are living constantly with stress and ongoing stress can make you ill; and no pill can fix that."[133]

Surveys and polls demonstrate the importance that Canadians place on health and, in particular, on home care. For instance, in 1998 85 percent of Canadians wanted to have home care included under the Canada Health Act.[134] In 1999 80 percent supported the inclusion of home care under Medicare.[135] The Romanow Commission also reported that "Canadians have said that home care services are too important to be excluded from the definition of insured health services under the *Canada Health Act*."[136] The current state of affairs does not reflect these priorities. Nor have we seen any changes addressing caregiver needs reflected in provincial standards or guidelines,[137] even though informal caregivers are on the front lines and have the knowledge to improve home care policies. They are consistently asking for the opportunity to share their knowledge and to have that knowledge reflected in policy decision making. Caregivers request "more choice in what we think is appropriate for our loved ones, more involvement in the decision making."[138] They also think that "the health care system ... should access [the] ... knowledge ... of the caretaker."[139] Indeed, caregivers, as citizens, should be engaged in all stages of the policy process and at all levels of decision making – municipal, provincial, and federal.

From the perspective of the care ethic, weighing the consequences of policy choices is integral to alleviating preventable suffering and improving citizens' quality of life. Taking into account the consequences of choice means evaluating the implications of choosing not to respond to the voices of those affected by policy. To date, this has resulted in home care policies and other related policies that are not as effective and humane as they could be. At the same time, such an analysis opens the door to seeing possible alternatives – namely, the potential for home care policies to be transformed if policy makers were to respond to the self-expressed needs of caregivers. From the perspective of a care ethic, there is much to be learned from informal caregivers in terms of what good care might look like and of how social policy can be developed to support such care. Seeing informal caregivers in this light is, as Harrington puts it, promoting "the idea that someone who *is* caring, who understands caretaking, who knows its importance, and who recognizes a caretaking crisis would be a highly valuable decision maker in government."[140] The result of the last principle of care is that we begin to think seriously about the social reality of care, the needs of caregivers, and the more general question about how care and policy making should interact. The hope is that those specifically responsible for policy making may be inspired to start moving in the direction of "judging with care."[141]

Most informal caregivers emphasize the need for a flexible system of home care that would allow for choice with regard to how care work is incorporated into one's life. This includes the ability to choose whether or not one wants to become a caregiver as well as the opportunity to assess whether one is capable of such an undertaking. For example, the National Forum on Health reported that, while informal caregivers are not opposed to providing care, they do not want to be "conscripted" into such a role.[142] And yet, more often than not, this is precisely what happens because there are no other options available for attending to care needs. In the words of a female informal caregiver in Saskatchewan: "I have not chosen to become a caregiver, I've been stuck with the job because no one else wants it."[143] Flexibility and choice also entail being able to decide what kinds of caring supports are required rather than being subject to the assumption that all requisite resources are available within the private realm.

Those who have been caregivers, whether through choice or conscription, agree that they need supports that will enable them to provide care with more ease and efficacy than is now the case. For instance, there are numerous examples of requests for increased knowledge and appropriate training: "Knowledge is power. We need to engage in learning all we can regarding a person's illness and home life conditions so that we can better meet their needs."[144] This knowledge and information should be appropriately tailored to the situation at hand. For example, one palliative caregiver explained, "There needs to be better preparation of the family for end of life care." Some caregivers gave other suggestions: "Just as there are parenting classes, there should be caregivers' classes which would enable the caregiver [to have] the confidence to do their best."[145] And "We need information and material to be made available in public places, libraries, clinics, and the internet ... a directory of information and a 1-800 number need to be created, for counselling, legal, break-through-red-tape, and medical information."[146]

Informal caregivers further emphasize the need for "a seamless system and structure"[147] as well as the need for advocates to assist them in navigating the system and gaining access to appropriate supports: "We need to have someone to call and talk about the person and the experience."[148] Support groups in which caregivers can share with others their experiences of care work also ranked high on the list. As one Nova Scotia caretaker explains: "Talking about [our] situations with other caregivers who have similar experiences is beneficial."[149] British Columbia caretakers have also given testimonials that underscore the importance of support initiatives: "You get motivated when you come to the group and I have learned to pay attention to my own needs as a person." And: "When I came to the group I was flat out. The group has helped me to build my self-esteem ... it is surprisingly open, better than I could have dreamed of."[150]

Rarely do informal caregivers report having enough formal supports and professionally trained personnel to relieve them.[151] Their accounts underscore the need for more respite "in the communities" and "for families." Without such relief, the negative consequences are significant. According to one unpaid caregiver, "Overnight care was unavailable and I would go to work on two hours of sleep."[152] Another reports, "I never get time alone. I am always on duty. The demands are hard to handle."[153] For others, there is a need to better coordinate existing services and to improve both informal and formal care. In the words of one unpaid caregiver in Newfoundland, "They [the government] need to provide better continuity of personnel. It's a big burden for the family to train someone new every day."[154] In general, caregivers believe that government should be providing better support for home care. Despite the widely held assumption that caregivers somehow have the financial wherewithal to undertake care work, caregivers themselves report that they require more help.

The conflicts of caregiving and work are enormous, but there are few supports to accommodate the need to undertake both activities. As one respondent to a study on rural female informal caregivers explains, "It's hard to keep on top of the work and caregiving responsibilities. Working less would make things easier but that's impossible because we really need the money right now."[155] Many caregivers have asked for some form of financial compensation: "There should be some kind of compensation, like minimum wage given to the family"; there should be "some way to give some sort of salary to caregivers in [the] form of direct payment."[156] Campbell et al. (1998) calculated that, if rural caregivers were compensated $10.90 for the hours that they spent on caregiving activities, then, on average, each caregiver would receive $92,000 annually.[157]

Financial remuneration aside, the majority of all informal caregivers feel frustrated because their work is not acknowledged and properly valued. Among all their recommendations for improving home care policies lies the demand that we, as a society, explicitly recognize the worth of care work: "Caregivers need to feel a sense of pride and recognition for their jobs in the community";[158] "Acknowledge, recognize and appreciate us please!"[159] Through the voices and narratives of informal caregivers we begin to see what is prerequisite to meaningful home care reform. The combined suggestions of informal caregivers point to the need to challenge social norms around caregiving and to fundamentally shift our thinking about the social contributions of caregiving. The act of making traditionally invisible work visible is the first step to confronting what values we want reflected in our public lives. As Deborah Stone explains, "we need to make the essence of caring visible, not so much in order to make it countable and rewardable, but rather, in order to render clear what it is that we want to provide in the public sphere."[160]

So, although recognizing how the work of caring specifically affects caregivers is crucial, no comprehensive policy changes will transpire unless we fundamentally shift our thinking about human beings and their basic needs. If we understood that caring is essential to human survival, then a concern for care would inform all aspects of social policy. This entails rejecting care as being a simple matter of personal responsibility, an issue to be relegated to the domestic sphere. It entails no longer defining good citizenship as being intimately associated with paid work and market responsibilities. It confronts us with the full scope of adult responsibilities.[161] This approach to care challenges the public/private divide, which currently distorts the primacy of care in human lives. And it encourages us to think about how government decisions and social institutions can be recreated to reflect care as a social policy priority.[162]

Such changes cannot be limited to home care: they need to extend to all other areas of social welfare policies as well. Reform would extend to a range of policy sectors, including health, social services, labour/employment, and the law. By drawing upon an ethic of care model, we can better understand what kinds of paradigm shifts need to occur for all Canadians – including policy makers and politicians – to "care about care." Tremendous transformations in policy and practice would occur if such a shift were to be realized. These changes would be far-reaching. According to West: "Any number of political practices, from the devaluation of housework and child care, to the quite general privatization of the practice of raising children, to the disdain in public life for 'caregiving' services from housework to social work to even health care, should be revealed as premised on false assumptions, injurious not only to the women most directly hurt but to the political life of the community as a whole."[163]

As part of such a policy transformation the boundaries between public and private caregiving – often referred to as the interface between formal and informal care – would be redrawn. There would be a more equitable division of care responsibilities between families, government, and other public institutions. Policy changes would include a kind of "life-plan" approach that would allow individuals to have more time for caring during their lifespan.[164]

There have been some explorations of how this life-plan approach might be realized in the redesign of the workplace. Attempts to balance the two conflicting models of citizenship – citizen as wage worker and citizen as caregiver – is key. Because caregiving labour affords a subsidy to society, the argument is premised on the notion that there should be public and corporate support, including institutional redesign to better accommodate persons to be both caregivers and breadwinners.[165] One proposal that stands out is Nancy Fraser's model of the "Universal Caregiver" welfare state. According to Fraser, this model would recognize the work of care and formal employment: "Its employment sector would not be divided into two different tacks; all jobs would be designed for workers who are caregivers, too; all would have a shorter workweek than full-time jobs have now; and all would have the support of employment-enabling services ... Some informal carework would be publicly supported and integrated on par with paid work ... Some would be performed in households by relatives and friends ... Other supported carework would be located outside households altogether – in civil society."[166] And although the possibilities of how one could include the work of care in our conception of citizenship are in their nascent stages of development, the point that needs to be made is that change is needed. And this change needs to reflect a new vision – one that incorporates care work, and government's obligation to support it, into any adequate concept of citizenship.

Moreover, if care becomes an integral part of citizenship, then gender equality, and in particular, the equality of marginalized women who are often charged with caregiving activities, would also be realized.[167] As Harrington has pointed out, any meaningful transformation would take care seriously, would take the need for women's equality seriously, and would recognize that there is a need to redistribute the responsibility for care between the public and the private, between women and men, and among families, employers, and governments.[168] An ethic of care allows us to see the importance of rebalancing public and private responsibilities for care as well as the importance of establishing more equitable caregiving between men and women. A fairer distribution of care in the public and private sphere, and between men and women, is a matter of social justice.

Conclusion
By applying an ethic of care to current home care policies we begin to see that, despite the role of care in fostering human life, social policy does not adequately prioritize it. Despite recent policy initiatives aimed at creating

more publicly funded home care services, most of the responsibility for caregiving still falls on the private sphere in general and on women in particular. The current crisis of care will continue to have enormous human costs both for those who struggle to provide care and for those who receive it. Within the current policy scenario, what is overlooked is the fact that we, as a society, directly benefit from the work of all caregivers. At the same time, if we consider the status quo, it would seem that we are comfortable with caregivers enduring the burdens of care and their associated sacrifices with no adequate support or assistance from the state.

McLain argues persuasively that the costs of care work ought to be a potential rallying point for efforts to instantiate care as a public value.[169] If we assume that, because of our interdependencies, we will all at some point engage in care work and that we will suffer tremendously as a result of this, then perhaps we will be inspired to take a different approach to how care should be accommodated within social policy. Indeed, the principles of a care ethic force us to confront the reality that government policies can either marginalize care and the work of caregiving or, alternatively, enhance our capacity to accommodate caring practices as a normal part of social life.[170] The outcome will depend upon whether the insights that the ethic of care offers into human dependence and the life-long need for care can be made compatible with the full equality of all citizens.[171]

Conclusion

In applying an ethic of care to a wide range of social policy issues, my goal has been to show the moral and political deficiencies of liberalism and its justice ethic while simultaneously demonstrating the transformative potential of an ethic of care. This project is intended to contribute to furthering the public viability of a care ethic in a time when we are experiencing rapid changes and reforms in policy. Most important, the exercise of bridging theory and practice ensures that each informs and enriches the another. We learn so much as theorists, Carens explains, "by confronting the abstract with the concrete and by inquiring into the relationship between the theoretical views we espouse and actual problems, practices, and debates in political life."[1] Such an examination enables us to uncover the inadequacies of the values system that underpins our current priorities and decisions, and allows us to explore approaches that may lead to greater social justice in social policy.

Returning to the question with which I began *Social Policy and the Ethic of Care* – What are the consequences of the human need for care in social policy? – I can now outline a number of conclusions. First, the problem is that our public priorities and decisions do not reflect the integral role that care and its distinct values play in our lives. Our decision-making processes do not properly contextualize humans and their needs, respond to those who articulate their needs, or consider the full consequences of pursuing certain social policy trajectories for the well-being of Canadian citizens, especially those who are vulnerable and marginalized. This is because social policy has been developed largely in accordance with a liberal ethic of justice, a normative orientation that at best supports an impoverished concern for others.

As has been shown, a liberal ethic of justice is highly individualistic and abstract, promoting self-sufficiency and self-regarding behaviour. The justice tradition does not require attending to the interdependencies that form the central bonds and relations of human life – interdependencies that give rise to varying needs in the private *as well as* in the public realms of our lives. To take these into account would require a significant departure for liberalism. The consequences of having policies developed solely in accordance with liberalism and its ethic of justice are considerable: impartial rules, principles, and standards do not properly identify, express, and value many fundamental characteristics of our lives, including our relational interdependencies and our constant need for care. The result is social policies that are deficient and fall short of what is needed to attend to basic human requirements. Thus, it can be seen that the normative climate within which policy develops matters a great deal.

An ethic of care defends principles that expand our moral domain. Social policy guided by the ethic of care differs sharply from social policy based entirely on the ethic of justice because it starts with different philosophical assumptions. These assumptions augment our understanding of human beings and, in particular, of their interconnections, context, experiences, and care-related needs. As I have argued, the principles of care – contextual sensitivity, responsiveness, and attention to the consequences of choice – serve as a point of departure from traditional principles of justice. They shift our modes of thinking and enable us to consider new information, ideas, and facts – facts that contrast with conventional liberal thinking but that are in accordance with what most humans value. A care ethic provides us with broader normative criteria that enable us to critically develop, evaluate, and transform social policy.

I have tried to demonstrate this by applying principles of a care ethic to a select number of social policy areas. In examining equality rights under Section 15 of the Canadian Charter of Rights and Freedoms I suggest that an ethic of care does not reject the liberal concept of rights but, rather, leads us to construe rights, and specifically a substantive model of equality, as originating in needs.[2] In the case of redress and compensation for victims of abuse, an ethic of care helps us to understand better the therapeutic requirements and expectations of claimants seeking social justice, thereby resulting in more effective legal responses and options for those who have experienced wrongdoing. In critically reviewing the dominant, neo-classical economic methods used for shaping social policy, I show how a care ethic reveals the need for decision-making processes to be informed by a plurality of values. Finally, in examining the practice of caregiving, I demonstrate how an ethic of care can transform home care policies. Applying the principles of care to this context makes visible the tangible costs to, and consequences for, those who perform caregiving work. It shows the need for better supports for those who provide care and, most notably, makes it clear that care needs to be more equitably distributed between the public and private realms.

What these case studies have in common is that they demonstrate concretely the limitations of liberal theory and the need for an alternative normative framework for social policy. These practical examples also illustrate the profound implications that an ethic of care can have for achieving social justice in social policy. An ethic of care, due to its distinct aims and virtues, has the potential to alter the tenets of citizenship and central priorities within social policy decision making. For example, if interdependence were seen as an integral component of citizenship, if the importance of care to the human condition were to be explicitly and systematically acknowledged, then we would approach decision making in our public lives very differently from how we do now. Public debates would include a different approach to human differences, vulnerability, dependency, suffering, and responsibility. This changing discourse would innovate and enrich our policy judgments by opening up new ways of looking at a wide range of problems about which decisions need to be made. By identifying what kinds of policies would be consistent with a care ethic, it is not difficult to conceive how very different our lives would be if an ethic of care were to be systematically integrated into the public sphere. Such social policy applications thus further support the viability and importance of care as a public ethic.

Clearly, the issues featured in this book are diverse and extend beyond social policy as welfare policy. As such, they demonstrate the breadth of the ethic of care and the potential for its wide applicability. As Kittay has correctly noted, "As feminist philosophers continue to explore the resources of a feminist ethic of care and offer it as a clear challenge to the paradigms which dominate public policy discussions, we can expect to see an ever-widening range of issues yielding to this approach."[3] The application of care within the Canadian context joins the emerging literature attempting to demonstrate more universal aspects of care.[4] It is from this analytic paradigm that we gain insights into why care should have public value worthy of societal and government support.[5]

In conclusion, an ethic of care provides us with a normative framework from which to investigate the extent to which social policies prioritize care and its concomitant values. Arguably, without care "no one would ensure that children were tended and educated, that the needy and powerless were protected against neglect and abandonment, [and] that we would receive attentive care when we were ill or downtrodden."[6] There are, in fact, a myriad of social issues that can be linked to the absence or neglect of care. The application of a care ethic in social policy reveals to us that it is not the need to receive or give care that is problematic; rather, it is that social policies and their related institutional contexts do not adequately attend to human needs. An ethic of care makes the case that what we need is not public retrenchment but, rather, more state responsibility directed towards care.[7]

Accordingly, a care ethic can help us to set different objectives and different measures for evaluating the success of any given policy. In the process, we will move beyond simply focusing on whether or not we should respond to the "needy" and "dependent" people in society. We will come to accept that policy changes are required because, by virtue of living interdependent lives, we all have care-related needs. Care allows us to be understood, responded to, and nurtured. It makes us better people.[8] Care is essential to preventing harm and to encouraging the flourishing and development of all human beings. An ethic of care makes care – the need, the practice, and its related priorities – an issue of public significance. If we accept that care is a central value, then public life and public decision making, including social policy, will be remade to become caring.[9] In these ways, the care ethic has the potential to instigate a principled debate on the values that should be incorporated into social policy.[10] It also shows, by virtue of its concrete transformative effects on social justice, that we should value care as much as we value justice.

Notes

Introduction

1 Joan Tronto, *Moral Boundaries: A Political Argument for an Ethic of Care* (New York: Routledge, 1993), 96.

2 Joan Tronto, "Care as a Basis for Radical Political Judgements," *Hypatia* 10 (Spring 1995): 141-49.

3 See Selma Sevenhuijsen, *Citizenship and the Ethics of Care: Feminist Considerations on Justice, Morality, and Politics* (London and New York: Routledge, 1998); Fiona Robinson, *Globalizing Care: Ethics, Feminist Theory, and International Relations* (Boulder, CO: Westview Press, 1999); Eva Feder Kittay and Diana T. Meyers, eds., *Women and Moral Theory* (Totowa, NJ: Rowman and Littlefield, 1987); Grace Clement, *Care, Autonomy, and Justice* (Boulder, CO: Westview Press, 1996).

4 Iris Marion Young, *Intersecting Voices: Dilemmas of Gender, Political Philosophy, and Policy* (Princeton: Princeton University Press, 1997).

5 Marilyn Friedman, "Beyond Caring: The De-Moralization of Gender," in *An Ethic of Care: Feminist and Interdisciplinary Perspectives,* ed. M.J. Larrabee, 87-110 (New York and London: Routledge, 1993).

6 John W. Kingdon, "The Reality of Public Policy Making," in *Ethical Dimensions of Health Policy,* ed. M. Davis, C. Clancy, and L. Churchill (Oxford: Oxford University Press, 2002), 113.

7 See Charles W. Anderson, "The Place of Principles in Policy Analysis," *American Political Science Review* 73 (1979): 713.

8 Keith Banting, "Keeping Our Balance: The Political Imperatives of Social Policy Reform," *Policy Options* 15 (July-August 1994): 66.

9 Pat Armstrong, "The Welfare State as History," in *The Welfare State in Canada: Past, Present, and Future,* ed. Raymond B. Blake, Penny E. Bryden, and J. Frank Strain, 52-74 (Concord, ON: Irwin Publishing, 1997).

10 Trudie Knijn and Monique Kremer, "Gender and the Caring Dimension of Welfare States: Toward Inclusive Citizenship," *Social Politics* 4 (1997): 328-61.

11 Gerard W. Boychuk, "Federal Spending in Health: Why Here? Why Now?" in *How Ottawa Spends, 2002-2003: The Security Aftermath and National Priorities,* ed. G. Bruce Doern (Don Mills, ON: Oxford University Press, 2002), 125.

12 Michael J. Prince, "From Health and Welfare to Stealth and Farewell: Federal Social Policy, 1980-2000," in *How Ottawa Spends, 1999-2000: Shape Shifting — Canadian Governance Toward the 21st Century,* ed. Leslie A. Pal (Don Mills, ON: Oxford University Press, 1999), referring to the December 1998 report of the United Nations Committee on Economic, Social and Cultural Rights, 188.

13 National Council of Welfare, *Poverty Profile 1998* (Ottawa: National Council of Welfare, 1998), 5.

14 Satya Brink and Allen Zeesman, *Measuring Social Well-Being: An Index of Social Health for Canada R-97-9E* (Hull, PQ: Applied Research Branch Strategic Policy, Human Resources Development Canada, June 1997).

15   Connie Hargrave, "Homelessness in Canada: From Housing to Shelters to Blankets," *Share International* (April 1999), <http://www.shareintl.org/archives/homelessness/hl-ch_Canada.htm>.
16   Canadian Association of Food Banks, 2001, <http://www.cafb-acba.ca/about_e.cfm> (accessed 15 March 2004).
17   Canadian Council on Social Development, *Gaining Ground: The Personal Security Index, 2001* (Ottawa: Canadian Council on Social Development, 2001).
18   See Arlie Russell Hochschild, "The Culture of Politics: Traditional, Post-Modern, Cold-Modern, and Warm-Modern Ideals of Care," *Social Politics* 2 (1995): 331-46.
19   See Pierre S. Pettigrew (former minister of Human Resources Development Canada), "A History of Trust, a Future of Confidence: Canada's Third Way," notes for an address to the Canadian Centre for Philanthropy, Toronto, Ontario, 26 April 1999.
20   For full details of Budget 2003, see <http://www.cbc.ca/budget2003> (accessed 9 July 2004).
21   See Matthew Mendelsohn, *Canada's Social Contract: Evidence from Public Opinion* (Ottawa: Canadian Policy Research Network, Discussion Paper No. P/01 Public Involvement Network, November 2002); Frank Graves, "Rethinking Government as if People Mattered: From 'Reagonomics' to 'Humanomics'"; and Michael J. Prince, "From Health and Welfare to Stealth and Farewell: Federal Social Policy, 1980-2000," both in *How Ottawa Spends, 1999-2000: Shape Shifting — Canadian Governance Toward the 21st Century*, ed. Leslie A. Pal (Don Mills, ON: Oxford University Press, 1999).
22   EWL/LEF, "Global Governance, Alternative Mechanisms and Gender Equality Mainstreaming," 6 June 2001, <http://www.womenlobby.org/Document.asp?DocID+318&tod+19714> (accessed 18 June 2002).
23   James J. Rice and Michael J. Prince, *Changing Politics of Canadian Social Policy* (Toronto: University of Toronto Press, 2000); Prince, "From Health and Welfare"; Graves, "Rethinking Government"; Blake et al., *Welfare State*.
24   Leslie Pal, *Beyond Policy Analysis: Public Issues Management in Turbulent Times* (Scarborough, ON: Nelson Thomson Learning, 2001), 16.
25   David Gil lists these as essential components of social policy. See *Unravelling Social Policy: Theory Analysis, and Political Action towards Social Equality* (Rochester: Schenkman Books, 1990).
26   Judith Squires, *Gender in Political Theory* (Cambridge: Polity Press, 1999), 168-69.
27   Tronto, *Moral Boundaries*, 162.
28   I take this term from Diana S. Ralph, André Régimbland, and Nérée St-Amand, eds., *Open for Business, Closed to People: Michael Harris's Ontario* (Halifax: Fernwood Publishing, 1997).
29   Janine Brodie, *Critical Concepts: An Introduction to Politics* (Scarborough, ON: Prentice Hall, 1999), 6.
30   Janine Brodie, *Politics on the Boundaries: Restructuring and the Canadian Women's Movement* (Toronto: Robarts Centre for Canadian Studies, 1994), 31-32.
31   Marina Morrow, Olena Hankivsky, and Colleen Varcoe, "Women and Violence: The Effects of Dismantling the Welfare State," *Critical Social Policy* 24, 3 (August 2004) (forthcoming).
32   Tronto, *Moral Boundaries*, 152.
33   Ibid., 178.
34   Lawrence Blum, *Friendship, Altruism, and Morality* (London: Routledge and Kegan Paul, 1980), 1.
35   Peta Bowden, *Caring: Gender-Sensitive Ethics* (London: Routledge Press, 1997), 154.
36   Deborah Stone, "Why We Need a Care Movement," *Nation* (New York), 13 March 2000, 13, 15.
37   Leslie A. Pal, ed., *How Ottawa Spends, 2000-2001*.
38   A number of feminist theorists have investigated themes consistent with the ethic of care in the works of Western philosophy. Alison Jaggar, in *Caring as Feminist Practice* (Boulder, CO: Westview Press, 1995), has noted similarities with Christian thinkers and Aristotle's *Nicomachean Ethics*. Annette Baier, in "Hume, the Women's Moral Theorist?" in *Women and Moral Theory*, ed. Eva Feder Kittay and Diana T. Meyers, 37-55 (Totowa,

NJ: Rowman and Littlefield, 1987), has made similar observations about David Hume. Joan Tronto, in *Moral Boundaries,* has examined the intersection between an ethic of care and the theories of Francis Hutcheson and Adam Smith.

39 See Sandra Harding, "The Curious Coincidence of Feminine and African Moralities: Challenges for Feminist Theory," in Kittay and Mayers, ed., *Women and Moral Theory,* 296-316; and Chenyang Li, *The Tao Encounters in the West: Explorations in Comparative Philosophy* (Albany: SUNY Press, 1999).

40 Carol Gilligan, *In a Different Voice: Psychological Theory and Women's Development* (Cambridge: Cambridge University Press, 1982).

41 Ibid., 19.

42 Ibid., 2.

43 Ibid.

44 Although Gilligan has attempted to argue that her "different voice" is neither biologically determined nor unique to women, her methodology has been challenged on the basis that, throughout her book, she makes generalizations based upon a very small number of unrepresentative samples and case studies. Gilligan utilizes results from three small studies (reinterpretation of the Heinz dilemma, a college student study of a class in moral development at Harvard, and an abortion study of twenty-nine women) to assert that women speak in a "different voice" from men and that their ethical choices are disposed to caring.

45 Gilligan, *In a Different Voice,* 4.

46 Ibid., 174.

47 See James P. Sterba, *Three Challenges to Ethics: Environmentalism, Feminism, and Multiculturalism* (New York: Oxford University Press, 2001); and Jeremy Waldron, "When Justice Replaces Affection: The Need for Rights," in *Liberal Rights: Collected Papers (1981-1991)* (Cambridge: Cambridge University Press, 1993), 379.

48 See Will Kymlicka, *Contemporary Political Philosophy,* 2nd ed. (New York: Oxford University Press, 2002); and Susan Moller Okin, "Reason and Feeling in Thinking about Justice," *Ethics* 99 (1989): 229-49.

49 See especially Joan Tronto, *Moral Boundaries;* Clement, *Care, Autonomy, and Justice;* and Selma Sevenhuijsen, *Citizenship and the Ethics of Care.*

50 Eva Feder Kittay, "Social Policy," in *A Companion to Feminist Philosophy,* ed. Alison M. Jaggar and Iris Marion Young (Oxford: Blackwell, 1998), 569.

51 Rice and Prince, *Changing Politics,* 80.

52 Martin Rein, "Value-Critical Policy Analysis," in *Ethics, the Social Science, and Policy Analysis,* ed. Bruce Jennings and Daniel Callahan (New York: Plenum Press, 1983), 83.

53 Joseph H. Carens, *Culture, Citizenship, and Community: A Contextual Exploration of Justice as Evenhandedness* (Oxford: Oxford University Press, 2000), 3.

Chapter 1: First-Generation Care Theorists

1 Nel Noddings, *Caring: A Feminine Approach to Ethics and Moral Education* (Berkeley: University of California Press, 1984).

2 Nel Noddings, *Starting at Home: Caring and Social Policy* (Berkeley: University of California Press, 2002).

3 Sara Ruddick, *Maternal Feminism: Toward a Politics of Peace* (Boston: Beacon Press, 1989).

4 Sara Ruddick, "Preservation, Love and Military Destruction," in *Mothering: Essays in Feminist Theory,* ed. J. Trebilcot (New Jersey: Rowman and Allanheld, 1983), 239.

5 Virginia Held, *Feminist Morality: Transforming Culture, Society and Politics* (Chicago: University of Chicago Press, 1993).

6 See Sara Ruddick, "Remarks on the Sexual Politics of Reason," in *Women and Moral Theory,* ed. Eva Feder Kittay and Diana T. Meyers (Totowa, NJ: Rowman and Littlefield, 1987), 242.

7 See Virginia Held, "Feminism and Moral Theory," in Kittay and Meyers, ed., *Women and Moral Theory,* 124-25.

8 Lawrence Walker, "Sex Differences in the Development of Moral Reasoning," *Child Development* 55 (1984): 677-91; Grace Clement, *Care, Autonomy, and Justice,* 3; Diane Romain,

"Care and Confusion," in *Explorations in Feminist Ethics: Theory and Practice,* ed. Eve Browning Cole and Susan Coultrap-McQuin (Bloomington: Indiana University Press, 1992), 35.

9 Onora O'Neill, "Justice, Gender and International Boundaries," in *International Justice and the Third World,* ed. Robin Attfield and Barry Wildins (London: Routledge, 1992), 55. See also Deborah Rhode, *Justice and Gender: Sex, Discrimination, and the Law* (Cambridge: Harvard University Press, 1989).

10 Monique Deveaux, "Shifting Paradigms: Theorizing Care and Justice in Political Theory," *Hypatia* 10, 2 (1995): 116.

11 Barbara Houston, "Rescuing Womanly Virtues: Some Dangers of Moral Reclamation," in *Science, Morality and Feminist Theory,* ed. Marcia Hanen and Kai Nielsen (Calgary: University of Calgary Press, 1987), 247.

12 For further discussion, see Sarah Lucia Hoagland, *Lesbian Ethics: Toward New Value* (Palo Alto: Institute of Lesbian Studies, 1990); and "Some Thoughts about 'Caring,'" in *Feminist Ethics,* ed. Claudia Card, 246-86 (Lawrence: University of Kansas Press, 1991).

13 See Michele Moody-Adams, "Gender and the Complexity of Moral Voices," in Card, ed., *Feminist Ethics,* 195-212.

14 Carol Stack, "The Culture of Gender: Women and Men of Color," *Signs* 11 (winter 1986): 321-24.

15 Noddings, *Caring: A Feminine Approach,* 36-37.

16 Ruddick, *Maternal Feminism,* 131.

17 Virginia Held, "The Meshing of Care and Justice," *Hypatia* 10, 2 (1995): 128-32.

18 Martha Minow, *Making All the Difference: Inclusion, Exclusion and American Law* (Ithaca: Cornell University Press, 1990), 228; and Mary Dietz, "Citizenship with a Feminist Face: The Problem with Maternal Thinking," *Political Theory* 13, 1 (1985): 19-37.

19 Some of these include Barbara Houston, "Rescuing Womanly Virtues"; Cynthia Card, "Gender and Moral Luck," in *Identity, Character and Morality,* ed. Owen Flanagan, 199-218 (Cambridge: MIT Press, 1990); Marilyn Friedman, *What Are Friends For? Feminist Perspectives on Personal Relationships and Moral Theory* (Ithaca: Cornell University Press, 1993); and Sarah Lucia Hoagland, "Some Thoughts about 'Caring.'"

20 Tronto, *Moral Boundaries,* 3.

21 Clement, *Care, Autonomy, and Justice,* 112.

22 Cheshire Calhoun, "Justice, Care, and Gender Bias," *Journal of Philosophy* 95 (September 1988): 452.

23 Clement, *Care, Autonomy, and Justice,* 5.

24 See Will Kymlicka, *Contemporary Political Philosophy,* 2nd ed. (New York: Oxford University Press, 2002).

25 See Susan Moller Okin, "Reason and Feeling in Thinking about Justice," *Ethics* 99 (1989): 229-49.

26 As White notes elsewhere, although Rawls's is not the only liberal theory of justice, his work continues to be the primary focus within justice/care debates. J.A. White, *Democracy, Justice, and the Welfare State: Reconstructing Public Care* (University Park: Pennsylvania State University Press, 2000), 48.

27 John Rawls, *A Theory of Justice* (Cambridge: Harvard University Press, 1971).

28 Ibid., 7.

29 John Rawls, "Justice as Fairness," *Philosophy and Public Affairs* 17 (1988): 484.

30 Rawls, *Theory of Justice,* 71.

31 Ibid., 137.

32 Friedman, *What Are Friends For?* 15.

33 Rawls, *Theory of Justice,* 12.

34 Ibid.

35 As quoted in Rob Martin, "The Charter and the Crisis in Canada," in *After Meech Lake: Lessons for the Future,* ed. D.E. Smith, P. MacKinnon, and J.C. Courtney (Saskatoon: Fifth House, 1991), 23.

36 John Rawls, "Social Unity and Primary Goods," in *Utilitarianism and Beyond,* ed. Amartya Sen and Bernard Williams (Cambridge, MA: Cambridge University Press, 1980), 526.

37   James P. Sterba, *Three Challenges to Ethics: Environmentalism, Feminism, and Multicultural-ism* (New York: Oxford University Press, 2001), 72.
38   Kymlicka, *Contemporary Political Philosophy*, 400.
39   Friedman, *What Are Friends For?* 135.
40   Kymlicka, *Contemporary Political Philosophy*, 402-3.
41   See Daryl Koehn, *Rethinking Feminist Ethics: Care, Trust and Empathy* (New York and London: Routledge, 1998).
42   Clement, *Care, Autonomy, and Justice*, 109.
43   Kymlicka, *Contemporary Political Philosophy*, 404.
44   Ibid., 407.
45   See Noddings, *Caring: A Feminine Approach.*
46   Robert E. Goodin, *Protecting the Vulnerable: A Reanalysis of Our Social Responsibilities* (Chicago: University of Chicago Press, 1985), 111.
47   Clement, *Care, Autonomy, and Justice*, 85.
48   Young, *Intersecting Voices*, 82.
49   Robinson, *Globalizing Care*, 23.
50   Kymlicka, *Contemporary Political Philosophy*, 408-9.
51   Okin, "Reason and Feeling," 230.
52   Susan Moller Okin, *Justice, Gender, and the Family* (New York: Basic Books, 1989), 15.
53   Friedman, *What Are Friends For?* 113.
54   Seyla Benhabib, "The Generalized and the Concrete Other," in *Women and Moral Theory*, ed. Eva Feder Kittay and Diana T. Meyers (Totowa, NJ: Rowman and Littlefield, 1987), 163-64.
55   Margaret Moore, "The Ethics of Care and Justice," *Women and Politics* 20 (1999): 11.
56   Kymlicka, *Contemporary Political Philosophy*, 409.
57   Rawls, *A Theory of Justice*, 13.
58   Nancy Fraser, "Toward a Discourse Ethic of Solidarity," *Praxis International* 5 (1986): 428.
59   Shane O'Neill, *Impartiality in Context: Grounding Justice in a Pluralist World* (Albany: State University of New York Press, 1997), 53.
60   Julie Anne White, *Democracy, Justice, and the Welfare State: Restructuring Public Care* (University Park: Pennsylvania State University Press, 2000), 103.
61   Kymlicka, *Contemporary Political Philosophy*, 417.
62   Ibid., 416.
63   Ibid., 411.
64   Uma Narayan, "Colonialism and Its Others: Considerations on Rights and Care Discourses," *Hypatia* 10 (1995): 133-41.
65   Sevenhuijsen, *Citizenship and the Ethics of Care.*
66   Nayaran, "Colonialism and Its Others," 133.
67   Friedman, "Beyond Caring," 267, emphasis in original.
68   Koehn, *Rethinking Feminist Ethics*, 5.
69   Sevenhuijsen, *Citizenship and the Ethics of Care*, 28.
70   Ruth Lister, *Citizenship: Feminist Perspectives*, 2nd ed. (New York: New York University Press, 2003), 115.
71   Young, *Intersecting Voices.*
72   Moore, "Ethics of Care and Justice."
73   Waldron, "When Justice Replaces Affection," 379.
74   Ibid.
75   Margaret Urban Walker, "Moral Understandings: Alternative 'Epistemology' for a Feminist Ethics," in Browning Cole and Coultrap-McQuin, ed., *Explorations in Feminist Ethics*, 171.
76   Friedman, *What Are Friends For?* 144.
77   Robinson, *Globalizing Care*, 150.
78   Iris Marion Young, *Justice and the Politics of Difference* (Princeton: Princeton University Press, 1990).
79   Kymlicka, *Contemporary Political Philosophy*, 418.
80   Ibid., 417.

81   Ibid., 419, emphasis in original.
82   Ibid., 420.
83   See Eva Feder Kittay, "Taking Dependency Seriously: The Family and Medical Leave Act Considered in Light of the Social Organization of Dependency Work and Gender Equality," *Hypatia* 10, 1 (1995): 8-29.
84   Linda C. McLain, "Care as a Public Value," *Chicago-Kent Law Review* 76 (2001): 1085, emphasis in original.
85   Kymlicka, *Contemporary Political Philosophy*, 419.
86   Charles Taylor, "Philosophical Reflections of Caring Practices," in *The Crisis of Care: Affirming and Restoring Caring Practices in the Helping Professions*, ed. S. Phillips and P. Benner (Washington, DC: Georgetown University Press, 1994), 177.
87   Judith Squires, *Gender in Political Theory* (Cambridge: Polity Press, 1999), 164.

Chapter 2: Second-Generation Care Theorists
1   Joan Tronto, *Moral Boundaries: A Political Argument for an Ethic of Care* (New York: Routledge, 1993), 103.
2   I believe that Joan Tronto's work marks a watershed in ethic of care theorizing because she was the first care theorist to persuasively challenge the essentialization of care as it relates to women and the first to critique persuasively the dichotomization of care and justice.
3   Tronto, *Moral Boundaries*, 158.
4   Ibid., 136.
5   Ibid., xi.
6   Ibid., 177.
7   Grace Clement, *Care, Autonomy, and Justice* (Boulder, CO: Westview Press, 1996), 121.
8   Ibid., 109.
9   Ibid., 107.
10   Ibid., 90.
11   Julie Anne White, *Democracy, Justice, and the Welfare State: Restructuring Public Care* (University Park: Pennsylvania State University Press, 2000), 7.
12   Selma Sevenhuijsen, *Citizenship and the Ethics of Care: Feminist Considerations on Justice, Morality, and Politics* (London and New York: Routledge, 1998), 34.
13   Ibid., 121.
14   Selma Sevenhuijsen, Vivienne Bozalek, Amanda Gouws, Marie Minnar-McDonald, "South African Social Welfare Policy: An Analysis Using the Ethic of Care," *Critical Social Policy* 23, 3 (2003): 299-321.
15   As quoted in ibid., 301.
16   Ibid., 318.
17   For example, The International Workshop, "The Use of the Ethics of Care Perspective in Social Policy," 14-15 January 2003, Hotel Turist, Ljubljana, Slovenia.
18   White, *Democracy, Justice, and the Welfare State*, 13.
19   Olena Hankivsky, "Social Justice and Women's Health: A Canadian Perspective," in *Made to Measure: Women, Gender, and Equity*, ed. C. Amaratunga (Maritime Centre of Excellence for Women's Health, 2000), 55.
20   Sevenhuijsen, *Citizenship and the Ethics of Care*.
21   Notable exceptions include Nancy Fraser's work on recognition and redistribution, Jürgen Habermas's work on law, and James Tully's work on dialogical conceptions of the public sphere.
22   Carol Gilligan, J. Ward, and J. Taylor, eds., *Mapping the Moral Domain* (Cambridge: Harvard University Press, 1988), 34.
23   Peta Bowden, *Caring: Gender-Sensitive Ethics* (London: Routledge, 1997), 168.
24   Tronto, *Moral Boundaries*, 124.
25   Ellen Moskowitz, "The Ethics of Government Bioethics," *Politics and the Life Sciences* 13 (1994): 96.
26   See Chris Crittenden, "The Principles of Care," *Women and Politics* 22 (2001): 81-106.

27 Seyla Benhabib, "The Generalized and the Concrete Other: The Kohlberg-Gilligan Controversy and Feminist Theory," in *Feminism as Critique*, ed. Seyla Benhabib and Drucilla Cornell (Minneapolis: University of Minnesota Press, 1987).

28 Deborah Rhode, "Feminist Critical Theories," in *Feminist Jurisprudence*, ed. Patricia Smith (New York: Oxford University Press, 1993), 598.

29 Clement, *Care, Autonomy, and Justice*, 80.

30 Fraser, "Toward a Discourse Ethic."

31 Selma Sevenhuijsen, "South African Policy and the Ethics of Care," paper presented at the annual meeting of the American Political Science Association, San Francisco, 30 August-2 September 2001, 16.

32 Ibid.

33 Alison Jaggar, "Caring as a Feminist Practice of Moral Reason," in *Justice and Care: Essential Readings in Feminist Ethics*, ed. Virginia Held (Boulder, CO: Westview Press, 1995), 194.

34 See Mary F. Rogers, "Caring and Community," in *Contemporary Feminist Theory*, ed. Mary F. Rogers (Boston: McGraw Hill Publishers, 1998), 329.

35 Sevenhuijsen et al., "South African Social Welfare Policy," 315.

36 Benhabib, "The Generalized and the Concrete Other," 92, emphasis in original.

37 Sevenhuijsen, *Citizenship and the Ethics of Care*, 60.

38 Ibid.

39 See, for example, Joan W. Scott, "The Evidence of Experience," *Critical Inquiry* 17 (1991): 773-97; and Shari Stone-Mediatore, "Chandra Mohanty and the Revaluing of Experience," in *Decentering the Center: Philosophy for a Multicultural, Postcolonial, and Feminist World*, ed. Uma Narayan and Sandra Harding, 110-27 (Bloomington: Indiana University Press, 2000).

40 Stone-Mediatore, "Chandra Mohanty," 110-11.

41 Aaron Wildavsky, *Speaking Truth to Power: The Art and Craft of Policy Analysis* (New Brunswick, USA: Transaction Books, 1987).

42 Martha Minow, *Making All the Difference: Inclusion, Exclusion, and American Law* (Ithaca: Cornell University Press, 1990), 379.

43 Richard Titmuss, *Essays on "The Welfare State"* (London: George Allen and Unwin, 1963), 39.

44 Tronto, "Care as a Basis," 145.

45 White, *Democracy, Justice, and the Welfare State*, 8.

46 Tronto, "Care as a Basis," 14.

47 Nancy Fraser, *Unruly Practices: Power Discourse and Gender in Contemporary Social Theory* (Minneapolis: University of Minneapolis Press, 1989) has made similar arguments, using the term "politics of needs interpretation."

48 Benhabib, "The Generalized and the Concrete Other."

49 James J. Rice and Michael J. Prince, *Changing Politics of Canadian Social Policy* (Toronto: University of Toronto Press, 2000), 24.

50 Frank Graves, "Rethinking Government as if People Mattered: From 'Reaganomics' to 'Humanomics,'" in *How Ottawa Spends, 1999-2000: Shape Shifting — Canadian Governance Toward the 21st Century*, ed. Leslie A. Pal (Don Mills: Oxford University Press, 1999), 45.

51 Carol Gilligan, *In a Different Voice: Psychological Theory and Women's Development* (Cambridge: Cambridge University Press, 1982).

52 Nel Noddings, *Starting at Home: Caring and Social Policy* (Berkeley: University of California Press, 1990).

53 This is a definition of public policy taken from Leslie A. Pal, *Public Policy Analysis: An Introduction* (Scarborough, ON: Nelson Canada, 1992), 2.

54 Fiona Robinson, *Globalizing Care: Ethics, Feminist Theory, and International Relations* (Boulder, CO: Westview Press, 1999), 149-50.

55 Ibid., 32.

56 Tronto, *Moral Boundaries*, 152.

Chapter 3: The Interpretation of Equality

1 Fiona Robinson, *Globalizing Care: Ethics, Feminist Theory and International Relations* (Boulder, CO: Westview Press, 1999), 126.

2 Lynne N. Henderson, "Legality and Empathy," *Michigan Law Review* 85 (1987): 1575.

3 Sandra Burt, "What's Fair? Changing Feminist Perceptions of Justice in English Canada," *Windsor Yearbook of Access to Justice* 12 (1992): 353.

4 Judy Fudge, "What Do We Mean by Law and Social Transformation?" *Canadian Journal of Law and Society* 5 (1990): 60.

5 According to the equality rights under Section 15(1), "every individual is equal before and under the law and has the right to the equal protection and equal benefit of the law without discrimination and, in particular, without discrimination based on race, national or ethnic origin, colour, religion, sex, age, or mental or physical disability." Further, Section 15(2) states: "Subsection (1) does not preclude any law, program or activity that has as its objective the amelioration of conditions of disadvantaged individuals or groups including those that are disadvantaged because of race, national or ethnic origin, colour religion, sex, age or mental or physical disability."

6 David Elliot, "Comments on *Andrews* v. *Law Society of British Columbia* and Section 15 (1) of the Charter: The Emperor's New Clothes?" *McGill Law Journal* 35 (1989): 251.

7 This phrase is taken from Judy Fudge's article, "The Public/Private Distinction: The Possibilities of and the Limits to the Use of Charter Litigation to Further Feminist Struggles," *Osgoode Hall Law Journal* 25, 3 (1987): 535.

8 Fudge, "The Public/Private Distinction," 551.

9 Paul Green, "The Logic of Special Rights," *Hypatia* 2, 1 (1987): 69.

10 Joel Bakan, *Just Words: Constitutional Rights and Social Wrongs* (Toronto: University of Toronto Press, 1997), 45.

11 Naomi Sharp, *Equality-Seeking Charter Litigation: Where to from Here? A Vision of Transformative Justice* (Ottawa: National Association of Women and the Law, May 1999).

12 S. Razack, *Canadian Feminism and the Law: The Women's Legal Education and Action Fund and the Pursuit of Equality* (Toronto: Second Story Press, 1991), 36.

13 For early work, see Leslie Bender, "A Lawyer's Primer on Feminist Theory and Tort," *Journal of Legal Education* 38 (1988): 58-74; Lynne N. Henderson, "Legality and Empathy," *Michigan Law Review* 85 (1987): 1574-1653; and Kenneth Karst, "Woman's Constitution," *Duke Law Review* 3 (June 1984): 447-510.

14 Martha Minow, *Making All the Difference: Inclusion, Exclusion, and American Law* (Ithaca: Cornell University Press, 1990).

15 Robin West, *Caring for Justice* (New York: New York University Press, 1997).

16 Colleen Sheppard, "Caring in Human Relations and Legal Approaches to Equality," *National Journal of Constitutional Law* 2 (1992-93): 2, emphasis in original.

17 Minow, *Making All the Difference*, 213, emphasis in original.

18 West, *Caring for Justice*, 24.

19 *Brown* v. *Board of Education* 347 U.S. at 483 (1954).

20 Sheppard, "Caring in Human Relations," 333.

21 E. Barker, trans., *The Politics of Aristotle* (London: Oxford University Press, c. 1946), Book 3, xii, 1282b.

22 It is important to highlight, as does Martha Minow, that "it is misleading to treat the implicit norm as consisting of all men ... for that obscures historical racial and class differences in the treatment of men themselves." *Making All the Difference*, 56.

23 Linda J. Krieger, "Through a Glass Darkly: Paradigms of Equality and the Search for Woman's Jurisprudence," *Hypatia* 2, 1 (1987): 47.

24 *A.G. Canada* v. *Lavell et al.*, [1974] S.C.R. 1349.

25 This section of the act stripped Indian women, upon marriage to a non-Indian, of their Indian status and all its benefits. This did not apply to Indian men.

26 See Sally Weaver's article, "First Nations Women and Government Policy, 1970-92: Discrimination and Conflict," in *Changing Patterns: Women in Canada*, ed. Sandra Burt et al. (Toronto: McClelland and Stewart, 1993). Weaver's list (94) of losses for a First Nations woman resulting from 12(1)(b) include: legal status as "Indian" under the Indian Act,

band membership, the right to transmit legal status and band membership to children, the right to reside on reserve, the right to own land on reserve, the right to inherit property on reserve, the right to vote and hold office in band council, the right to vote in band referendums, the right to collect band annuities and treaty payments, the benefits of special government programs for reserve and off-reserve residents, and the right to be buried on home reserve.

27 This phrase was used by dissenting Justice Laskin: *A.G. Canada* v. *Lavell et al.* [1974], S.C.R. 1349, 1386.

28 *Bliss* v. *Attorney General of Canada* (1978) 92 D.L.R. (3d) 417; [1979] 1 S.C.R. 183.

29 Unlike the Bill of Rights, which provided for "equality before the law," Section 15 guarantees four elements of equality: equality before the law, equality under the law, equal protection, and equal benefit of the law without discrimination.

30 In addition to Section 15, Section 28 was incorporated into the Charter to ensure that "notwithstanding anything in the Charter, the rights and freedoms referred to in it are guaranteed equally to male and female persons." Section 28 was intended to further substantiate the equality guarantees of Section 15.

31 See Gwen Brodsky and Shelagh Day for a comprehensive assessment of the impact of initial Charter equality rights litigation pertaining to women in *Canadian Charter Equality Rights for Women: One Step Forward or Two Steps Back?* (Ottawa: Canadian Advisory Council on the Status of Women, 1989). In this work they observe that, out of forty-four equality challenges, only nine were made by or on behalf of women (49) and that women were losing important laws affecting their welfare benefits, unemployment insurance, pregnancy benefits, and protection from sexual assault (56, 59).

32 Elizabeth Frazer, "Feminism and Liberalism," in *Liberal Political Tradition: Contemporary Reappraisals*, ed. J. Meadowcroft (Cheltenham: Edward Elgar Publishing Limited, 1996), 132.

33 *Andrews* v. *Law Society of British Columbia*, [1989] 1 S.C.R. at 170.

34 Kathleen Mahoney has described the approach established in *Andrews* as "purposeful, contextual" in "The Constitutional Law of Equality in Canada," *International Law and Politics* 24 (1992): 761; Colleen Sheppard has explained that it "examines the contextual realities of subordinate groups, classes and individuals." See Colleen Sheppard, "Recognition of the Disadvantaging of Women: The Promise of *Andrews* v. *Law Society of British Columbia*," *McGill Law Review* 35 (1989): 48.

35 *Andrews* v. *Law Society of British Columbia*, [1989] 1 S.C.R. note 7 at 169.

36 This is not to say that comparisons will no longer be necessary. After all, McIntyre clearly stated that equality is comparative: "It is a comparative concept, the condition of which may only be attained or discerned by comparison with the condition of others in the social and political setting in which the question arises."

37 *Andrews* v. *Law Society of British Columbia*, [1989] 1 S.C.R. at 165.

38 *Symes* v. *Canada*, [1993] 4 S.C.R. 695.

39 Lesley D. Harman, "The Feminization of Poverty: An Old Problem with a New Name," in *Gender in the 1990s: Images, Realities and Issues*, ed. Adie Nelson and Barrie W. Robinson (Scarborough, ON: Nelson Canada, 1995), 407.

40 *Thibaudeau* v. *Canada*, [1995] 2 S.C.R. 627.

41 Ibid., at 3.

42 Ibid., at 7.

43 Ellen B. Zweibel, "*Thibaudeau* v. *R.*: Constitutional Challenge to the Taxation of Child Support Payments," *National Journal of Constitutional Law* 4 (1994): 329.

44 Statistics Canada, *Women in Canada 2000: A Gender-Based Statistical Report* (Ottawa: Minister of Industry, 2000), 139.

45 Amy Bartholomew, "Achieving a Place for Women in a Man's World: Or Feminism with No Class," *Canadian Journal of Women and the Law* 6 (1993): 474.

46 West, *Caring for Justice*, 57.

47 Christine Littleton, "Reconstructing Sexual Equality," in *Feminist Legal Theory: Foundations*, ed. K. Weisberg (Philadelphia: Temple University Press, 1993), 260.

48 Sheppard, *Caring in Human Relations*, 342.

49 Sharp, *Equality-Seeking,* 24.
50 Sheppard, *Caring in Human Relations,* 327.
51 Henderson, "Legality and Empathy."
52 See Carol Lee Bacchi, *Same Difference: Feminism and Sexual Difference* (Sydney, Australia: Allen and Unwin Ltd., 1990), 179.
53 Bakan, *Just Words,* 60.
54 West, *Caring for Justice,* 32.
55 Madam Justice B. Wilson, "Will Women Judges Really Make a Difference?" The Fourth Annual B. Betcherman Memorial Lecture, Osgoode Hall Law School, York University, 8 February 1992, note 105.
56 Clement, *Care, Autonomy, and Justice,* 118.
57 As Joan Tronto has explained: "a care perspective ... would make facts about inequality more difficult to dismiss. Questions such as: at what point do inequalities ... prevent citizens from equal power would become important political questions; they would not remain simply theoretical questions." See *Moral Boundaries: A Political Argument for an Ethic of Care* (New York: Routledge, 1993), 164.
58 Uma Narayan, "Colonialism and Its Others: Considerations on Rights and Care Discourses," *Hypatia* 10 (1995): 139.
59 *Symes* v. *Canada* (1993), 110 D.L.R. (4th) 470; [1993] 4 S.C.R. 695; 19 C.R.R. (2d) 1 at 6037.
60 Debra M. McAllister, "The Supreme Court in Symes: Two Solitudes," *National Journal of Constitutional Law* 4 (1994): 260.
61 At the trial of the *Symes* case, Patricia Armstrong, a sociologist at York University, elaborated in great detail upon the facts and statistics regarding how working women with childcare responsibilities were negatively affected.
62 Here I am specifically referring to *Lavell* v. *Attorney General of Canada* (1971), 22 D.L.R. (3d) 182 (Ont. Co. Ct.), where the court maintained that, as long as all Indian women as a group were treated the same under the law, equality was being preserved.
63 As quoted by McAllister, "The Supreme Court," 260.
64 *Thibaudeau* v. *Canada,* [1995] 2 S.C.R. 9 at 5.
65 Ibid.
66 Zwiebel, "*Thibaudeau* v. *R.*: Constitutional Challenge," 347.
67 *Thibaudeau* v. *Canada,* [1995] 2 S.C.R. 195 at 17.
68 Ibid., at 5.
69 Ibid., at 9.
70 Ibid., at 7.
71 See Ellen B. Zweibel and Richard Shillington, *Child Support Policy: Income Tax Treatment of Child Support and Child Support Guidelines* (Toronto: Policy Research Centre on Children, Youth and Families, 1993).
72 Ibid., 21n44.
73 See Leslie Bender, "A Lawyer's Primer on Feminist Theory and Tort," *Journal of Legal Education* 38, 3 (1988): 58-74.
74 [1995] 2 S.C.R. 636.
75 *Eldridge* v. *British Columbia (Attorney General),* [1997] 3 S.C.R. 624.
76 *Thibaudeau* v. *Canada,* [1997] 3 S.C.R. at 56.
77 *Vriend* v. *Alberta,* [1998] 1 S.C.R. 493.
78 Ibid., 57.
79 Ibid., 50.
80 Ibid., 65.
81 Ibid., 66.
82 *Law* v. *Canada,* [1999] 1. S.C.R. 497 at 5.
83 Ibid., 40.
84 Ibid., 9.
85 Ibid., 6.
86 Rita Manning, *Speaking from the Heart: A Feminist Perspective on Ethics* (Lanham, MD: Rowman and Littlefield, 1992), 154.

Chapter 4: Therapeutic Jurisprudence

1 Law Commission of Canada, *Restoring Dignity: Responding to Child Abuse in Canadian Institutions* (Ottawa: Minister of Public Works and Government Services, 2000), 17.

2 Findings first appeared in Bruce Feldthusen, Olena Hankivsky, and Lorraine Greaves, "Therapeutic Consequences of Civil Actions for Damages and Compensation Claims by Victims of Sexual Abuse," *Canadian Journal of Women and the Law* 12, 1 (2000): 66-116.

3 Institute for Human Resource Development (IHRD), *Review of the Needs of Victims of Institutional Abuse* (Ottawa: Law Commission of Canada, 1998).

4 Peggy Fulton Hora and William G. Schma, "Therapeutic Jurisprudence," *Judicature* 82, 9 (1998): 8-12.

5 See Susan Daicoff, "The Role of Therapeutic Jurisprudence within the Comprehensive Law Movement," in *Practicing Therapeutic Jurisprudence: Law as a Helping Profession,* ed. Dennis P. Stolle, David B. Wexler, and Bruce J. Winick (Durham, NC: Carolina Academic Press, 2000).

6 David B. Wexler and Bruce J. Winick, *Essays in Therapeutic Jurisprudence* (Durham, NC: Carolina Academic Press, 1991).

7 Christopher Slobogin, "Therapeutic Jurisprudence: Five Dilemmas to Ponder," in *Law in a Therapeutic Key: Developments in Therapeutic Jurisprudence,* ed. David B. Wexler and Bruce J. Winick (Durham, NC: Carolina Academic Press, 1996), 775.

8 Charles Barton and Karen van den Broek, "Restorative Justice Conferencing and the Ethic of Care," *Ethics and Justice* 2, 2 (1999): 2.

9 David Wexler, "Therapeutic Jurisprudence: An Overview," *Thomas M. Cooley Law Review* 17, 1 (2000): 126.

10 See Bruce J. Winick, "The Jurisprudence of Therapeutic Jurisprudence," in *Law in a Therapeutic Key,* ed. David B. Wexler and Bruce J. Winick (Durham, NC: Carolina Academic Press, 1996), 645-68.

11 Ken Kress, "Therapeutic Jurisprudence and the Resolution of Value Conflicts: What We Can Realistically Expect, in Practice, from Theory," *Behavioral Sciences and the Law* 17 (1999): 571.

12 See William Schma, "Judging for the New Millenium," *Court Review* 37 (2000): 4-6; Pamela Casey and David B. Rottman, "Therapeutic Jurisprudence in the Courts," *Behavioral Sciences and the Law* 18 (2000): 445-57; M.W. Patry, D.B. Wexler, et al., "Better Legal Counseling through Empirical Research: Identifying Psycholegal Soft Spots and Strategies," in *Practicing Therapeutic Jurisprudence: Law as a Helping Profession,* ed. Dennis P. Stolle, David B. Wexler, and Bruce J. Winick (Durham, NC: Carolina Academic Press, 2000), 69-79.

13 Mark Gannage, *An International Perspective: A Review and Analysis of Approaches to Addressing Past Institutional or Systemic Abuse in Selected Countries* (Ottawa: Law Commission of Canada, 1998), Section 5, 11.

14 Martha Minow, *Between Vengeance and Forgiveness: Facing History after Genocide and Mass Violence* (Boston: Beacon Press, 1998).

15 Law Commission of Canada, *Restoring Dignity*, 83.

16 Gannage, *An International Perspective,* Section 5, 15.

17 These include the following: Newfoundland: Mount Cashel Orphanage, Belvedere Orphanage, Whitbourne Boys' School; Nova Scotia: the Shelburne School for Boys, the Nova Scotia School for Girls, the Nova Scotia Youth Training Centre; New Brunswick: the New Brunswick Training School at Kingsclear; Quebec: Les Enfants Duplessis, the Batshaw Youth and Family Centres; Ontario: the Grandview Training School for Girls, St. Joseph's Training School for Boys, St. John's Training School for Boys, The Syl Apps Campus at Thistletown Regional Centre, Father George Epoch and the Jesuit Fathers of Upper Canada, the Ernest C. Drury School for the Deaf, the Robarts School for the Deaf, the Sir James Whitney School for the Deaf; Alberta: the Westfield Diagnostic and Treatment Centre, the Provincial School for Mentally Defectives [sic] (the Michener Institute), the Northern Regional Treatment Residence; British Columbia: Jericho Provincial School for the Deaf, the Children's Park Youth Ranch, Arden Park Youth Ranch. See Ronda Bessner, *Institutional Child Abuse in Canada* (Ottawa: Law Commission of Canada, 1998).

18   Rhonda Claes and Deborah Clifton, *Needs and Expectations for Redress of Victims of Abuse at Native Residential Schools* (Ottawa: Law Commission of Canada, 1998), 2-3.
19   Feldthusen et al., "Therapeutic Consequences"; Deborah K. Hepler, "Providing Creative Remedies to Bystander Emotional Distress Victims: A Feminist Perspective," *Northern Illinois University Law Review* 14 (1994): 71-104.
20   The list includes Alberta (Victims of Crime Financial Benefits Program), British Columbia (Criminal Injury Section), Manitoba (the Criminal Injuries Compensation Board), New Brunswick (Victim Services Program), Nova Scotia (Criminal Injuries Compensation Program), Ontario (Criminal Injuries Compensation Board), Prince Edward Island (Victim Services), Quebec (Direction de l'indemnisation des victimes d'actes criminels), and Saskatchewan (Victims Services).
21   A detailed analysis of the methodology and findings of this study can be found in Feldthusen et al., "Therapeutic Consequences."
22   Compensation for Victims of Crime Act, R.S.O. 1990, c. 24.
23   The Training Schools Act was originally enacted as the Boys' Welfare Act, S.O. 1925, c. 80. It was eventually superseded by the Training Schools Act, S.O. 1931, c.60. It was last consolidated as R.S.O. 1980, c. 508 and repealed by S.O. 1984, c. 19, s. 12.
24   While at the facility, many Grandview residents had tattooed themselves with sewing needles and India ink. These tattoos were permanent reminders of the abuse they had received and their removal was an important part of the healing process.
25   See IHRD, *Review of the Needs of Victims.*
26   Feldthusen et al., "Therapeutic Consequences," 107 and 87.
27   Christopher Bagley and Kathleen King, *Committee on Sexual Offences against Children and Youths: Sexual Offences against Children* (Ottawa: Supply and Services Canada, 1984), 215.
28   H.L. MacMillan et al., "Prevalence of Child Physical and Sexual Abuse in the Community: Results from the Ontario Health Supplement," *Journal of the American Medical Association* 278, 2 (1997): 131-35.
29   Federal/Provincial/Territorial Working Group on Child and Family Services Information, *Child Welfare in Canada: The Role of Provincial and Territorial Authorities in Cases of Child Abuse* (Ottawa: Federal/Provincial/Territorial Working Group on Child and Family Services Information, 1994).
30   S.E. Romans, "Childhood Sexual Abuse: Concerns and Consequences," *Medical Journal of Australia* 166, 2 (1997): 59-60; D. Finkelhor, G. Hotaling, I.A. Lewis, and C. Smith, "Sexual Abuse in a National Survey of Adult Men and Women: Prevalence, Characteristics, and Risk Factors," *Child Abuse and Neglect* 14 (1997): 19-28; D. Finkelhor and A. Brown, "Impact of Child Sexual Abuse: A Review of the Research," *Psychological Bulletin* 99, 1 (1986): 66-77. This may be especially true for male victims. See D. Elliot and J. Briere, "The Sexually Abused Boy: Problems in Manhood," *Medical Aspects of Human Sexuality* 26, 2 (1992): 68.
31   D.E.H. Russell, "The Incidence and Prevalence of Intra-Familial and Extra-Familial Sexual Abuse of Female Children," *Child Abuse and Neglect* 7 (1983): 133-46.
32   W. Maltz and B. Holman, *Incest and Sexuality: A Guide to Understanding and Healing* (Toronto: Lexington Books, 1987).
33   Law Commission of Canada, *Restoring Dignity,* 14.
34   Ibid., 32.
35   Ibid., 28.
36   Robin West, *Caring for Justice* (New York: New York University Press, 1997), 219.
37   Agnes Grant, *No End of Grief: Indian Residential Schools in Canada* (Winnipeg: Pemmican Publishers, 1996), 224-25.
38   IHRD, *Review of the Needs of Victims,* 31.
39   W.N. Friedrich and L.C. Schafer, "Somatic Symptoms in Sexually Abused Children," *Journal of Pediatric Psychology* 20, 5 (1995): 661.
40   Law Commission of Canada, *Restoring Dignity,* 45.
41   J. Briere and D. Elliot, "Immediate and Long-Term Impacts of Child Sexual Abuse," *The Future of Children* 4, 2 (1994): 54-69; K.A. Kendall-Tackett, L. Meyer-Williams, and D. Finkelhor, "Impact of Sexual Abuse on Children: A Review and Synthesis of Recent Empirical

Studies," *Psychological Bulletin* 113, 1 (1993): 164-80; A.H. Green, "Child Sexual Abuse: Immediate and Long-Term Effects and Intervention," *Journal of the American Academy and Child Adolescent Psychiatry* 32, 5 (1993): 890-903; J. Beitchman, K. Zucker, et al., "A Review of the Long-Term Effects of Child Sexual Abuse," *Child Abuse and Neglect* 16 (1992): 101-18; D. Finkelhor, "Early and Long-Term Effects of Child Sexual Abuse: An Update," *Professional Psychology* 21 (1990): 325-30.

42 C. Ponée, "Child Abuse Programming at Work," in *Women, Work, and Wellness*, ed. V. Carver and C. Ponée (Toronto: Addiction Research Foundation, 1989); S.P. Widom, *Victims of Childhood Sexual Abuse: Later Criminal Consequences* (Washington, DC: US Department of Justice, Office of Justice Programs, National Institute of Justice, 1995); C. Cyr, *Modèle conceptuel: Programmation de la violence familiale dans un cadre correctionnel* (Ottawa: Service correctionnel du Canada, 1994); M.J. Rotheram-Borus et al., "Sexual Abuse History and Associated Multiple Risk Behavior in Adolescent Runaways," *American Journal of Orthopsychiatry* 66, 3 (1996): 390-400.

43 Claes and Clifton, *Needs and Expectations*.

44 Barton and van den Broek, "Restorative Justice," 4.

45 IHRD, *Review of the Needs of Victims* (Ottawa: Law Commission of Canada, 1998), 26.

46 Quoted in Doug Roche and Ben Hoffman, *The Vision to Reconcile: Process Report on the Helpline Reconciliation Model Agreement* (Waterloo, ON: Conflict Resolution Network Canada: Fund for Dispute Resolution, 1993), 21.

47 K.M. Fox and B.O. Gilbert, "The Interpersonal and Psychological Functioning of Women Who Experienced Childhood Physical Abuse, Incest, and Parental Alcoholism," *Child Abuse and Neglect* 18, 10 (1994): 849-58; G.E. Wyatt, D. Guthrie, and C.M. Notgrass, "Differential Effects of Women's Child Sexual Abuse and Subsequent Sexual Revictimization," *Journal of Consulting and Clinical Psychology* 60, 2 (1992): 167-73.

48 R.R. Hilton and G.C. Mezey, "Victims and Perpetrators of Child Sexual Abuse," *British Journal of Psychiatry* 189 (1996): 411-15; J. Kaufman and E. Ziegler, "Do Abused Children Become Abusive Parents?" *American Journal of Orthopsychiatry* 57, 2 (1987): 186-92; and D. Finkelhor, *Child Sexual Abuse: New Theory and Research* (New York: Free Press, 1984).

49 Law Commission of Canada, *Restoring Dignity*, 58.

50 O. Hankivsky and D. Draker, "The Economic Costs of Child Sexual Abuse in Canada: A Preliminary Analysis," *Journal of Health and Social Policy* 17, 2 (2003): 1-82.

51 Bruce J. Winick, "Applying the Law Therapeutically in Domestic Violence Cases," *Kansas City Law Review* 69, 33 (2000): 43.

52 Joan Tronto, *Moral Boundaries: A Political Argument for an Ethic of Care* (New York: Routledge, 1993), 134.

53 See Martha Minow, *Between Vengeance and Forgiveness: Facing History after Genocide and Mass Violence* (Boston: Beacon Press, 1998), 24.

54 Law Commission of Canada, *Restoring Dignity*.

55 West, *Caring for Justice*, 91.

56 Kate Paradine, "The Importance of Understanding Love and Other Feelings in Survivors' Experiences of Domestic Violence," *Court Review* 37 (Spring 2000): 40-7.

57 Tom Tyler, "The Psychological Consequences of Judicial Procedures: Implications for Civil Commitment Hearings," in *Law in a Therapeutic Key*, ed. David B. Wexler and Bruce J. Winick (Durham, NC: Carolina Academic Press, 1996); and Linda E. Allen et al., "In the Eye of the Beholder: Tort Litigants' Evaluations of their Experiences in the Civil Justice System," *Law and Society Review* 24 (1990): 953.

58 Feldthusen et al., "Therapeutic Consequences," 76.

59 Winick, "Applying the Law Therapeutically," 63.

60 Gannage, *An International Perspective*, 45.

61 Lukas Baba Kikwepere as recorded in *Reconciliation, Chapter 5, Final Report* (South Africa: The Truth and Reconciliation Commission, 2000), 2-3.

62 Feldthusen et al., "Therapeutic Consequences," 96.

63 Ibid., 89.

64 Ibid.

65 Ibid.

66 Law Commission of Canada, *Restoring Dignity*, 2.
67 Ibid., 68.
68 Feldthusen et al., "Therapeutic Consequences," 106.
69 Ibid.
70 Ibid.
71 Mount Cashel survivor, IHRD, *Review of the Needs of Victims*.
72 Judith Lewis Herman, *Trauma and Recovery* (New York: Basic Books, 1997), 215.
73 Feldthusen et al., "Therapeutic Consequences," 106-7, 107, 109.
74 Ibid., 109.
75 For instance, in their research for the Law Commission, the IHRD was unable to deter-
    mine how compensation amounts were chosen.
76 Feldthusen et al., "Therapeutic Consequences," 109.
77 See Daniel W. Shuman, "The Psychology of Compensation in Tort Law," in *Law in a
    Therapeutic Key*, ed. David B. Wexler and Bruce J. Winick (Durham, NC: Carolina Aca-
    demic Press, 1996), 439.
78 Feldthusen et al., "Therapeutic Consequences," 110.
79 Ibid., 100.
80 Ibid., 99.
81 As quoted in Minow, *Between Vengeance*, 91.
82 Feldthusen et al., "Therapeutic Consequences," 111.
83 Barton and van den Broek, "Restorative Justice," 3.
84 Daniel W. Shuman, "The Role of Apology in Tort Law," *Judicature* 83, 4 (2000): 180.
85 Feldthusen et al., "Therapeutic Consequences," 75 and 76.
86 Ibid., 97.
87 Fiona Bawdon, "Putting a Price on Rape: Increasing Compensation Awards," *New Law Jour-
    nal* 143 (1993): 372. For a provocative discussion of the inadequacy of financial compen-
    sation, especially for non-pecuniary losses, see Hepler, "Providing Creative Remedies," 71.
88 Feldthusen et al., "Therapeutic Consequences," 75-76.
89 Susan Alter, *Apologizing for Serious Wrongdoing: Social, Psychological and Legal Considera-
    tions* (Ottawa: Law Commission of Canada, May 1999), 5.
90 D. Henton and D. McCann, *Boys Don't Cry: The Struggle for Justice and Healing in Canada's
    Biggest Sex Abuse Scandal* (Toronto: McClelland and Stewart, 1995), 169.
91 Alter, *Apologizing*, 2.
92 Shuman, "Role of Apology."
93 Ibid., 183.
94 Alter, *Apologizing*, 4.
95 Minow, *Between Vengeance*, 17.
96 Shuman, "Role of Apology," 183.
97 Law Commission of Canada, *Restoring Dignity*, 76.
98 Alter, *Apologizing*, 3.
99 Feldthusen et al., "Therapeutic Consequences," 77..
100 As quoted in Steven Keeva, "Does the Law Mean Never Having to Say You're Sorry?"
    American Bar Association Journal 95 (December 1999): 67.
101 Alter, *Apologizing*, 16.
102 Minow, *Between Vengeance*, 116.
103 Feldthusen et al., "Therapeutic Consequences," 111.
104 Ibid., 100.
105 Herman, *Trauma*, 193.
106 IHRD, *Review of the Needs of Victims*, 15.
107 Feldthusen et al., "Therapeutic Consequences," 111.
108 Shelbourne survivor; Mount Cashel survivor.
109 IHRD, *Review of the Needs of Victims*, 7.
110 Ibid., 26.
111 Feldthusen et al., "Therapeutic Consequences," 111.
112 IRHD, *Review of the Needs of Victims*.
113 Ibid., 70.

114 L. Sky and V. Sparks, *Until Someone Listens (Work Book)* (Toronto: Skyworks Charitable Foundation, 1999), 7.
115 Herman, *Trauma*, 208.
116 Richard J. Goldstone, "Foreword," in Minow, *Between Vengeance*, x.
117 Neil S. Kritz, *Transitional Justice: How Emerging Democracies Reckon with Former Regimes* (Washington, DC: US Institute of Peace Press, 1995): 126-27.
118 Herman, *Trauma*, 211.
119 Barton and van den Broek, "Restorative Justice," 6.

Chapter 5: Economic Costing in Social Policy

1 M. Teresa Lunati, *Ethical Issues in Economics: From Altruism to Cooperation to Equity* (Hampshire: MacMillan Press, 1997), 74-75.
2 Margaret J. Radin, *Contested Commodities* (Cambridge: Harvard University Press, 1996); Elizabeth Anderson, *Value in Ethics and Economics* (Cambridge: Harvard University Press, 1993); Amartya Sen, *Commodities and Capabilities* (New York: Elsevier Science Publishing Co., 1985).
3 Virginia Held, "Liberalism and the Ethics of Care," in *On Feminist Ethics and Politics*, ed. Claudia Card (Lawrence: University Press of Kansas, 1999), 307.
4 Radin, *Contested Commodities*, xii.
5 Julie A. Nelson, "Feminism and Economics," *Journal of Economic Perspectives* 9, 2 (1995): 135.
6 Virginia Held, "Feminism and Moral Theory," in *Women and Moral Theory*, ed. Eva Feder Kittay and Diane T. Meyers (Totowa, NJ: Rowman and Littlefield, 1987), 116.
7 Anderson, *Value in Ethics*, 212.
8 Radin, *Contested Commodities*, 5.
9 Thomas S. Kuhn, *The Structure of Scientific Revolutions* (Chicago: University of Chicago Press, 1970), 206.
10 Radin, *Contested Commodities*, 5.
11 Joseph Heath, *The Efficient Society: Why Canada Is as Close to Utopia as It Gets* (Toronto: Penguin, 2001), 7.
12 Held, "Liberalism and the Ethics of Care," 305.
13 Elizabeth Anderson, "Is Women's Labour a Commodity?" in *Economics, Ethics, and Public Policy*, ed. Charles K. Wilber (Lanham, MD: Rowman and Littlefield, 1998), 217.
14 R. Moore et al., *Economic Burden of Illness in Canada, 1993* (Ottawa: Health Canada, 1997).
15 Eric Single et al., *The Costs of Substance Abuse in Canada: A Cost Estimation Study* (Ottawa: Canadian Centre on Substance Abuse, 1997).
16 M. Kasierman, "The Cost of Smoking in Canada, 1991," *Chronic Diseases in Canada* 18, 1 (1997): 15-22.
17 T. Albert and G. Williams, *The Economic Burden of HIV/AIDS in Canada* (Ottawa: Canadian Policy Research Networks, 1998).
18 Cassidy M. Klymasz, "Economic Costs of Schizophrenia in Canada: A Preliminary Study" (Ottawa: Schizophrenia Society of Canada and Health Canada, 1995).
19 National Crime Prevention Council, *Money Well Spent: Investing in Preventing Crime* (Ottawa: National Crime Prevention Council, 1996), l; Ted Miller et al., "Crime in the United States: Victim Costs and Consequences (1995)," unpublished manuscript.
20 A. Sherman, *Wasting America's Future: The Children's Defense Fund Report on the Costs of Child Poverty* (Boston: Beacon Press, 1994).
21 These include: L. Greaves, O. Hankivsky and J. Kingston-Riechers, *Selected Estimates of the Costs of Violence against Women in Canada: The Tip of the Iceberg* (London: Centre for Research on Violence Against Women and Children, 1995).
22 Dorothy P. Rice, *Estimating the Cost of Illness* (Washington, DC: US Department of Health, Education, and Welfare, Public Health Service, Division of Medical Care Administration, Health Economics Branch, 1966).
23 In cost-benefit analysis, both the program costs and results (benefits) are measured in monetary terms. This indicates whether or not society would reap a monetary benefit due to the implementation of a given policy, program, and/or service.

24   Unlike cost-benefit analysis, cost-effectiveness analysis does not require outcomes to be measured in dollar figures; instead, it considers benefits usually measured by changes in mortality and morbidity measured by common denominators such as life years saved or improvements in quality of life (e.g., QALs).

25   Alan Shiell, K. Gerard, and Cam Donaldson, "Cost of Illness Studies: An Aid to Decision-Making?" *Health Policy* 8, 3 (1987): 317.

26   Dorothy P. Rice, "Cost of Illness Studies: Fact or Fiction?" *Lancet* 344, 8936 (1994): 1519.

27   Leona VanRoijen et al., "Indirect Costs of Disease: An International Comparison," *Health Policy* 33 (1995): 16.

28   Thomas Hobbes, *Leviathan; or, the Matter, Forme, and Power of a Common Wealth, Ecclesiastical and Civil* (London: Andrew Cooke, 1651), 42.

29   Dorothy P. Rice et al., "Health Economic and Cost Implications of Anxiety and Other Mental Disorders in the United States," *British Journal of Psychiatry* 173, 34 (1998): 6.

30   Shiell, Gerard, and Donaldson, *Cost of Illness Studies*.

31   Steven Grover et al., "Prostate Cancer: The Economic Burden," *Canadian Medical Association Journal* 160, 5 (1999): 685.

32   See Radin, *Contested Commodities*, 3.

33   T.R. Miller et al., "Highway Crash Costs in the United States by Driver Age, Blood Alcohol Level, Victim Age, and Restraint Use," *Accident Analysis and Prevention* 30 (1998) 137-50; T.R. Miller and M. Galbraith, "Estimating the Costs of Occupational Injury in the United States," *Accident Analysis and Prevention* 27 (1995): 741-47; Miller et al., "Crime in the United States"; M.A. Cohen, "Pain, Suffering and Jury Awards: A Study of the Cost of Crime to Victims," *Law and Society Review* 22, 3 (1988): 537-55.

34   Miller and Galbraith, "Estimating the Costs of Occupational Injury," 744.

35   See Miller et al., "Highway Crash Costs."

36   Andrew Jay McClurg, "It's a Wonderful Life: The Case for Hedonic Damages in Wrongful Death Cases," *Notre Dame Law Review* 66, 57 (1990): 68.

37   See, for example, Miller and Cohen, "Victim Costs of Violent Crime and Resulting Injuries," *Health Affairs* 12, 4 (Winter 1993): 186-97; and Cohen, "Pain, Suffering."

38   The most popular of these measures — QALs — are collective scores that emerge from surveys that ask people to rank their preferred state of health in terms of the mobility and distress levels that affect normal daily life. Treatments are then assessed in terms of whether they lead to increased or decreased misery on the scale of values that has been derived.

39   Single et al., *The Costs of Substance Abuse*, 18.

40   See Dan Usher, "The Value of Life for Decision Making in the Public Sector," in *Ethics and Economics*, ed. Ellen Frankel Paul, Fred D. Miller, and Jeffrey Paul (Oxford: Basil Blackwell, 1985), 168-91.

41   Robert Evans, *Strained Mercy: The Economics of Canadian Health Care* (Toronto: Butterworths, 1984).

42   Radin, *Contested Commodities*, 2.

43   See Kenneth J. Arrow, "Invaluable Goods," *Journal of Economic Literature* 35 (June 1997): 756.

44   This phrase is taken from Elizabeth Anderson, "The Ethical Limitations of the Market," *Economics and Philosophy* 6 (1990): 179-205.

45   Elizabeth Anderson, *Value in Ethics and Economics* (Cambridge, MA: Harvard University Press, 1993), 143-44.

46   Joshua Cohen, "Value in Ethics and Economics," *Journal of Economic Literature* 33, 1 (1995): 192.

47   See, for example, E.J. Mishan, "Consistency in the Valuation of Life: A Wild Goose Chase?" in *Ethics and Economics*, ed. Ellen Frankel Paul, Fred D. Miller, and Jeffrey Paul (Oxford: Basil Blackwell, 1985); and Kenneth Henley, "The Value of Individuals," *Philosophy and Phenomenological Research* 37 (1977): 345-52.

48   Kurt W. Rothschild, *Ethics and Economic Theory: Ideas, Models, Dilemmas* (Aldershot, UK: Edward Elgar, 1993), 106.

49   D.J. Reynolds, "The Cost of Road Accidents," *Journal of the Royal Statistical Society* 119 (1956): 393-408.

50 Deborah Stone, *Policy Paradox and Political Reason* (New York: HarperCollins, 1988), 136.
51 Reynolds, "Cost of Road Accidents."
52 Albert and Williams, *The Economic Burden of HIV/AIDS*.
53 Larry E. Ruff, "The Economic Sense of Pollution," *Public Interest* 19 (Spring 1970): 69.
54 V. Kerry Smith, *Estimating Economic Values for Nature: Methods for Non-Market Valuation* (Cheltenham, UK: Edward Elgar, 1996), xvi.
55 Anderson, "Ethical Limitations," 193.
56 Marilyn Waring, *What Men Value and What Women Are Worth* (Toronto: University of Toronto Press, 1999), xlii.
57 Amartya Sen, *On Ethics and Economics* (Oxford: Basil Blackwell, 1987).
58 Rothschild, *Ethics and Economic Theory*, 2.
59 Daniel Hausman and Michael McPherson, "Taking Ethics Seriously: Economics and Contemporary Moral Philosophy," *Journal of Economic Literature* 31 (1993): 672.
60 Sen, *Commodities and Capabilities*; Peter D. Groenewegen, *Economics and Ethics?* (London and New York: Routledge, 1996).
61 Charles K. Wilber, *Economics, Ethics and Public Policy* (Lanham, MD: Rowman and Littlefield, 1998); Daniel Hausman and Michael McPherson, *Economic Analysis and Moral Philosophy* (Cambridge: Cambridge University Press, 1996); Lunati, *Ethical Issues in Economics*.
62 Frank Knight, *Risk, Uncertainty and Profit* (Chicago: University of Chicago Press, 1921), 454.
63 Westin, cited in Rothschild, *Ethics and Economic Theory*, 23.
64 Ibid., 16.
65 P.J. Cook and D.A. Graham, "The Demand for Insurance and Protection: The Case of Irreplaceable Commodities," *Quarterly Journal of Economics* 91, 1 (February 1977): 143.
66 Radin, *Contested Commodities*, 56.
67 Anderson, "Is Women's Labour a Commodity?" 269.
68 Radin, *Contested Commodities*, xiii.
69 Nancy Hartsock, *Money Sex, and Power: Toward a Feminist Historical Materialism* (New York: Longman, 1983), 39.
70 Anderson, "Is Women's Labour a Commodity?" 218.
71 Amartya Sen, *On Ethics and Economics* (New York: Basil Blackwell, 1987), 99.
72 See Nancy Folbre, *The Invisible Heart: Economics and Family Values* (New York: The New Press, 2001).
73 Scott Altman, "Com(Modifying)Experience," *Southern California Law Review* 65 (1991): 333.
74 Henry J. Aaron, "Distinguished Lecture on Economics in Government: Public Policy, Values, and Consciousness," *Journal of Economic Perspectives* 8, 2 (1994): 15.
75 Altman, "Com(Modifying) Experience," 333.
76 See "At the Shrine of Our Lady of Fatima, or Why Political Questions Are Not Economic," in Donald Van de Veer and Christine Pierce, *The Environmental Ethics and Policy Book* (Belmont: Wadsworth, 1994).
77 Radin, *Contested Commodities*, 59.
78 Martha C. Nussbaum, "Human Functioning and Social Justice: In Defense of Aristotelian Essentialism," *Political Theory* 20 (1992): 231.
79 Anderson, *Value in Ethics*, 267.
80 Anderson, "Is Women's Labour a Commodity?"
81 Radin, *Contested Commodities*, 21.
82 Held, "Liberalism and the Ethics of Care," 306.
83 Radin, *Contested Commodities*, 62.
84 Nussbaum, "Human Functioning and Social Justice," 231.
85 Anderson, *Value in Ethics*, 268.
86 Cohen, "Value in Ethics and Economics," 192.
87 Immanuel Kant, *Foundations of the Metaphysics of Morals with Critical Essays,* trans. Lewis White Beck, ed. Robert Paul Wolff (Indianapolis: Boss-Merrill, 1969), 60.
88 Anderson, *Value in Ethics*, 8-10.

89   Radin, *Contested Commodities*, 6.
90   Anderson, *Value in Ethics*, 211.
91   Tineke A. Abma, "Voices from the Margins: Political and Ethical Dilemmas in Evaluation," *CRSP/RCPS* 39 (1997): 42.
92   Martha C. Nussbaum, "Plato on Commensurability and Desire," in *Love's Knowledge: Essays on Philosophy and Literature* (New York: Oxford University Press, 1990), 106, 123.
93   Amartya Sen, *Objectivity and Position*, Lindley Lecture, University of Kansas, 1992.
94   Anderson, *Value in Ethics*, 194.
95   Ibid., 211.
96   Susan Donath, "The Other Economy: A Suggestion for Distinctively Feminist Economics," *Feminist Economics* 6, 1 (2000): 122.
97   Janice Gross Stein, *The Cult of Efficiency* (Don Mills, ON: Anansi, 2001), 62-63.
98   Romanow Commission, *Building on Values: The Future of Health Care in Canada* (Saskatoon: Commission on the Future of Health Care in Canada, 2002), xx.
99   Ibid., xvi.
100 Ibid., 120.
101 Robin West, *Caring for Justice* (New York: New York University Press, 1997), 55.
102 Ibid., 59.
103 Robert Rowe and Lauraine G. Chestnut, *The Value of Visibility: Economic Theory and Applications for Air Pollution Control* (Cambridge: Abt Books, 1982), 10.
104 See O. Hankivsky and D. Draker, "The Economic Costs of Child Sexual Abuse in Canada: A Preliminary Analysis," *Journal of Health and Social Policy* 17, 2 (2003): 1-33; and unpublished material in the possession of the authors.
105 Here I am specifically referring to QALs now being widely utilized in cost-effectiveness and cost-utility analyses.
106 Aaron, "Distinguished Lecture," 4.
107 Similar arguments have been made by Michèle Pujol, "Introduction: Broadening Economic Data and Methods," *Feminist Economics* 3, 2 (1997): 119-20; and Günseli Berik, "The Need for Crossing the Method Boundaries in Economic Research," *Feminist Economics* 3, 2 (1997): 1-33.
108 Joyce P. Jacobson and Andrew R. Newman, "What Data Do Economists Use? The Case of Labour Economics and Industrial Relations," *Feminist Economics* 3, 2 (1997): 129-30.
109 Berik, "The Need for Crossing the Method Boundaries," 122.
110 Radin, *Contested Commodities*, 215.
111 Daniel Engster, "The Political Economy of Care," paper presented at the 2003 Annual Meeting of the American Political Science Association, 28-31 August 2003, 2.
112 Janet L. Storch, "Foundational Values in Canadian Health Care," in *Efficiency Versus Equality: Health Reform in Canada*, ed. Michael Stingle and Donna Wilson (Halifax: Fernwood, 1996), 24.
113 Stein, *Cult of Efficiency*, 58.
114 Waring, *What Men Value*, xxiv.
115 BBC News, "Smoking Is Cost-Effective Says Report," 17 July 2001, 1.
116 According to Radin, a fungible object can pass in and out of a person's possession without having any effect on that person as long as its market equivalent is given in exchange, *Contested Commodities*, 87-88.
117 Nussbaum, "Human Functioning and Social Justice," 231.
118 Ibid., 271.
119 Victor R. Fuchs, *Who Shall Live? Health, Economics, and Social Choice* (New York: Basic Books, 1974), 148.
120 Adam Smith, *An Inquiry into the Nature and Causes of the Wealth of Nations* (London: Strahan and Cadell, 1776). Republished in *The Wealth of Nations*, ed. Edwin Canada (New York: Modern Library, 1937), 821.
121 Romanow, *Building on Values*, 49.
122 United Nations Development Programme, *Human Development Report 1996* (New York: Oxford University Press, 1997), 57.
123 E.F. Schumacher, *Small Is Beautiful* (New York: Harper and Row, 1974).

124 Michael J. Sandel, *Democracy's Discontent: America in Search of a Public Philosophy* (Cambridge: Harvard University Press, 1996).
125 Stein, *Cult of Efficiency*, 225-26.
126 Michael Bayles, "The Price of Life," *Ethics* 89, 1 (1978): 20-34.
127 Anderson, *Value in Ethics*, 207.
128 Radin, *Contested Commodities*, 103.
129 Ibid.
130 Ibid., 192.
131 Joan Tronto, *Moral Boundaries: A Political Argument for an Ethic of Care* (New York: Routledge, 1993), 172.
132 Patrick G. Welle, "Public Policy and the Quality of Life: How Relevant Is Economics?" *Atlantic Economic Journal* 27, 1 (1999): 103.
133 Tronto, *Moral Boundaries*, 105.
134 Richard Abel, "A Critique of Torts," 37 *University of California Law Review* 785 (1990): 804-6.
135 Anderson, *Value in Ethics*, 2.
136 David Seedhouse, *Ethics: The Heart of Health Care* (West Sussex, UK: John Wiley and Sons, 1998), 139.

Chapter 6: Caregiving
1 Robin West, *Caring for Justice* (New York: New York University Press, 1997).
2 Marilyn Friedman, "Beyond Caring," in *An Ethic of Care: Feminist and Interdisciplinary Perspectives*, ed. M.J. Larrabee (New York: Routledge, 1993), 183.
3 Joan Tronto, "Women and Caring: What Can Feminists Learn about Morality from Caring?" in *Justice and Care: Essential Readings in Feminist Ethics*, ed. V. Held (Boulder, CO: Westview Press, 1995), 102.
4 In *Moral Boundaries: A Political Argument for an Ethic of Care* (New York: Routledge, 1993), 118, Joan Tronto also argues that care is both an activity and a disposition.
5 This is a phrase from Rosemarie Tong, *Feminine and Feminist Ethics* (Belmont, CA: Wadsworth Publishing, 1993).
6 Tronto, *Moral Boundaries*, 178.
7 Janice McLaughlin, "An Ethic of Care: A Valuable Tool?" *Politics* 17, 1 (1997): 17.
8 See Will Kymlicka, *Contemporary Political Philosophy*, 2nd ed. (New York: Oxford University Press, 2002) for a discussion of how the ethic of justice relates to caring for others.
9 Carol Baines, Patricia M. Evans, and Sheila Neysmith, *Women's Caring: Feminist Perspectives on Social Welfare*, 2nd ed. (Toronto: Oxford University Press, 1998), 3.
10 Carol Thomas, "De-Constructing Concepts of Care," *Sociology* 27, 4 (1993): 654.
11 Lorraine Greaves et al., *Final Payments: Socioeconomic Costs of Palliative Home Caregiving in the Last Month of Life* (Ottawa: Centres of Excellence for Women's Health Program, Women's Health Bureau, Health Canada, 2002).
12 See Canadian Institute for Health Information, *Home Care: Health Information Standards and Related Initiatives* (Ottawa: CIHI, 1999), 2.
13 Pat Armstrong and Hugh Armstrong, *Thinking It Through: Women, Work and Caring in the New Millennium* (Nova Scotia: Maritime Centre of Excellence for Women's Health, Healthy Balance Project, 2001), 41.
14 Hilary Rose, "Hand, Brain, and Heart: A Feminist Epistemology for the Natural Sciences," *Signs* 9, 1 (1983): 75-90.
15 Pat Armstrong and Olga Kits, *Hundred Years of Caregiving* (Ottawa: Law Commission of Canada, 2001), 11.
16 The process of deinstitutionalization is not, in fact, altogether new. It began in the late 1960s, with patients suffering from psychiatric disorders. See H.G. Simmons, *Unbalanced: Mental Health Policy in Ontario, 1930-1989* (Toronto: Wall and Thompson, 1990).
17 P. Armstrong, "Fads and Foibles in Modern Health Care," paper presented at the 29th Annual Sorokin Lecture, University of Saskatchewan, 6 February 1997.
18 C. Ungerson, "Gender, Cash and Informal Care: European Perspectives and Dilemmas," *Journal of Social Policy* 24, 1 (1999): 44.

19   Sheila M. Neysmith, "From Home Care to Social Care: The Value of a Vision," in Baines et al., ed. *Women's Caring* (Toronto: Oxford University Press, 1998), 238.
20   For example, the Canadian Home Care Association has noted that the provincial government in Alberta cut $749 million from health care but added only $110 million to community care. Campbell et al., *Caregivers' Support Needs: Insights from the Experiences of Women Providing Care in Rural Nova Scotia* (Halifax: Maritime Centre of Excellence for Women's Health, Dalhousie University, 1998), 3.
21   M. Maltoni et al., "Evaluation of Cost of Home Therapy for Patients with Terminal Diseases," *Current Opinion in Oncology* 10 (1998): 302-9; M. Lane et al., "Location of Death as an Indicator of End-of-Life Costs for the Person with Dementia," *American Journal of Alzheimer's Disease* 13, 4 (1998): 208-10; J. Fast et al., *Conceptualizing and Operationalizing the Costs of Informal Elder Care* (Ottawa: Report to the National Health Research Development Program, 1997); H. Birnbaum and D. Kidder, "What Does Hospice Cost?" *American Journal of Public Health* 74, 7 (1984): 689-97.
22   See Health Canada, *Public Home Care Expenditures in Canada 1975-76 to 1997-98: Fact Sheets* (Ottawa: Health Canada, 1998), 3.
23   Sherry Hoppe and Edna Harder Mattson, "Bridging Care from Hospital to Home: An Innovative Joint Project," *Canadian Nursing Management* 95 (1996): 5-8.
24   Health Services Utilization and Research Commission, *Hospital and Home Care Study* (Saskatoon, SK: Health Services Utilization and Research Commission, 1998).
25   J.M. Gomas, "Palliative Care at Home: A Reality or Mission Impossible?" *Palliative Medicine* 14, 3 (1993): 47.
26   Martha Albertson Fineman, "Contract and Care," *Chicago-Kent Law Review* 76 (2001): 1421.
27   See J.E. Fast and J.A. Frederick, "Informal Eldercare: Is It Really Cheaper?" paper presented at the International Association of Time Use Researchers Conference, Colchester, England, October 1999.
28   Shelagh Day and Gwen Brodsky, *Women and the Equality Deficit: The Impact of Restructuring Canada's Social Programs* (Ottawa: Status of Women Canada, 1998).
29   Deborah Stone, "Care and Trembling," *The American Prospect* 10, 43 (1999): 61-67.
30   By 2041 it is expected that more than 22 percent of the population will be over sixty-five. Statistics Canada, "Snapshot No. 1: A Growing Population," at <http://www.hc-sc.gc.ca/seniors-aines/pubs/factoids/2001/no01_e.htm> (accessed 15 March 2004).
31   Romanow Commission, *Building on Values: The Future of Health Care in Canada* (Saskatoon: Commission on the Future of Health Care in Canada, 2002), 184.
32   "Health Care Renewal Accord 2003," at <http://www.hc-sc.gc.ca/english/hca2003/accord.html> (accessed 20 February 2003).
33   The National Coordinating Group on Health Care Reform and Women — Pat Armstrong, Madeline Boscoe, Barbara Chow, Karen Grant, Ann Pederson, Kay Wilson with Olena Hankivsky, Beth Jackson and Marina Morrow, *Reading Romanow: The Implications of the Final Report of the Commission on the Future of Health Care in Canada for Women* (Canadian Women's Health Network, 2003), 34.
34   Arlie Russell Hochschild, "The Culture of Politics: Traditional, Post-Modern, Cold-Modern, and Warm-Modern Ideals of Care," *Social Politics* 2, 3 (1995): 335.
35   Eva Feder Kittay, *Love's Labor: Essays on Women's Equality and Dependency* (New York: Routledge, 1999), 133.
36   Kymlicka, *Contemporary Political Philosophy*.
37   See Berenice Fisher and Joan Tronto, "Toward a Feminist Theory of Caring," in *Circles of Care: Work and Identity in Women's Lives*, ed. Emily K. Abel and Margaret K. Nelson (New York: State University of New York Press, 1990).
38   Fisher and Tronto, "Toward a Feminist Theory of Caring," 35.
39   Selma Sevenhuijsen, *Citizenship and the Ethics of Care: Feminist Considerations on Justice, Morality and Politics* (London and New York: Routledge, 1998), 131.
40   Alison Jaggar, *Feminist Politics and Human Nature* (Totowa, NJ: Rowman and Allanheld, 1988).
41   See Susan Sherwin, "A Relational Approach to Autonomy in Health Care," in *The Politics*

of Women's Health: Exploring Agency and Autonomy, ed. Susan Sherwin et al. (Philadelphia: Temple University Press, 1998).

42 Kittay, *Love's Labor,* 29.
43 Fineman, "Contract and Care," 1403.
44 Arnlaug Leira, "Concepts of Caring: Loving, Thinking, and Doing," *Social Service Review* 68 (June 1994): 197.
45 Ibid., 198.
46 Joan Tronto, "Politics, Plurality and Purpose: How to Investigate and Theorize Care in an Institutional Context," in *Care, Citizenship and Social Cohesion: Towards a Gender Perspective,* ed. T. Knijn and S. Sevenhuijsen (Utrecht: Netherlands School for Social and Economic Policy, 1998), 27.
47 M.L. Johnson, "Interdependency and the Generational Compact," *Ageing and Society* 15 (1995): 262.
48 Joan Tronto, "An Ethic of Care," *Generations* 22, 3 (1998): 19.
49 Sevenhuijsen, *Citizenship and the Ethics of Care,* 139.
50 Similar arguments have been made by Trudie Knijn and Monique Kremer, "Gender and the Caring Dimension of Welfare States: Toward Inclusive Citizenship," *Social Politics* 4, 3 (1997): 328-61.
51 Canadian Institute for Health Information, *Home Care: Health Information Standards and Related Initiatives* (Ottawa: Canadian Institute for Health Information, 1999).
52 These include Marika Morris et al., *The Changing Nature of Home Care and Its Impact on Women's Vulnerability to Poverty* (Ottawa: Status of Women Canada, November 1999); Bonnie Blakley and JoAnn Jaffe, *Coping as a Rural Caregiver: The Impact of Health Care Reforms on Rural Women Informal Caregivers — A Saskatchewan Study* (Winnipeg: Prairie Women's Health Centre of Excellence, 2000); Campbell et al., *Caregivers' Support Needs.*
53 R. Eliasson Lappalainen and I. Nilsson Motevasel, "Ethics of Care and Social Policy," *Scandinavian Journal of Social Welfare* 6 (1997): 193.
54 See Karen S. Lyons and Steven H. Zarit, "Formal and Informal Support: The Great Divide," *International Journal of Geriatric Psychiatry* 14 (1999): 183-92.
55 See Ontario Ministry of Community and Social Services, *Redirection of Long-Term Care and Support Service in Ontario* (Toronto: Queen's Printer for Ontario, 1991), 210; M. Denton, "The Linkages between Informal and Formal Care of the Elderly," *Canadian Journal on Aging* 16, 1 (1997): 30-50; and Kelly Cranswick, *Canada's Caregivers* (Ottawa: Statistics Canada, 1997).
56 It is estimated that approximately one-fifth of caregiving is done by friends and neighbours. See N.C. Keating et al., *Eldercare in Canada: Context, Content, and Consequences* (Ottawa: Statistics Canada Housing Family and Social Statistics Division, 1999), 53.
57 See S. Neysmith and J. Aronson, "Working Conditions in Home Care: Negotiating Issues of Race and Class in Gendered Work," *International Journal of Health Services* 27, 3 (1997): 479-99.
58 Ann Shola Orloff, "Gender and the Social Rights of Citizenship," *American Sociological Reviews* 58 (June 1993): 313.
59 Statistics Canada, *Who Cares? Caregiving in the 1990s: General Social Survey* (Ottawa: unpublished data, 1996) as quoted in Campbell et al., *Caregivers' Support Needs,* 9.
60 National Advisory Council on Ageing, *Ageing Vignettes: "A Quick Portrait of Dementia in Canada"* (Ottawa: NACA, 1996), 34-50.
61 Marika Morris, *Gender-Sensitive Home and Community Care and Caregiving Research: A Synthesis Paper* (Ottawa: Health Canada Women's Health Bureau, 2001), 2.
62 Keating et al., *Eldercare in Canada.*
63 The findings of this particular study have been challenged by Keating et al. for a number of reasons. The authors question whether the survey captured work that is not always considered "caregiving," and they also pointed out that statistics did not include care for persons under the age of sixty-five, thus underestimating the number of women caregivers.
64 See Cranswick, *Canada's Caregivers.*

65   Annette Baier, "The Need for More Than Justice," in *Science, Morality, and Feminist Theory*, ed. Marcia Hanen and Kai Nielsen, *Canadian Journal of Philosophy* 13, Suppl. (1987): 41-56.
66   See, for example, A. Snowden and D. Kane, "Parental Needs Following the Discharge of a Hospitalized Child," *Pediatric Nurse* 21 (1995): 425-28.
67   Keating et al., *Eldercare in Canada*.
68   Ibid.
69   Karen Parent and Malcolm Anderson, *CARP's Report Card on Home Care in Canada, 2001* (Toronto: CARP, 2001), 31; see Monique A.M. Gignac, E. Kevin Kelloway, and Benjamin H. Gottlieb, "The Impact of Caregiving on Employment: A Mediational Model of Work-Family Conflict," *Canadian Journal on Aging* 15, 4 (1996): 525-42.
70   J.E. Fast and J.A. Frederick, "Working Arrangements and Time Stress," *Canadian Social Trends* 45 (1996): 14-19.
71   J.E. Fast and M. DaPont, "Changes in Women's Employment Continuity," *Canadian Social Trends* 46 (1997): 2-7.
72   Janet Fast, Jaquie Eales, and Norah Keating, *Economic Impact of Health, Income Security and Labour Policies on Informal Caregivers of Frail Seniors* (Ottawa: Status of Women Canada: Policy Research Fund, March 2001), 38.
73   J. Jenson and J. Jacobzone, *Care Allowances for the Frail Elderly and Their Impact on Women Care-Givers* (Paris: Organisation for Economic Co-operation and Development, Directorate for Education Employment Labour and Social Affairs, 2000), 26.
74   Armstrong and Kits, *Hundred Years of Caregiving*, 12; J.M. Keefe and P. Facney, "Financial Compensation or Home Help Services: Examining Differences among Program Recipients," *Canadian Journal on Aging/La Revue Canadienne du Vieillissement* 16, 2 (1997): 256.
75   James J. Rice and Michael J. Prince, *Changing Politics of Canadian Social Policy* (Toronto: University of Toronto Press, 2000), 166.
76   The components of the two lists are derived from Armstrong and Kits, *Hundred Years of Caregiving*; and Keating et al., *Eldercare in Canada*.
77   A.E. Joseph and B.C. Hallman, "Over the Hill and Far Away: Distance as a Barrier to the Provision of Assistance to Elderly Relatives," *Social Science and Medicine* 46, 6 (1998): 631-39; J. Kaden and S.A. McDaniel, "Caregiving and Care-Receiving: A Double Bind for Women in Canada's Aging Society," *Journal of Women and Aging* 2, 3 (1990): 3-26.
78   Colleen Flood, *Unpacking the Shift to Home Care* (Halifax: Maritime Centre of Excellence for Women's Health, 2002), 18.
79   Pat Armstrong and Hugh Armstrong, *Take Care: Warning Signals for Canada's Health System* (Toronto: Garamond, 1994), 98.
80   Armstrong and Kits, *Hundred Years of Caregiving*, 34.
81   See J. Aronson and S. Neysmith, "The Retreat of the State and Long-Term Provision: Implementations for Frail Elderly People, Unpaid Family Carers and Paid Home Care Workers," *Studies in Political Economy* 53 (Summer 1997): 37-66.
82   See Campbell et al., *Caregivers' Support Needs*.
83   Blakley and Jaffe, *Coping as a Rural Caregiver*, 2.
84   Ibid.
85   G.G. Giarchi, "Distance Decay and Information Deprivation: Health Implications for People in Rural Isolation," in *New Directions in the Sociology of Health*, ed. P. Abbott and G. Payne (New York: Famler Press, 1990).
86   Kathleen Connors, personal interview, 4 June 1998, quoted in Morris et al., *The Changing Nature of Home Care*, 64.
87   Sharon Tennstedt, "Family Caregiving in an Aging Society," paper presented at the US Administration on Aging Symposium, entitled "Longevity in the New American Century," Baltimore, Maryland, 29 March 1999, 9.
88   Matthew Sanger, *Reckless Abandon: Canada, the GATS and the Future of Health Care* (Ottawa: Canadian Centre for Policy Alternatives, 2001); Aleck Ostry, "The New International Trade Regime: Problems for Publicly Funded Healthcare in Canada?" *Canadian Journal of Public Health* 31, 3 (2000): 475-80.
89   See O. Hankivsky, M. Morrow, P. Armstrong, with L. Galvin and H. Grinvalds, *Trade Agreements, Home Care and Women's Health* (Ottawa: Status of Women Canada, forthcoming).

90 See Campbell et al., *Caregivers' Support Needs;* P.G. Hawranik and L.A. Strain, *Health of Informal Caregivers: Effects of Gender, Employment and Use of Home Care Services* (Winnipeg: Centre of Aging and Faculty of Nursing, University of Manitoba, 2000); Aronson and Neysmith, "The Retreat of the State"; and Shauna-Vi Harlton, Norah Keating, and Janet Fast, "Defining Eldercare for Policy and Practice: Perspectives Matter," *Family Relations* 47, 3 (1998): 1-8.

91 See Mona Harrington, *Care and Equality: Inventing a New Family Politics* (New York: Routledge, 2000), 179.

92 Clement, *Care, Autonomy, and Justice,* 25.

93 Ann Robertson, "Beyond Apocalyptic Demography: Toward a Moral Economy of Interdependence," *Aging and Society* 17 (1997): 441.

94 Nancy Fraser, *Unruly Practices: Power, Discourse and Gender in Contemporary Social Theory* (Minneapolis: University of Minneapolis Press, 1989).

95 Selma Sevenhuijsen, "South African Social Policy and the Ethic of Care," paper prepared for the annual meeting of the American Political Science Association, San Francisco, 30 August-2 September 2001, 14-15.

96 Sevenhuijsen, *Citizenship and the Ethics of Care,* 85.

97 N.R. Hooyman and J. Gonyea, *Feminist Perspectives on Family Care: Policies for Gender Justice* (Thousand Oaks, CA: Sage Publications, 1995), 346.

98 Campbell et al., *Caregivers' Support Needs,* 3.

99 See A. Noonan, S. Tennstedt, and F. Rebelsky, "Making the Best of It: Themes of Meaning among Informal Caregivers to the Elderly," *Journal of Aging Society* 10, 4 (1996): 313-28.

100 Greaves et al., *Final Payments.*

101 Ibid.

102 As quoted in Campbell et al., *Caregivers' Support Needs,* 59.

103 Hilary Graham, "Caring: A Labour of Love," in *A Labour of Love,* ed. J. Finch and D. Groves (London: Routledge and Kegan Paul, 1993), 16.

104 Fineman, "Contract and Care," 1412.

105 Statistics Canada, *Who Cares?*

106 Keating et al., *Eldercare in Canada.*

107 Statistics Canada, *Who Cares?*

108 Blakley and Jaffe, *Coping as a Rural Caregiver,* 6.

109 Ibid., 6.

110 The Roeher Institute, *Beyond the Limits: Mothers Caring for Children with Disabilities* (Toronto: The Roeher Institute, 2000); The Roeher Institute, *When Kids Belong: Supporting Children with Complex Needs — At Home and in the Community* (Toronto: The Roeher Institute, 2000); The Roeher Institute, *Agenda for Action: Policy Directions for Children with Disabilities and Families* (Toronto: The Roeher Institute, 2000); The Roeher Institute, *Finding a Way In: Parents on Social Assistance Caring for Children with Disabilities* (Toronto: The Roeher Institute, 2000).

111 As quoted in Campbell et al., *Caregivers' Support Needs,* 21.

112 Ibid., 20.

113 Greaves et al., *Final Payments.*

114 Blakley and Jaffe, *Coping as a Rural Caregiver,* 9.

115 See Janice M. Keefe and Sheva Medjuck, "The Contribution of Long Term Economic Costs and Predicting Strain among Employed Women Caregivers," *Journal of Women and Aging* 9, 3 (1997): 3-25.

116 Morris et al., *Changing Nature of Home Care,* 52.

117 Greaves, et al., *Final Payments;* and Cranswick, *Canada's Caregivers.*

118 Cranswick, *Canada's Caregivers,* 6.

119 H.C. Northcott and B.R. Northcott, *The 1999 Survey about Health and the Health Care System in Alberta* (Edmonton: Alberta Health and Wellness through the Population Research Laboratory at the University of Alberta, 1999).

120 See G. Meshefedjian et al., "Factors Associated with Symptoms of Depression among Informal Caregivers of Demented Elders in the Community," *Gerontologist* 38, 2 (1998):

247-53; and S. Dhawan, "Caregiving Stress and Acculturation in East Indian Immigrants: Caring for Their Elders" (PhD diss., Queen's University, Kingston, 1998), 25.
121 Armstrong and Kits, *Hundred Years of Caregiving*, 15.
122 These quotes taken from Greaves et al., *Final Payments*.
123 Alisa L. Carse and Hilde Lindemann Nelson, "Rehabilitating Care," *Kennedy Institute of Ethics Journal* 6, 1 (1996): 26.
124 Victoria Davion, "Integrity and Radical Change," in *Feminist Ethics*, ed. Claudia Card (Lawrence: University of Kansas Press, 1991).
125 Greaves et al., *Final Payments*.
126 Cranswick, *Canada's Caregivers*, 6.
127 Keating et al., *Eldercare in Canada*.
128 Greaves et al., *Final Payments*, 49.
129 Tronto, *Moral Boundaries*, 117.
130 Armstrong and Armstrong, *Thinking It Through*.
131 Pat Armstrong and Hugh Armstrong, *Wasting Away: The Undermining of Canadian Health Care* (Toronto: Oxford University Press, 1996), 145.
132 C. Ward-Griffin and P. McKeever, "Relationships between Nurses and Family Caregivers: Partners in Care?" *Advances in Nursing Science* 22, 3 (2000): 101.
133 Greaves et al., *Final Payments*.
134 Price WaterhouseCoopers, *Canada Health Monitor*, Fall 1998.
135 Health Canada and the Hay Group, *The Berger Monitor* (Ottawa: Health Canada, 1999).
136 Romanow, *Building on Values*, 177.
137 Parent has made a similar argument.
138 As quoted in Campbell et al., *Caregivers' Support Needs*.
139 Ibid., 22.
140 Harrington, *Care and Equality*, 23.
141 Sevenhuijsen, "Caring in the Third Way," 4.
142 National Forum on Health (Canada), *Canada Health Action: Building on the Legacy*, vol. 2: *Synthesis Report and Issues Papers* (Ottawa: National Forum on Health, 1997), 19.
143 Blakley and Jaffe, *Coping as a Rural Caregiver*.
144 Campbell et al., *Caregivers' Support Needs*.
145 Ibid.
146 Greaves et al., *Final Payments*.
147 Ibid.
148 Nova Scotia Centre on Aging, *Both Puzzle and Paradox: Support for Informal Caregivers in Atlantic Canada* (Halifax: Mount Saint Vincent University, 1998).
149 Campbell et al., *Caregivers Support Needs*.
150 As quoted in Health Canada, Division of Aging and Seniors, "The Future of Caregiving," *Seniors Info Exchange* 7, 1 (1997-98): 1-16.
151 See National Forum on Health (Canada), *Canada Health Action: Building on the Legacy*, vol. 2: *Synthesis Report and Issues Papers* (Ottawa: National Forum on Health, n.d.).
152 Morris et al., *Changing Nature of Home Care*, 36.
153 Ibid., 42 (unpaid caregiver in Winnipeg).
154 Ibid., 34.
155 Blakley and Jaffe, *Coping as a Rural Caregiver*, 9.
156 As quoted in Campbell et al., *Caregivers' Support Needs*, 20.
157 Ibid.
158 Ibid., 23.
159 Ibid.
160 Deborah Stone, "Caring by the Book," in *Care Work: Gender, Labour, and the Welfare State*, ed. Madonna Harrington Meyer (London: Routledge, 2000), 91.
161 See Linda C. McClain, "Care as a Public Value," *Chicago-Kent Law Review* 76 (2001): 1679.
162 Rita Manning, "Just Caring," in *Explorations in Feminist Ethics: Theory and Practice*, ed. Eve Browning Cole and Susan Coultrap-McQuin (Bloomington: Indiana University Press, 1992), 52.
163 West, *Caring for Justice*, 35.

164   Sevenhuijsen, "Caring in the Third Way," 26.
165   McClain, "Care as a Public Value," 1706.
166   Nancy Fraser, *Justice Interruptus: Critical Reflections on the "Postsocialist" Condition* (New York: Routledge, 1997), 41, 61.
167   This claim is also made by Knijn and Kremer in "Gender and the Caring Dimension of Welfare States."
168   Harrington, *Care and Equality*.
169   McClain, "Care as a Public Value," 1673.
170   Sevenhuijsen, "Caring in the Third Way," 27.
171   Kittay, *Love's Labor*.

Conclusion

1   Joseph H. Carens, *Culture, Citizenship, and Community: A Contextual Exploration of Justice as Evenhandedness* (Oxford: Oxford University Press, 2000), 2.
2   Nel Noddings, *Starting at Home: Caring and Social Policy* (Berkeley: University of California Press, 2002), 53.
3   Eva Feder Kittay, "Social Policy," in *A Companion to Feminist Philosophy*, ed. Alison M. Jaggar and Iris Marion Young (Oxford: Blackwell, 1998), 578.
4   Selma Sevenhuijsen, *Citizenship and the Ethics of Care: Feminist Considerations on Justice, Morality, and Politics* (London and New York: Routledge, 1998), ix.
5   Linda C. McLain, "Care as a Public Value," *Chicago-Kent Law Review* 76 (2001): 1677.
6   Alisa L. Carse and Hilde Lindemann Nelson, "Rehabilitating Care," *Kennedy Institute of Ethics Journal* 6, 1 (1996): 30-31.
7   Gillian Dalley, *Ideologies of Caring: Rethinking Community and Collectivism* (London: Macmillan Press, 1996).
8   Emily K. Abel and Margaret K. Nelson, eds., *Circles of Care: Work and Identity in Women's Lives* (New York: State University of New York Press, 1990).
9   A similar argument is made by Robin West, *Caring for Justice* (New York: New York University Press, 1997), 35.
10   I borrow this phrase from Parent and Anderson, *CARP's Report Card*, 37.

Bibliography

Aaron, Henry J. "Distinguished Lecture on Economics in Government: Public Policy, Values and Consciousness." *Journal of Economic Perspectives* 8, 2 (1994): 3-21.

Abel, Emily K., and Margaret K. Nelson. *Circles of Care: Work and Identity in Women's Lives.* Albany: State University of New York Press, 1990.

Abel, Richard. "A Critique of Torts." *University of California Law Review* 37, 785 (1990): 804-6.

Abma, Tineke A. "Voices from the Margins: Political and Ethical Dilemmas in Evaluation." *CRPS/RCPS* 39 (1997): 41-53.

A.G. Canada v. *Lavell et al.,* [1974] S.C.R. 1349.

Albert, T., and G. Williams. *The Economic Burden of HIV/AIDS in Canada.* Ottawa: Canadian Policy Research Network, CPRN Study no. H/02, 1998.

Allan, Lind, Robert MacCoun, Patricia Ebener, William Felstiner, Deborah Hensler, Judith Resnick, and Tom Tyler. "In the Eye of the Beholder: Tort Litigants' Evaluations of Their Experiences in the Civil Justice System." *Law and Society Review* 24 (1990): 953-96.

Allers, C.T., K.J. Benjack, and J.T. Rousey. "HIV Vulnerability and the Adult Survivor of Childhood Sexual Abuse." *Child Abuse and Neglect* 17 (1993): 291-98.

Alter, Susan. *Apologizing for Serious Wrongdoing: Social, Psychological and Legal Considerations.* Ottawa: Law Commission of Canada, May 1999.

Altman, Scott. "Com(Modifying) Experience." *Southern California Law Review* 65 (1991): 293-340.

Anderson, Charles W. "The Place of Principles in Policy Analysis." *American Political Science Review* 73 (1979): 711-23.

Anderson, Elizabeth. "The Ethical Limitations of the Market." *Economics and Philosophy* 6 (1990): 179-205.

–. *Value in Ethics and Economics.* Cambridge, MA: Harvard University Press, 1993.

–. "Is Women's Labour a Commodity?" In *Economics, Ethics, and Public Policy,* ed. Charles K. Wilber, 267-86. Lanham, MD: Rowman and Littlefield, 1998.

Andrews v. *Law Society of British Columbia,* [1989] 1 S.C.R. 143.

Armstrong, Pat. "Fads and Foibles in Modern Health Care." Paper presented at the 28th Annual Sorokin Lecture, University of Saskatchewan, 6 February 1997.

–. "The Welfare State as History." In *The Welfare State in Canada: Past, Present, and Future,* ed. Raymond B. Blake, Penny E. Bryden, and J. Frank Strain, 52-73. Concord, ON: Irwin Publishing, 1997.

Armstrong, Pat, and Hugh Armstrong. *Take Care: Warning Signals for Canada's Health System.* Toronto: Garamond, 1994.

–. *Wasting Away: The Undermining of Canadian Health Care.* Toronto: Oxford University Press, 1996.

–. *Thinking It Through: Women, Work and Caring in the New Millennium.* Halifax, NS: Maritime Centre of Excellence for Women's Health: Healthy Balance Project, 2001.

Armstrong, Pat, and Olga Kits. *Hundred Years of Caregiving*. Ottawa: Law Commission of Canada, 2001.

Arnold, Peter. *Sport, Ethics and Education*. London: Cassel, 1997.

Aronson, J., and S. Neysmith. "The Retreat of the State and Long-Term Provision: Implementations for Frail Elderly People, Unpaid Family Carers and Paid Home Care Workers." *Studies in Political Economy* 53 (Summer 1997): 37-66.

Arrow, Kenneth J. "Invaluable Goods." *Journal of Economic Literature* 35, 2 (1997): 756-65.

Bacchi, Carol Lee. *Same Difference: Feminism and Sexual Difference*. Sidney, Australia: Allen and Unwin, 1990.

Badgley, Robin F. *Sexual Offences against Children: Report of the Committee on Sexual Offences against Children and Youths*. Ottawa: Supply and Services Canada, 1984.

Bagley, Christopher, and Kathleen King. *Committee on Sexual Offences against Children and Youths: Sexual Offences against Children*. Ottawa: Supply and Services Canada, 1984.

Baier, Annette C. "Hume, the Women's Moral Theorist." In *Women and Moral Theory*, ed. Eva Feder Kittay and Diana T. Meyers, 37-55. Totowa: Rowman and Littlefield, 1987.

–. "The Need for More Than Justice." In *Science, Morality and Feminist Theory*, ed. Marcia Hanen and Kai Nielsen. *Canadian Journal of Philosophy* 13, Supp. (1987): 41-56.

Baines, Carol, Patricia M. Evans, and Sheila M. Neysmith, eds. *Women's Caring: Feminist Perspectives on Social Welfare*. Toronto: Oxford University Press, 1998.

Bakan, Joel. *Just Words: Constitutional Rights and Social Wrongs*. Toronto: University of Toronto Press, 1997.

Banting, Keith. "Keeping Our Balance: The Political Imperatives of Social Policy Reform." *Policy Options* 15 (July-August 1994): 64-69.

Barker, E. *The Politics of Aristotle*. Book 3, xii. London: Oxford University Press, 1946.

Barry, J. "Care-Need and Care-Receivers: Views from the Margin." *Women's Studies International Forum* 18, 3 (1995): 361-74.

Bartholomew, Amy. "Achieving a Place for Women in a Man's World: Or Feminism with No Class." *Canadian Journal of Women and the Law* 6 (1993): 465-90.

Barton, Charles, and Karen van den Broek. "Restorative Justice Conferencing and the Ethic of Care." *Ethics and Justice* 2, 2 (1999): 55-66.

Bawdon, Fiona. "Putting a Price on Rape: Increasing Compensation Awards." *New Law Journal* 143 (1993): 371-72.

Bayles, Michael. "The Price of Life." *Ethics* 89, 1 (1978): 20-34.

Beane, J.A. *Affect in the Curriculum: Toward Democracy, Dignity, and Diversity*. New York: Teachers College Press, 1990.

Beitchman, J., K. Zucker, J. Hood, G. DaCosta, D. Akman, and E. Cassavia. "A Review of the Long-Term Effects of Child Sexual Abuse." *Child Abuse and Neglect* 16 (1992): 101-18.

Bender, Leslie. "A Lawyer's Primer on Feminist Theory and Tort." *Journal of Legal Education* 38, 3 (1988): 58-74.

–. "From Gender Difference to Feminist Solidarity: Using Carol Gilligan and an Ethic of Care in Law." *Vermont Law Review* 15, 1 (1990): 1-50.

Benhabib, Seyla. "The Generalized and the Concrete Other: The Kohlberg-Gilligan Controversy and Moral Theory." In *Women and Moral Theory*, ed. Eva Feder Kittay and Diana T. Meyers, 154-77. Totowa: Rowman and Littlefield, 1987.

–. "The Generalized and the Concrete Other: The Kohlberg-Gilligan Controversy and Feminist Theory." In *Feminism as Critique*, ed. Seyla Benhabib and Drucilla Cornell, 77-95. Minneapolis: University of Minnesota Press, 1987.

Berik, Gunseli. "The Need for Crossing the Method Boundaries in Economic Research." *Feminist Economics* 3, 2 (1997): 121-27.

Bessner, Ronda. *Institutional Child Abuse in Canada*. Ottawa: Law Commission of Canada, fall 1998.

Birnbaum, H., and D. Kidder. "What Does Hospice Cost?" *American Journal of Public Health* 74, 7 (1984): 689-97.

Blake, Raymond B., Penny E. Bryden,, and J. Frank Strain, eds. *The Welfare State in Canada: Past, Present, and Future*. Concord, ON: Irwin Publishing, 1997.

Blakley, Bonnie, and JoAnn Jaffe. *Coping as a Rural Caregiver: The Impact of Health Care Reforms on Rural Women Informal Caregivers – A Saskatchewan Study.* Winnipeg: Prairie Women's Health Centre of Excellence, 2000.

Bliss v. *A.G. Canada* (1978), 92 D.L.R. (3d) 417; [1979] 1 S.C.R. 183.

Blum, Lawrence. *Friendship, Altruism, and Morality.* London: Routledge and Kegan Paul, 1980.

Bowden, Peta. *Caring: Gender-Sensitive Ethics.* London: Routledge, 1997.

Boychuk, Gerard W. "Federal Spending in Health: Why Here? Why Now?" In *How Ottawa Spends 2002-2003: The Security Aftermath and National Priorities,* ed. G. Bruce Doern, 121-36. Don Mills, ON: Oxford University Press, 2002.

Briere, J. "Methodological Issues in the Study of Sexual Abuse Effects." *Journal of Counselling and Clinical Psychology* 60, 2 (1992): 196-203.

Briere, J., and D. Elliot. "Immediate and Long-Term Impacts of Child Sexual Abuse." *The Future of Children* 4, 2 (1994): 54-69.

Brink, Satya, and Allen Zeesman. *Measuring Social Well-Being: An Index of Social Health for Canada R-97-9e.* Hull, QC: Applied Research Branch Strategic Policy Human Resources Development Canada, 1997.

British Broadcasting Corporation. "Smoking Is Cost-Effective Says Report." 2001.

Brodie, Janine. *Politics on the Boundaries: Restructuring and the Canadian Women's Movement.* Toronto: Robarts Centre for Canadian Studies, 1994.

–. *Critical Concepts: An Introduction to Politics.* Scarborough, ON: Prentice Hall, 1999.

Brodsky, Gwen, and Shelagh Day. *Canadian Charter Equality Rights for Women: One Step Forward or Two Steps Back?* Ottawa: Canadian Advisory Council on the Status of Women, 1989.

Brooks, Roy L., ed. *When Sorry Isn't Enough: The Controversy over Apologies and Reparations for Human Injustice.* New York: New York University Press, 1999.

Brown v. *Board of Education.* 347 U.S., 483 (1954) (USSC+).

Burt, Sandra. "What's Fair? Changing Feminist Perceptions of Justice in English Canada." *Windsor Yearbook of Access to Justice* 12 (1992): 337-55.

Calhoun, Cheshire. "Justice, Care, Gender Bias." *Journal of Philosophy* 85, 9 (1988): 451 63.

Campbell, J., Gail Bruhm, and Susan Lilley. *Caregivers' Support Needs: Insights from the Experiences of Women Providing Care in Rural Nova Scotia.* Halifax: Maritime Centre of Excellence for Women's Health, Dalhousie University, 1998.

Canadian Association of Food Banks, 2001, <http://www.cafb-acba.ca/about_e.cfm> (accessed 15 March 2004).

Canadian Council on Social Development. *Gaining Ground: The Personal Security Index, 2001.* Ottawa: Canadian Council on Social Development, 2001.

Canadian Institute for Health Information. *Home Care: Health Information Standards and Related Initiatives.* Ottawa: Canadian Institute for Health Information, 1999.

Card, Cynthia. "Gender and Moral Luck." In *Identity, Character and Morality,* ed. Owen Flanagan, 199-218. Cambridge, MA: MIT Press, 1990.

Carens, Joseph H. *Culture, Citizenship, and Community: A Contextual Exploration of Justice as Evenhandedness.* Oxford and New York: Oxford University Press, 2000.

Carse, Alisa, and Hilde Lindemann Nelson. "Rehabilitating Care." *Kennedy Institute of Ethics Journal* 6, 1 (1996): 19-35.

Casey, Pamela, and David B. Rottman. "Therapeutic Jurisprudence in the Courts." *Behavioral Sciences and the Law* 18 (2000): 445-57.

Claes, Rhonda, and Deborah Clifton. *Needs and Expectations for Redress of Victims of Abuse at Native Residential Schools.* Ottawa: Law Commission of Canada, 1998.

Clement, Grace. *Care, Autonomy, and Justice.* Boulder: Westview Press, 1996.

Cohen, Joshua. "Value in Ethics and Economics." *Journal of Economic Literature* 33, 1 (1995): 192-276.

Cohen, Mark A. "Pain, Suffering and Jury Awards: A Study of the Cost of Crime to Victims." *Law and Society Review* 22, 3 (1988): 537-55.

Cole, Eve Browning, and Susan Coultrap-McQuin. *Explorations in Feminist Ethics: Theory and Practice.* Bloomington: Indiana University Press, 1992.

Compensation for Victims of Crime Act. In R.S.O. 1990, c. 24.

Cook, P.J., and D.A. Graham. "The Demand for Insurance and Protection: The Case of Irreplaceable Commodities." *Quarterly Journal of Economics* 91, 1 (1977): 143-56.

Cranswick, Kelly. *Canada's Caregivers*. Vol. 11-008 XPE, *Canadian Social Trends*. Ottawa: Statistics Canada, 1997.

Crittenden, Chris. "The Principles of Care." *Women and Politics* 22 (2001): 81-106.

Cyr, C. *Modèle conceptuel: Programmation de la violence familiale dans un cadre correctionnel*. Ottawa: Service correctionnel du Canada, 1994.

Daicoff, Susan. "The Role of Therapeutic Jurisprudence within the Comprehensive Law Movement." In *Practicing Therapeutic Jurisprudence: Law as a Helping Profession*, ed. Dennis P. Stolle, David B. Wexler, and Bruce J. Winick, 465-92. Durham, NC: Carolina Academic Press, 2000.

Dalley, Gillian. *Ideologies of Caring: Rethinking Community and Collectivism*. London: Macmillan Press, 1996.

Davion, Victoria. "Integrity and Radical Change." In *Feminist Ethics*, ed. Claudia Card, 180-92. Lawrence: University of Kansas Press, 1991.

Day, Shelagh, and Gwen Brodsky. *Women and the Equality Deficit: The Impact of Restructuring Canada's Social Programs*. Ottawa: Status of Women Canada, 1998.

Denton, M. "The Linkages between Informal and Formal Care of the Elderly." *Canadian Journal on Aging* 16, 1 (1997): 30-50.

Deveaux, Monique. "Shifting Paradigms: Theorizing Care and Justice in Political Theory." *Hypatia* 10, 2 (1995): 115-19.

Dhawan, S. "Caregiving Stress and Acculturation in East Indian Immigrants: Caring for their Elders." Ph.D. diss., Queen's University, Kingston, 1998.

Dietz, Mary. "Citizenship with a Feminist Face: The Problem with Maternal Thinking." *Political Theory* 13 (1985): 19-37.

Dillon, Robin S. "Respect and Care: Toward Moral Integration." *Canadian Journal of Philosophy* 22, 1 (1992): 105-33.

Donath, Susan. "The Other Economy: A Suggestion for Distinctively Feminist Economics." *Feminist Economics* 6, 1 (2000): 115-25.

Eldridge v. *British Columbia*, [1997] 3 S.C.R. 624.

Elliot, D., and J. Briere. "The Sexually Abused Boy: Problems in Manhood." *Medical Aspects of Human Sexuality* 26, 2 (1992): 68-71.

Elliot, David. "Comment on *Andrews* v. *Law Society of British Columbia* and Section 15(1) of the Charter: The Emperor's New Clothes?" *McGill Law Journal* 35 (1989): 235-52.

Engster, Daniel. "The Political Economy of Care." Paper delivered at the 2003 annual meeting of the American Political Science Association, 28-31 August 2003.

Evans, Robert. *Strained Mercy: The Economics of Canadian Health Care*. Toronto: Butterworths, 1984.

EWL/LEF. "Global Governance, Alternative Mechanisms and Gender Equality Mainstreaming," 6 June 2001, at <http://www.womenlobby.org/Document.asp?DocID+318&tod+19714> (accessed 18 June 2002).

Fast, J., N.C. Keating, and L. Oakes. *Conceptualizing and Operationalizing the Costs of Informal Elder Care*. Ottawa: Report to the National Health Research Development Program, 1997.

Fast, J.E., and M. DaPont. "Changes in Women's Employment Continuity." *Canadian Social Trends* 46 (1997): 2-7.

Fast, J.E., and J.A. Frederick. "Working Arrangements and Time Stress," *Canadian Social Trends* 45 (1996): 14-19.

–. "Informal Eldercare: Is It Really Cheaper?" Paper presented at the International Association of Time Use Researchers Conference, Colchester, England, October 1999.

Fast, Janet, Jaquie Eales, and Norah Keating. *Economic Impact of Health, Income Security and Labour Policies on Informal Caregivers of Frail Seniors*. Ottawa: Status of Women Canada, Policy Research Fund, 2001.

Federal/Provincial/Territorial Working Group on Child and Family Services Information.

Child Welfare in Canada: The Role of Provincial and Territorial Authorities in Cases of Child Abuse. Ottawa: Federal/Provincial/Territorial Working Group on Child and Family Services Information, 1994.

Feldthusen, Bruce. "The Civil Action for Sexual Battery: Therapeutic Jurisprudence?" *Ottawa Law Review* 25, 2 (1993): 205-34.

Feldthusen, Bruce, O. Hankivsky, and L. Greaves. "Therapeutic Consequences of Civil Actions for Damages and Compensation Claims by Victims of Sexual Abuse." *Canadian Journal of Women and the Law* 12, 1 (2000): 66-116.

Fineman, Martha Albertson. "Contract and Care." *Chicago-Kent Law Review* 76 (2001): 1403-40.

Finkelhor, D. *Child Sexual Abuse: New Theory and Research.* New York: Free Press, 1984.

–. "Early and Long-Term Effects of Child Sexual Abuse: An Update." *Professional Psychology* 21 (1990): 325-30.

–. "The International Epidemiology of Child Sexual Abuse." *Child Abuse and Neglect* 18, 5 (1994): 409-17.

Finkelhor, D., and A. Brown. "Impact of Child Sexual Abuse: A Review of the Research." *Psychological Bulletin* 99, 1 (1986): 66-77.

Finkelhor, D., G. Hotaling, I.A. Lewis, and C. Smith. "Sexual Abuse in a National Survey of Adult Men and Women: Prevalence, Characteristics, and Risk Factors." *Child Abuse and Neglect* 14 (1997): 19-28.

Finlay, Lucinda. "Transcending Equality Theory: A Way out of the Maternity and Workplace Debate." *Columbia Law Review* 86, 118 (1986): 571-81.

Fisher, Berenice, and Joan Tronto. "Toward a Feminist Theory of Caring." In *Circles of Care: Work and Identity in Women's Lives,* ed. Emily K. Abel and Margaret K. Nelson, 35-62. New York: State University of New York Press, 1990.

Flood, Colleen. *Unpacking the Shift to Home Care.* Halifax: Maritime Centre of Excellence for Women's Health, 2002.

Folbre, Nancy. *The Invisible Heart: Economics and Family Valves.* New York: The New Press, 2001.

Fox, K.M., and B.O. Gilbert. "The Interpersonal and Psychological Functioning of Women Who Experienced Childhood Physical Abuse, Incest, and Parental Alcoholism." *Child Abuse and Neglect* 18, 10 (1994): 849-58.

Fraser, Nancy. "Toward a Discourse Ethic of Solidarity." *Praxis International* 5 (1986): 425-29.

–. *Unruly Practices: Power Discourse and Gender in Contemporary Social Theory.* Minneapolis: University of Minneapolis Press, 1989.

–. *Justice Interruptus: Critical Reflections on the "Postsocialist" Condition.* New York: Routledge, 1997.

Frazer, Elizabeth. "Feminism and Liberalism." In *Liberal Political Tradition: Contemporary Reappraisals,* ed. James Meadowcroft, 115-37. Cheltenham, UK: E. Elgar Publishers, 1986.

Friedman, Marilyn. "Beyond Caring." In *An Ethic of Care: Feminist and Interdisciplinary Perspectives,* ed. M.J. Larrabee, 87-110. New York: Routledge, 1993.

–. *What Are Friends For? Feminist Perspectives on Personal Relationships and Moral Theory.* Ithaca: Cornell University Press, 1993.

–. "Beyond Caring: The De-Moralization of Gender." In *Justice and Care: Essential Readings in Feminist Ethics,* ed. Virginia Held, 61-78. Boulder: Westview Press, 1995.

Friedrich, W.N., and L.C. Schafer. "Somatic Symptoms in Sexually Abused Children." *Journal of Pediatric Psychology* 20, 5 (1995): 661-70.

Fuchs, Victor R. *Who Shall Live? Health, Economics, and Social Choice.* New York: Basic Books, 1974.

Fudge, Judy. "The Public/Private Distinction: The Possibilities of and the Limits to the Use of Charter Litigation for Further Feminist Struggles." *Osgoode Hall Law Journal* 25, 3 (1987): 485-547.

–. "What Do We Mean by Law and Social Transformation?" *Canadian Journal of Law and Society* 5 (1990): 47-69.

Gannage, Mark. "Introduction." In *An International Perspective: A Review and Analysis of Approaches to Addressing Past Institutional or Systemic Abuse in Selected Countries.* Ottawa: Law Commission of Canada, 1998. Available at <http://www.lcc.gc.ca/en/themes/mr/ica/ganrep/ganrep1.asp> (accessed 7 October 2002).

Giarchi, G.G. "Distance Decay and Information Deprivation: Health Implications for People in Rural Isolation." In *New Directions in the Sociology of Health,* ed. P. Abbott and G. Payne, 57-69. New York: Famler Press, 1990.

Gignac, Monique A.M., Kevin Kelloway, and Benjamin H. Gottlieb. "The Impact of Caregiving on Employment: A Meditational Model of Work-Family Conflict." *Canadian Journal on Aging* 15, 4 (1996): 525-42.

Gil, David. *Unravelling Social Policy: Theory, Analysis, and Political Action Towards Social Equality.* Rochester: Schenkman Books, 1990.

Gilligan, Carol. *In a Different Voice: Psychological Theory and Women's Development.* Cambridge: Cambridge University Press, 1982.

Gilligan, Carol, J. Ward, and J. Taylor, eds. *Mapping the Moral Domain.* Cambridge: Harvard University Press, 1988.

Gold, Marc. "Moral and Political Theories in Equality Rights Adjudication." In *Litigating the Values of a Nation: The Canadian Charter of Rights and Freedoms,* ed. Joseph M. Weiler and Robin M. Elliot, 85-103. Toronto: Carswell, 1986.

Goldstone, Richard J. "Foreword." In *Between Vengeance and Forgiveness: Facing History after Genocide and Mass Violence,* ed. Martha Minow, ix-xiii. Boston: Beacon Press, 1998.

Gomas, J.M. "Palliative Care at Home: A Reality or Mission Impossible?" *Palliative Medicine* 14, 3 (1993): 62-68.

Goodin, Robert E. *Protecting the Vulnerable: A Reanalysis of Our Social Responsibilities.* Chicago: University of Chicago Press, 1985.

–. *Reasons for Welfare: The Political Theory of The Welfare State.* Princeton: Princeton University Press, 1988.

Graham, Hilary. "Caring: A Labour of Love." In *A Labour of Love,* ed. J. Finch and D. Groves, 13-29. London: Routledge and Kegan Paul, 1983.

Grant, Agnes. *No End of Grief: Indian Residential Schools in Canada.* Winnipeg: Pemmican Publishers, 1996.

Graves, Frank. "Rethinking Government as if People Mattered: From 'Reaganomics' to 'Humanomics.'" In *How Ottawa Spends, 1999-2000 – Shape Shifting: Canadian Governance Toward the 21st Century,* ed. Leslie A. Pal, 37-74. Don Mills, ON: Oxford University Press, 1999.

Greaves, L., O. Hankivsky, and J. Kingston-Riechers. *Selected Estimates of the Costs of Violence against Women in Canada: The Tip of the Iceberg.* London: Centre for Research on Violence Against Women and Children, 1995.

Greaves, Lorraine, Olena Hankivsky, Georgia Lividiotakis, and Renée Cormier. *Final Payments: Socioeconomic Costs of Palliative Home Caregiving in the Last Month of Life.* Ottawa: Health Canada, forthcoming.

Green, A.H. "Child Sexual Abuse: Immediate and Long-Term Effects and Intervention." *Journal of the American Academy of Child and Adolescent Psychiatry* 32, 5 (1993): 890-903.

Green, P. "The Logic of Special Rights." *Hypatia* 2, 1 (1987): 67-71.

Groenewegen, Peter D., ed. *Economics and Ethics?* London, New York: Routledge, 1996.

Grover, Steven A., H. Zowall, L. Coupal, and M.D. Krahn. "Prostate Cancer: The Economic Burden," *Canadian Medical Association Journal* 160, 5 (1999): 685.

Gutmann, Amy, and Dennis Thompson. *Ethics and Politics: Cases and Comments.* 3rd ed. Chicago: Nelson-Hall Publishers, 1997.

Hankivsky, Olena. "Enhancing Therapeutic Jurisprudence for Victims of Institutional Abuse: The Potential for an Ethic of Care." *Journal of Nursing Law* 8, 5 (2002): 31-55.

–. "Social Justice and Women's Health: A Canadian Perspective." In *Made to Measure: Women, Gender, and Equity,* vol. 3, ed. Carol Amaratunga, 54-64. Maritime Centre of Excellence for Women's Health, 2002.

Hankivsky, Olena, and Debbie Draker. "The Economic Costs of Child Sexual Abuse in Canada: A Preliminary Analysis." *Journal of Health and Social Policy* 17, 2 (2003): 1-82.

Hankivsky, Olena, Marina Morrow, Pat Armstrong, with Lindsey Galvin and Holly Grinvalds. *Trade Agreements, Home Care, and Women's Health*. Ottawa: Status of Women
Canada (forthcoming).

Harding, Sandra. "The Curious Coincidence of Feminine and African Moralities: Challenges for Feminist Theory." In *Women and Moral Theory*, ed. Eva Feder Kittay and
Diana T. Meyers, 296-316. Totowa, NJ: Rowman and Littlefield, 1987.

Hargrave, Connie. "Homelessness in Canada: From Housing to Shelters to Blankets."
Share International (April 1999). <http://www.shareintl.org/archives/homelessness/hl-
ch_Canada.htm> (accessed 15 March 2004).

Harlton, Shauna-Vi, Norah Keating, and Janet Fast. "Defining Eldercare for Policy and
Practice: Perspectives Matter." *Family Relations* 47, 3 (1998): 1-8.

Harman, Lesley D. "The Feminization of Poverty: An Old Problem with a New Name."
In *Gender in the 1990s: Images, Realities and Issues*, ed. Adie Nelson and B.W. Robinson, 404-10. Scarborough, ON: Nelson Canada, 1995.

Harrington, Mona. *Care and Equality: Inventing a New Family Politics*. New York: Routledge, 2000.

Hartsock, Nancy. *Money, Sex, and Power: Toward a Feminist Historical Materialism*. New
York: Longman, 1983.

Hartunian, N.S., C.N. Smart, and M.S. Thompson. "The Incidents and Economic Costs
of Cancer, Motor Vehicle Incidents, Coronary Heart Disease, and Stroke: A Comparative Analysis." *American Journal of Public Health* 70 (1980): 1249-60.

Harwood, Henrick J., Peter Reuter, Mark A.R. Kleiman, Pierre Kopp, and Mark A. Cohen.
"A Report and Commentaries: Cost Estimates for Alcohol and Drug Abuse." *Addiction*
94, 5 (1999): 631-47.

Hausman, Daniel, and Michael McPherson. "Taking Ethics Seriously: Economics and
Contemporary Moral Philosophy." *Journal of Economic Literature* 31 (1993): 671-731.

–. *Economic Analysis and Moral Philosophy*. Cambridge: Cambridge University Press, 1996.

Hawranik, P.G., and L.A. Strain. *Health of Informal Caregivers: Effects of Gender, Employment and Use of Home Care Services*. Winnipeg: Centre of Aging and Faculty of Nursing, University of Manitoba, 2000.

Health Canada. *Public Home Care Expenditures in Canada, Fact Sheets*. Ottawa: Health
Canada, 1998.

Health Canada, Division of Aging and Seniors. "The Future of Caregiving." *Seniors Info
Exchange* (winter 1997-98).

Health Canada and the Hay Group. *The Berger Monitor* (Ottawa: Health Canada, 1999).

Health Care Renewal Accord 2003. Available at <http://www.hc-sc.gc.ca/english/
hca2003/accord.html> (accessed 20 February 2003).

Health Services Utilization and Research Commission. *Hospital and Home Care Study*
(Saskatoon, SK: Health Services Utilization and Research Commission, 1998).

Heath, Joseph. *The Efficient Society: Why Canada Is as Close to Utopia as It Gets*. Toronto:
Penguin, 2001.

Held, Virginia. "Feminism and Moral Theory." In *Women and Moral Theory*, ed. Eva Feder
Kittay and Diana T. Meyers, 111-28. Totowa, NJ: Rowman and Littlefield, 1987.

–. *Feminist Morality: Transforming Culture, Society and Politics*. Chicago: University of
Chicago Press, 1993.

–. "The Meshing of Care and Justice." *Hypatia* 10, 2 (1995): 128-32.

–. *Justice and Care: Essential Readings in Feminist Ethics*. Boulder: Westview Press, 1995.

–. "Liberalism and the Ethics of Care." In *On Feminist Ethics and Politics*, ed. Claudia
Card, 288-309. Lawrence: University Press of Kansas, 1999.

Henderson, Lynne N. "Legality and Empathy." *Michigan Law Review* 85 (1987): 1574-653.

Henley, Kenneth. "The Value of Individuals." *Philosophy and Phenomenological Research*
37 (1977): 345-52.

Henton, D., and D. McCann. *Boys Don't Cry: The Struggle for Justice and Healing in Canada's
Biggest Sex Abuse Scandal*. Toronto: McClelland and Stewart, 1995.

Hepler, Deborah K. "Providing Creative Remedies to Bystander Emotional Distress Victims: A Feminist Perspective." *Northern Illinois University Law Review* 14 (1994): 71-104.

Herman, Judith Lewis. *Trauma and Recovery*. New York: Basic Books, 1997.

Hill, Rick. "Repatriation Must Heal Old Wounds." In *Reckoning with the Dead*, ed. Tamara L. Bray and Thomas K. Killion, 184-86. Washington, DC: Smithsonian Institution, 1994.

Hilton, R.R., and G.C. Mezey. "Victims and Perpetrators of Child Sexual Abuse." *British Journal of Psychiatry* 189 (1996): 411-15.

Himmelweit, Susan. "Gender, Care and Emotions." *Work, Employment, and Society* 12, 3 (1998): 551-53.

Hoagland, Sarah Lucia. *Lesbian Ethics: Toward New Value*. Palo Alto: Institute of Lesbian Ethics, 1988.

Hobbes, Thomas. *Leviathan; or, the Matter, Forme, and Power of a Common Wealth, Ecclesiastical and Civil*. London: Andrew Cooke, 1651.

–. "Some Thoughts about 'Caring.'" In *Feminist Ethics*, ed. Claudia Card, 246-86. Lawrence: University Press of Kansas, 1991.

Hochschild, A.R. "The Culture of Politics: Traditional, Post-Modern, Cold-Modern, and Warm-Modern Ideals of Care." *Social Politics* 2, 3 (1995): 331-46.

Hodgson, T.A., and M.R. Meiners. "Cost of Illness Methodology: A Guide to Current Practices and Procedures." *Milbank Memorial Fund Quarterly/Health and Society* 60 (1982): 429-61.

Hooyman, N.R., and J. Gonyea. *Feminist Perspectives on Family Care: Policies for Gender Justice*. Thousand Oaks, CA: Sage Publications, 1995.

Hoppe, Sherry, and Edna Harder Mattson. "Bridging Care from Hospital to Home: An Innovative Joint Project." *Canadian Nursing Management* 95 (1996): 5-8.

Hora, Peggy Fulton, and William G. Schma. "Therapeutic Jurisprudence." *Judicature* 82, 9 (1998): 8-12.

Houston, Barbara. "Rescuing Womanly Virtues: Some Dangers of Moral Reclamation." In *Science, Morality and Feminist Theory*, ed. Marcia Hanen and Kai Nielsen, 237-62. Calgary: University of Calgary Press, 1987.

Institute for Human Resource Development (IHRD). *Review of the Needs of Victims of Institutional Abuse*. Ottawa: Law Commission of Canada, 1998.

Jacobson, Joyce P., and Andrew R. Newman. "What Data Do Economists Use? The Case of Labour Economics and Industrial Relations." *Feminist Economics* 3, 2 (1997): 129-30.

Jaggar, Alison. *Feminist Politics and Human Nature*. Totowa, NJ: Rowman and Allanheld, 1988.

–. "Caring as a Feminist Practice of Moral Reason." In *Justice and Care: Essential Readings in Feminist Ethics*, ed. Virginia Held, 179-202. Boulder: Westview Press, 1995.

Jenson, J., and J. Jacobzone. *Care Allowances for the Frail Elderly and Their Impact on Women Care-Givers*. Paris, France: Organisation for Economic Co-operation and Development, Directorate for Education Employment Labour and Social Affairs, 2000.

Johnson, M.L. "Interdependency and the Generational Compact." *Ageing and Society* 15 (1995): 243-65.

Joseph, A.E., and B.C. Hallman. "Over the Hill and Far Away: Distance as a Barrier to the Provision of Assistance to Elderly Relatives." *Social Science and Medicine* 46, 6 (1998): 631-39.

Kaden, J., and S.A. McDaniel. "Caregiving and Care-Receiving: A Double Bind for Women in Canada's Aging Society." *Journal of Women and Aging* 2, 3 (1990): 3-26.

Kaiserman, M.R. "The Cost of Smoking in Canada, 1991." *Chronic Diseases in Canada* 18, 1 (1997): 15-22.

Kant, Immanuel. *Foundations of the Metaphysics of Morals with Critical Essays*. Trans. Lewis White Beck, ed. Robert Paul Wolff. Indianapolis: Boss-Merrill Co., 1969.

Karst, Kenneth. "Woman's Constitution." *Duke Law Journal* 3 (1984): 447-510.

Kaufman, J., and E. Ziegler. "Do Abused Children Become Abusive Parents?" *American Journal of Orthopsychiatry* 57, 2 (1987): 186-92.

Keating, N.C., J.E. Fast, J.A. Frederick, K. Cranswick, and C. Perrier. *Eldercare in Canada: Context, Content, and Consequences*. Ottawa: Statistics Canada Housing Family and Social Statistics Division, 1999.

Keefe, J.M., and P. Fancey. "Financial Compensation or Home Help Services: Examining Differences among Program Recipients." *Canadian Journal on Aging/La Revue Canadienne du Vieillissement* 16, 2 (1997): 254-77.

Keefe, Janice M., and Sheva Medjuck. "The Contribution of Long-Term Economic Costs and Predicting Strain among Employed Women Caregivers." *Journal of Women and Aging* 9, 3 (1997): 3-25.

Keeva, Steven. "Does the Law Mean Never Having to Say You're Sorry?" *American Bar Association Journal* 95 (December 1999): 64-67.

Kendall-Tackett, K.A., L. Meyer-Williams, and D. Finkelhor. "Impact of Sexual Abuse on Children: A Review and Synthesis of Recent Empirical Studies." *Psychological Bulletin* 113, 1 (1993): 164-80.

Kikwepere, Lukas Baba. *Reconciliation, Chapter 5, Final Report*. South Africa: The Truth and Reconciliation Commission, 2000.

Kingdon, John W. "The Reality of Public Policy Making." In *Ethical Dimensions of Health Policy*, ed. Marion Danis, Carolyn Clancy, and Larry Churchill, 97-119. Oxford: Oxford University Press, 2002.

Kittay, Eva Feder. "Taking Dependency Seriously: The Family and Medical Leave Act Considered in Light of the Social Organization of Dependency Work and Gender Equality." *Hypatia* 10, 1 (1995): 8-29.

–. "Social Policy." In *A Companion to Feminist Philosophy*, ed. Alison M. Jaggar and Iris Marion Young, 581-90. Oxford: Blackwell, 1998.

–. *Love's Labor: Essays on Women's Equality and Dependency*. New York: Routledge, 1999.

Kittay, Eva Feder, and Diana T. Meyers, eds. *Women and Moral Theory*. Totowa, NJ: Rowman and Littlefield, 1987.

Klymasz, Cassidy M. "Economic Costs of Schizophrenia in Canada: A Preliminary Study." Ottawa: Schizophrenia Society of Canada and Health Canada, 1995.

Knight, Frank. *Risk, Uncertainty, and Profit*. Chicago: University of Chicago Press, 1921.

Knijn, Trudie, and Monique Kremer. "Gender and the Caring Dimension of Welfare States: Toward Inclusive Citizenship." *Social Politics* 4 (Fall 1997): 328-61.

Koehn, Daryl. *Rethinking Feminist Ethics: Care, Trust, and Empathy*. London and New York: Routledge, 1998.

Koniak, Susan P. "Law and Ethics in a World of Rights and Unsuitable Wrongs." *Canadian Journal of Law and Jurisprudence: An International Journal of Legal Thought* 9, 1 (1996): 11-32.

Kress, Ken. "Therapeutic Jurisprudence and the Resolution of Value Conflicts: What We Can Realistically Expect, in Practice, from Theory." *Behavioral Sciences and the Law* 17 (1999): 555-88.

Krieger, Linda J. "Through a Glass Darkly: Paradigms of Equality and the Search for Woman's Jurisprudence." *Hypatia* 2, 1 (1987): 45-61.

Kritz, Neil S., ed. *Transitional Justice: How Emerging Democracies Reckon with Former Regimes*. Washington DC: US Institute of Peace Press, 1995.

Kroeger-Mappes, Joe. "The Ethic of Care vis-à-vis the Ethic of Rights: A Problem for Contemporary Moral Theory." *Hypatia* 9 (1994): 108-31.

Kuhn, Thomas S. *The Structure of Scientific Revolutions*. Chicago: University of Chicago Press, 1970.

Kymlicka, Will. "Approaches to Ethical Issues Raised by the Royal Commission's Mandate." In *New Reproductive Technologies: Ethical Aspects*, ed. Research Studies of the Royal Commission on New Reproductive Technologies, 1-46. Ottawa: Supply and Services Canada, 1993.

–. *Contemporary Political Philosophy*. 2nd ed. New York: Oxford University Press, 2002.

Lahey, Kathleen. "Feminist Theories of (in)Equality." In *Equality and Judicial Neutrality*, ed. K.E. Mahoney and S.L. Martin, 71-86. Toronto: Carswell, 1987.

Lake, E.S. "Exploration of the Violent Victim Experiences of Female Offenders." *Violence and Victims* 8, 1 (1993): 41-52.

Lane, M., D.R. Davis, C.B. Cornman, C.A. Macera, and M. Sanderson. "Location of Death as an Indicator of End-of-Life Costs for the Person with Dementia." *Journal of Alzheimer's Disease* 13, 4 (1998): 208-10.

La Novara, Pina. *A Portrait of Families in Canada*. Ottawa: Statistics Canada, 1993.

Lappalainen, R. Eliasson, and I. Nilsson Motevasel. "Ethics of Care and Social Policy." *Scandinavian Journal of Social Welfare* 6 (1997): 189-96.

Lavell v. *Attorney General of Canada* (1971), 22 D.L.R. (3d) 182 (Ont. Co. Ct.).

Law v. *Canada*, [1999] 1 S.C.R. 497.

Law Commission of Canada. *Restoring Dignity: Responding to Child Abuse in Canadian Institutions*. Ottawa: Minister of Public Works and Government Services, 2000.

Leira, Arnlaug. "Concepts of Caring: Loving, Thinking, and Doing." *Social Service Review* 68 (1994): 185-201.

Levi, D. "The Role of Apology in Mediation." *New York University Law Review* 72 (1997): 1165-80.

Li, Chenyang. "Ethics: Confucian Jen and Feminist Care." In *The Tao Encounters the West: Explorations in Comparative Philosophy*. Albany, NY: SUNY Press, 1999.

Lieder, Michael, and Jake Page. *Wild Justice: The People of Geronimo vs. the United States*. New York: Random House, 1997.

Lister, Ruth. *Citizenship: Feminist Perspectives*. 2nd ed. New York: New York University Press, 2003.

Littleton, Christine. "Reconstructing Sexual Equality." In *Feminist Legal Theory,* ed. K. Weisberg, 248-63. Philadelphia: Temple University Press, 1993.

Lunati, Teresa M. *Ethical Issues in Economics: From Altruism to Cooperation to Equity*. Hampshire: McMillan Press, 1997.

Lyons, Karen S., and Steven H. Zarit. "Formal and Informal Support: The Great Divide." *International Journal of Geriatric Psychiatry* 14 (1999): 183-92.

MacMillan, H.L., J.E. Fleming, N. Trocme, M.H. Boyle, M. Wong, Y.A. Racine, W.R. Beardslee, and D.R. Offord. "Prevalence of Child Physical and Sexual Abuse in the Community: Results from the Ontario Health Supplement." *Journal of the American Medical Association* 278, 2 (1997): 131-35.

Magee, Rhonda V. "The Master's Tools, from the Bottom Up: Responses to American Reparations Theory in Mainstream and Outsider Remedies Discourse." *Virginia Law Review* 79 (1993): 863-907.

Mahoney, Kathleen. "The Constitutional Law of Equality in Canada." *International Law and Politics* 24 (1992): 759-93.

Maltoni, M., O. Nanni, M. Naldoni, P. Serra, and D. Amadori. "Evaluation of Cost of Home Therapy for Patients with Terminal Diseases." *Current Opinion in Oncology* 10 (1998): 302-9.

Maltz, W., and B. Holman. *Incest and Sexuality: A Guide to Understanding and Healing*. Toronto: Lexington Books, 1987.

Manning, Rita. *Speaking from the Heart: A Feminist Perspective on Ethics*. Lanham, MD: Rowman and Littlefield, 1992.

–. "Just Caring." In *Explorations in Feminist Ethics: Theory and Practice,* ed. Eve Browning Cole and Susan Coultrap-McQuin, 45-56. Bloomington: Indiana University Press, 1992.

Martin, Rob. "The Charter and the Crisis in Canada." In *After Meech Lake, Lessons for the Future,* ed. D.E. Smith, P. MacKinnon, and J.C. Courtney, 121-38. Saskatoon, SK: Fifth House, 1991.

McAllister, Debra M. "The Supreme Court in Symes: Two Solitudes." *National Journal of Constitutional Law* 4 (1994): 248-63.

McClain, Linda C. "Atomistic Man Revisited: Liberalism, Connection, and Feminist Jurisprudence." *Southern California Law Review* 65 (1992): 1171-264.

–. "Care as a Public Value." *Chicago-Kent Law Review* 76 (2001): 1673-731.

McClurg, Andrew Jay. "It's a Wonderful Life: The Case for Hedonic Damages in Wrongful Death Cases." *Notre Dame Law Review* 66, 57 (1990): 57-116.

McKinnon, Catherine. *Sexual Harassment of Working Women*. New Haven: Yale University Press, 1979.

McLaughlin, Janice. "An Ethic of Care: A Valuable Political Tool?" *Politics* 17, 1 (1997): 17-23.

Mendelsohn, Matthew. *Canada's Social Contract: Evidence from Public Opinion*. Ottawa:

Canadian Policy Research Network, Discussion Paper No. P/01 Public Involvement Network, November 2002.

Menkel-Meadow, C. "Portia in a Different Voice: Speculations on a Woman's Lawyering Process." *Berkeley Women's Law Journal* 1 (1985): 39-63.

Meshefedjian, G., J. McCusker, F. Bellavance, and M. Baumgartner. "Factors Associated with Symptoms of Depression among Informal Caregivers of Demented Elders in the Community." *Gerontologist* 38, 2 (1998): 247-53.

Miller, T.R., D.C. Lestina, and R.S. Spicer. "Highway Crash Costs in the United States by Driver Age, Blood Alcohol Level, Victim Age, and Restraint Use." *Accident Analysis and Prevention* 30 (1998): 137-50.

Miller, T.R., and M.A. Cohen. "Victim Costs of Violent Crime and Resulting Injuries." *Health Affairs* 12, 4 (Winter 1993): 186-97.

Miller, T.R., M.A. Cohen, and B. Wiersema. "Crime in the United States: Victim Costs and Consequences." Washington, DC: National Institute of Justice, 1995.

Miller, T.R., and M. Galbraith. "Estimating the Costs of Occupational Injury in the United States." *Accident Analysis and Prevention* 27 (1995): 741-47.

Minow, Martha. *Making All the Difference: Inclusion, Exclusion, and American Law*. Ithaca: Cornell University Press, 1990.

–. *Between Vengeance and Forgiveness: Facing History after Genocide and Mass Violence*. Boston: Beacon Press, 1998.

Mishan, E.J. "Consistency in the Valuation of Life: A Wild Goose Chase?" In *Ethics and Economics*, ed. Ellen Frankel Paul, Fred D. Miller, and Jeffrey Paul, 152-67. Oxford: Basil Blackwell, 1985.

Moody-Adams, Michele. "Gender and the Complexity of Moral Voices." In *Feminist Ethics*, ed. Claudia Card, 195-212. Lawrence: University of Kansas Press, 1991.

Moore, Margaret. "The Ethics of Care and Justice." *Women and Politics* 20, 2 (1999): 1-15.

Moore, R., Y. Mao, J. Zhang, and K. Clarke. *Economic Burden of Illness in Canada, 1993*. Ottawa: Health Canada, 1997.

Morris, Marika. *Gender-Sensitive Home and Community Care and Caregiving Research: A Synthesis Paper*. Ottawa: Health Canada Women's Health Bureau, 2001.

Morris, Marika, Jane Robinson, Janet Simpson with Sherry Galey, Sandra Kirby, Lise Martin, and Martha Muzychka. *The Changing Nature of Home Care and Its Impact on Women's Vulnerability to Poverty*. Ottawa: Status of Women Canada, 1999.

Morrow, Marina, Olena Hankivsky, and Colleen Varcoe. "Women and Violence: The Effects of Dismantling the Welfare State," *Critical Social Policy* 24, 3 (August 2004) (forthcoming).

Moskowitz, Ellen H. "The Ethics of Government Bioethics." *Politics and the Life Sciences* 13 (1994): 96.

Naffine, Ngair. *Law and the Sexes: Explorations in Feminist Jurisprudence*. New Zealand: Allen and Unwin, 1990.

Narayan, Uma. "Colonialism and Its Others: Considerations on Rights and Care Discourses." *Hypatia* 10 (1995): 133-41.

National Advisory Council on Aging. *Aging Vignettes: A Quick Portrait of Dementia in Canada*. Ottawa: National Advisory Council on Aging, 1996.

National Coordinating Group on Health Care Reform and Women: P. Armstrong, Madeline Boscoe, Barbara Chow, Karen Grant, Ann Pederson, Kay Wilson with Olena Hankivsky, Beth Jackson, and Marina Morrow. *Reading Romanow: The Implications of the Final Report of the Commission on the Future of Health Care in Canada for Women*. Canadian Women's Health Network, 2003.

National Council of Welfare. *Poverty Profile 1998*. Ottawa: National Council of Welfare, 1998.

National Crime Prevention Council. *Money Well Spent: Investing in Preventing Crime*. Ottawa: National Crime Prevention Council, 1996.

National Forum on Health (Canada). *Canada Health Action: Building on the Legacy*. Vol. 2: *Synthesis Reports and Issue Papers*. Ottawa: National Forum on Health, 1997.

Nelson, Julie A. "Feminism and Economics." *Journal of Economic Perspectives* 9, 2 (1995): 131-48.

Neysmith, S., and J. Aronson. "Working Conditions in Home Care: Negotiating Issues of Race and Class in Gendered Work." *International Journal of Health Services* 27, 3 (1997): 479-99.

Neysmith, Sheila M. "From Home Care to Social Care: The Value of a Vision." In *Women's Caring: Feminist Perspectives on Social Welfare*, ed. Carol T. Baines, Patricia M. Evans, and Sheila M. Neysmith, 233-49. Don Mills, ON: Oxford University Press, 1998.

Noddings, Nel. *Caring: A Feminine Approach to Ethics and Moral Education*. Berkeley, CA: University of California Press, 1984.

–. "Ethics from the Standpoint of Women." In *Theoretical Perspectives on Sexual Difference*, ed. Deborah L. Rhode, 160-73. New Haven: Yale University Press, 1990.

–. *Starting at Home: Caring and Social Policy*. Berkeley, CA: University of California Press, 2002.

Noonan, A.E., S.L. Tennstedt, and F.G. Rebelsky. "Making the Best of It: Themes of Meaning among Informal Caregivers to the Elderly." *Journal of Aging Society* 10, 4 (1996): 313-28.

Northcott, H.C., and B.R. Northcott. *The 1999 Survey about Health and the Health Care System in Alberta*. Edmonton: Alberta Health and Wellness through the Population Research Laboratory at the University of Alberta, 1999.

Nova Scotia Centre on Aging. *Both Puzzle and Paradox: Support for Informal Caregivers in Atlantic Canada*. Halifax: Mount Saint Vincent University, 1998.

Nussbaum, Martha C. "Plato on Commensurability and Desire." In *Love's Knowledge: Essays on Philosophy and Literature*, 106-24. Oxford and New York: Oxford University Press, 1990.

–. "Human Functioning and Social Justice: In Defense of Aristotelian Essentialism." *Political Theory* 20 (1992): 202-46.

Okin, Susan Moller. *Justice, Gender, and the Family*. Princeton: Princeton University Press, 1989.

–. "Reason and Feeling in Thinking about Justice." *Ethics* 99 (1989): 229-49.

O'Neill, Onora. "Justice, Gender and International Boundaries." In *International Justice and the Third World*, ed. Robin Attfield and Barry Wildins, 439-60. London: Routledge, 1992.

O'Neill, Shane. *Impartiality in Context: Grounding Justice in a Pluralist World*. Albany: State University of New York Press, 1997.

Ontario Ministry of Community and Social Services. *Redirection of Long-Term Care and Support Services in Ontario*. Toronto: Queen's Printer, 1991.

Orloff, Ann Shola. "Gender and the Social Rights of Citizenship." *American Sociological Reviews* 58 (June 1993): 303-28.

Orton, Helena. "Litigating for Equality: LEAF's Approach to Section 15 of the Charter." In *Equality Issues in Family Law: Considerations for Test Case Litigation*, ed. Karen Busby, Lisa Fainstein, and Holly Penner, 7-20. Winnipeg: Legal Research Institute, University of Manitoba, 1990.

Ostry, A. "The New International Trade Regime: Problems for Publicly Funded Healthcare in Canada?" *Canadian Journal of Public Health* 31, 3 (2000): 475-80.

Pal, Leslie A. *Public Policy Analysis: An Introduction*. Scarborough, ON: Nelson Canada, 1992.

–. *How Ottawa Spends, 2000-2001*. Don Mills, ON: Oxford University Press, 2000.

–. *Beyond Policy Analysis: Public Issues Management in Turbulent Times*. Scarborough, ON: Nelson Thomson Learning, 2001.

Paradine, Kate. "The Importance of Understanding Love and Other Feelings in Survivors' Experiences of Domestic Violence." *Court Review* 37 (Spring 2000): 40-47.

Parent, Karen, and Malcolm Anderson. *Carp's Report Card on Home Care in Canada, 2001: Home Care by Default Not by Design*. Toronto: CARP, 2001.

Patry, M.W., D.B. Wexler, D.P. Stolle, and A.J. Tomkins. "Better Legal Counseling through Empirical Research: Identifying Psycholegal Soft Spots and Strategies." In *Practicing Therapeutic Jurisprudence: Law as a Helping Profession*, ed. Dennis P. Stolle, D.B. Wexler, and B.J. Winick, 69-82. Durham, NC: Carolina Academic Press, 2000.

Pettigrew, Pierre S. "A History of Trust, a Future of Confidence: Canada's Third Way." Notes for a paper presented by the Honourable Pierre S. Pettigrew, Minister of Human

Resources Development Canada, to the Canadian Centre for Philanthropy. Toronto, 26 April 1999.

Ponée, C. "Child Abuse Programming at Work." In *Women, Work, and Wellness,* ed. V. Carver and C. Ponée, 141-56. Toronto: Addiction Research Foundation, 1989.

Prince, Michael J. "From Health and Welfare to Stealth and Farewell: Federal Social Policy, 1980-2000." In *How Ottawa Spends, 1999-2000 – Shape Shifting: Canadian Governance toward the 21st Century,* ed. Leslie A. Pal, 151-96. Don Mills, ON: Oxford University Press, 1999.

Pringle, R., and S. Watson. "Feminist Theory and the State: Needs, Rights, and Interests." In *Gender, Politics, and Citizenship in the 1990s,* ed. W. Sullivan and G. Whitehouse, 64-80. Sydney: University of New South Wales, 1996.

Pujol, Michèle. "Introduction: Broadening Economic Data and Methods." *Feminist Economics* 3, 2 (1997): 119-20.

Radin, Margaret Jane. *Contested Commodities.* Cambridge: Harvard University Press, 1996.

Ralph, Diana S., André Régimbland, and Nérée St-Amand, eds. *Open for Business, Closed to People: Michael Harris's Ontario.* Halifax: Fernwood Publishing, 1997.

Rawls, John. *A Theory of Justice.* Cambridge: Harvard University Press, 1971.

–. "Social Unity and Primary Goods." In *Utilitarianism and Beyond,* ed. Amartya Sen and Bernard Williams, 159-87. Cambridge: Cambridge University Press, 1980.

–. "Justice as Fairness." *Philosophy and Public Affairs* 17 (1988): 223-51.

Razack, S. *Canadian Feminism and the Law: The Woman's Legal Education and Action Fund and the Pursuit of Equality.* Toronto: Second Story Press, 1991.

Rein, Martin. "Value-Critical Policy Analysis." In *Ethics, the Social Sciences, and Policy Analysis,* ed. Bruce Jennings and Daniel Callahan, 83-111. New York: Plenum Press, 1983.

Reynolds, D.J. "The Cost of Road Accidents." *Journal of the Royal Statistical Society* 119 (1956): 393-408.

Rhode, Deborah. *Justice and Gender: Sex, Discrimination, and the Law.* Cambridge: Harvard University Press, 1989.

–. "Feminist Critical Theories." In *Feminist Jurisprudence,* ed. Patricia Smith, 594-610. New York: Oxford University Press, 1993.

Rice, Dorothy P. *Estimating the Cost of Illness.* Washington, DC: US Department of Health, Education, and Welfare, Public Health Service, Division of Medical Care Administration, Health Economics Branch, 1966.

–. "Cost of Illness Studies: Fact or Fiction?" *Lancet* 344 (1994): 1519–21.

Rice, Dorothy P., and L.S. Miller. "Health Economics and Cost Implications of Anxiety and Other Mental Disorders in the United States." *British Journal of Psychiatry* 172, 34 (1998): 4-9.

Rice, James J., and Michael J. Prince. *Changing Politics of Canadian Social Policy.* Toronto: University of Toronto Press, 2000.

Robbins, Lionel. *An Essay on the Nature and Significance of Economic Science.* 2nd ed. London: Macmillan Press, 1935.

Robertson, Ann. "Beyond Apocalyptic Demography: Toward a Moral Economy of Interdependence." *Aging and Society* 17 (1997): 245-65.

Robinson, Fiona. *Globalizing Care: Ethics, Feminist Theory, and International Relations.* Boulder, CO: Westview Press, 1999.

Robinson, Lori S. "Growing Movement Seeks Reparations for U.S. Blacks," *Arizona Republic,* 22 June 1997, H1.

Roche, Doug, and Ben Hoffman. *The Vision to Reconcile: Progress Report on the Helpline Reconciliation Model Agreement.* Waterloo, ON: Conflict Resolution Network Canada, Fund for Dispute Resolution, 1993.

The Roeher Institute: *Agenda for Action: Policy Directions for Children with Disabilities and Families.* Toronto: The Roeher Institute, 2000.

–. *Beyond the Limits: Mothers Caring for Children with Disabilities.* Toronto: The Roeher Institute, 2000.

–. *Finding a Way In: Parents on Social Assistance Caring for Children with Disabilities.* Toronto: The Roeher Institute, 2000.

–. *When Kids Belong: Supporting Children with Complex Needs at Home and in the Community.* Toronto: The Roeher Institute, 2000.

Rogers, Mary F. "Caring and Community." In *Contemporary Feminist Theory,* ed. Mary F. Rogers, 327-40. Boston: McGraw Hill Publishers, 1998.

Romain, Diane. "Care and Confusion." In *Explorations in Feminist Ethics: Theory and Practice,* ed. Eve Browning Cole and Susan Coultrap-McQuin, 27-37. Bloomington: Indiana University Press, 1991.

Romanow Commission. *Building on Values: The Future of Health Care in Canada.* Final Report. Saskatoon: Commission on the Future of Health Care in Canada, 2002.

Romans, S.E., and Paul E. Mullen. "Childhood Sexual Abuse: Concerns and Consequences." *Medical Journal of Australia* 166, 2 (1997): 59.

Rose, Hilary. "Hand, Brain, and Heart: A Feminist Epistemology for the Natural Sciences." *Signs* 9, 1 (1983): 75-90.

Rotheram-Borus, M.J., K.A. Mahler, C. Koopman, and K. Langabeer. "Sexual Abuse History and Associated Multiple Risk Behavior in Adolescent Runaways." *American Journal of Orthopsychiatry* 66, 3 (1996): 390-400.

Rothschild, Kurt W. *Ethics and Economic Theory: Ideas, Models, Dilemmas.* Aldershot, UK: E. Elgar, 1993.

Rowe, Robert D., and Lauraine G. Chestnut. *The Value of Visibility: Economic Theory and Applications for Air Pollution Control.* Cambridge: Abt Books, 1982.

Ruddick, Sara. "Maternal Thinking." In *Mothering: Essays in Feminist Theory,* ed. J. Trebilcot, 213-30. Totowa, NJ: Rowman and Allanheld, 1983.

–. "Preservation, Love, and Military Destruction." In *Mothering: Essays in Feminist Theory,* ed. J. Trebilcot, 231-62. Totowa, NJ: Rowman and Allanheld, 1983.

–. "Remarks on the Sexual Politics of Reason." In *Women and Moral Theory,* ed. Eva Feder Kittay and Diana T. Meyers, 237-60. Totowa, NJ: Rowman and Littlefield, 1987.

–. *Maternal Feminism: Toward a Politics of Peace.* Boston: Beacon Press, 1989.

Ruff, Larry E. "The Economic Sense of Pollution." *The Public Interest* 19 (Spring 1970): 69-85.

Russell, D.E.H. "The Incidence and Prevalence of Intra-Familial and Extra-Familial Sexual Abuse of Female Children." *Child Abuse and Neglect* 7 (1983): 133-46.

Sandel, Michael J. *Democracy's Discontent: America in Search of a Public Philosophy.* Cambridge: Harvard University Press, 1996.

Sanger, M. *Reckless Abandon: Canada, the GATS and the Future of Health Care.* Ottawa: Canadian Centre for Policy Alternatives, 2001.

Scales, Ann. "The Emergence of Feminist Jurisprudence: An Essay." In *Feminist Legal Theory Foundations,* ed. K. Weisberg, 40-57. Philadelphia: Temple University Press, 1993.

Schma, William G. "Judging for the New Millennium." *Court Review* 37 (2000): 4-6.

Schumacher, E.F. *Small Is Beautiful.* New York: Harper and Row, 1974.

Scott, Joan W. "The Evidence of Experience." *Critical Inquiry* 17 (1991): 773-97.

Seedhouse, David. *Ethics: The Heart of Health Care.* 2nd ed. West Sussex: John Wiley and Sons, 1998.

Sen, Amartya. *Commodities and Capabilities.* New York: Elsevier Science Pub. Co., 1985.

–. *On Ethics and Economics.* Oxford: Basil Blackwell, 1987.

–. "Objectivity and Position." Paper presented at the Lindley Lecture, University of Kansas, 1992.

Sevenhuijsen, Selma. *Citizenship and the Ethics of Care: Feminist Considerations on Justice, Morality, and Politics.* London and New York: Routledge, 1998.

–. "Caring in the Third Way: The Relation between Obligation, Responsibility, and Care in Third Way Discourse." *Critical Social Policy* 20, 1 (2000): 5-37.

–. "South African Social Policy and the Ethic of Care." Paper presented at the annual meeting of the American Political Science Association, San Francisco, 30 August-2 September 2001.

Sevenhuijsen, Selma, Vivienne Bozalek, Amanda Gouws, and Marie Minnar-McDonald. "South African Social Welfare Policy: An Analysis Using the Ethic of Care." *Critical Social Policy* 23, 3 (2003): 299-321.

Sharp, Naomi. *Equality-Seeking Charter Litigation: Where to from Here? A Vision of Trans-formative Justice.* Ottawa: National Association of Women and the Law, 1999.

Sheppard, Colleen. "Recognition of the Disadvantaging of Women: The Promise of *Andrews* v. *Law Society of British Columbia.*" *McGill Law Journal* 35 (1989): 207-34.

–. "Caring in Human Relations and Legal Approaches to Equality." *National Journal of Constitutional Law* 2 (1992-93): 305-45.

Sherman, A. *Wasting America's Future: The Children's Defense Fund Report on the Costs of Child Poverty.* Boston: Beacon Press, 1994.

Sherwin, Susan. "A Relational Approach to Autonomy in Health Care." In *The Politics of Women's Health: Exploring Agency and Autonomy,* ed. Susan Sherwin and the Feminist Health Care Ethics Research Network, 19-47. Philadelphia: Temple University Press, 1998.

Shiell, Alan, K. Gerard, and Cam Donaldson. "Cost of Illness Studies: An Aid to Decision-Making." *Health Policy* 8 (1987): 317-23.

Shuman, Daniel W. "The Psychology of Compensation in Tort Law." In *Law in a Therapeutic Key: Developments in Therapeutic Jurisprudence,* ed. D.B. Wexler and B.J. Winick, 433-66. Durham, NC: Carolina Academic Press, 1996.

–. "The Role of Apology in Tort Law." *Judicature* 83, 4 (2000): 180-89.

Sigurdson, Richard. "The Left-Legal Critique and the Charter: A Critical Assessment." *Windsor Yearbook of Access to Justice* 13 (1992): 117-55.

Silbert, M.H., and A.M. Pines. "Sexual Child Abuse as an Antecedent to Prostitution." *Child Abuse and Neglect* 5 (1981): 407-11.

Simmons, H.G. *Unbalanced: Mental Health Policy in Ontario, 1930-1989.* Toronto: Wall and Thompson, 1990.

Single, E., L. Robson, X. Xie, J.W. Rehm, R. Moore, B. Choi, S. Desjardins, and J. Anderson. *The Costs of Substance Abuse in Canada: A Cost Estimation Study.* Ottawa: Canadian Centre for Substance Abuse, 1997.

Sky, L., and V. Sparks. *Until Someone Listens.* Toronto: Skyworks Charitable Foundation, 1999.

Slobogin, Christopher. "Therapeutic Jurisprudence: Five Dilemmas to Ponder." In *Law in a Therapeutic Key: Developments in Therapeutic Jurisprudence,* ed. D.B. Wexler and B.J. Winick, 763-93. Durham, NC: Carolina Academic Press, 1996.

Smart, R.G., E.M. Adlaf, G.W. Walsh, and Y.M. Zdanowicz. *Drifting and Doing: Changes in Drug Use among Toronto Street Youth.* Toronto: Addiction Research Foundation, 1992.

Smith, Adam. *An Inquiry into the Nature and Causes of the Wealth of Nations.* London: Strahan and Cadell, 1776.

Smith, Kerry V. *Estimating Economic Values for Nature: Methods for Non-Market Valuation.* Cheltenham: Edward Elgar, 1996.

Snowden, A., and D. Kane. "Parental Needs Following the Discharge of a Hospitalized Child." *Pediatric Nurse* 21 (1995): 425-28.

Squires, Judith. *Gender in Political Theory.* Cambridge: Polity Press, 1999.

Stack, Carol. "The Culture of Gender: Women and Men of Color." *Signs* 11 (Winter 1986): 321-24.

Statistics Canada. *Snapshot No. 1: A Growing Population.* Online at <http://www.hc-sc.gc.ca/seniors-aines/pubs/factoids/2001/no01_e.htm> (accessed 15 March 2004).

–. "Women in Canada 2000: A Gender-Based Statistical Report." Ottawa: Minister of Industry, 2000.

Stein, Janice Gross. *The Cult of Efficiency.* Don Mills, ON: Anansi, 2001.

Sterba, James P. *Three Challenges to Ethics: Environmentalism, Feminism, and Multiculturalism.* New York: Oxford University Press, 2001.

Stone, Deborah. *Policy Paradox and Political Reason.* New York: HarperCollins, 1988.

–. "Care and Trembling." *The American Prospect* 10, 43 (1999): 61-67.

–. "Caring by the Book." In *Care Work: Gender, Labour, and the Welfare State,* ed. Madonna Harrington Meyer, 89-111. London: Routledge, 2000.

–. "Why We Need a Care Movement." *Nation* (New York), 13 March 2000, 13-15.

Stone-Mediatore, Shari. "Chandra Mohanty and the Revaluing of Experience." In

Decentering the Center: Philosophy for a Multicultural, Postcolonial, and Feminist World, ed. Uma Narayan and Sandra Harding, 110-27. Bloomington: Indiana University Press, 2000.

Storch, Janet L. "Foundational Values in Canadian Health Care." In *Efficiency Versus Equality: Health Care Reform in Canada,* ed. Michael Stingl and Donna Wilson, 21-26. Halifax: Fernwood, 1996.

Street, L. *The Screening Handbook: Protecting Clients, Staff, and the Community.* Ottawa: Canadian Association of Volunteer Bureau and Centres, 1996.

Symes v. *Canada,* [1993] 4 S.C.R. 695.

Taub, Nadine. "Book Review." *Columbia Law Review* 80 (1980): 1686-96.

Taylor, Charles. "Philosophical Reflections of Caring Practices." In *The Crisis of Care: Affirming and Restoring Caring Practices in the Helping Professions,* ed. S. Phillips and P. Benner, 174-88. Washington, DC: Georgetown University Press, 1994.

Tennstedt, Sharon. "Family Caregiving in an Aging Society." Paper presented at the US Administration on Aging Symposium entitled "Longevity in the New American Century," Baltimore, MD, 29 March 1999.

Thibaudeau v. *Canada,* [1995] 2 S.C.R. 627.

Thomas, Carol. "De-Constructing Concepts of Care." *Sociology* 27, 4 (1993): 649-69.

Titmuss, Richard. *Essays on "the Welfare State."* London: George Allen and Unwin, 1963.

Tong, Rosemarie. *Feminine and Feminist Ethics.* Belmont, CA: Wadsworth Publishing Company, 1993.

Tronto, Joan. *Moral Boundaries: A Political Argument for an Ethic of Care.* New York: Routledge Press, 1993.

–. "Care as a Basis for Radical Political Judgements." *Hypatia* 10, 2 (1995): 141-49.

–. "Women and Caring: What Can Feminists Learn about Morality from Caring?" In *Justice and Care: Essential Readings in Feminist Ethics,* ed. Virginia Held, 101-16. Boulder: Westview Press, 1995.

–. "An Ethic of Care." *Generations* 22, 3 (1998): 15-21.

–. "Politics, Plurality, and Purpose: How to Investigate and Theorize Care in an Institutional Context." In *Care, Citizenship, and Social Cohesion: Towards a Gender Perspective,* ed. Trudie Knijn and Selma Sevenhuijsen, 19-30. Utrecht: Netherlands School for Social and Economic Policy, 1998.

Tyler, Tom. "The Psychological Consequences of Judicial Procedures: Implications for Civil Commitment Hearings." In *Law in a Therapeutic Key: Developments in Therapeutic Jurisprudence,* ed. D.B. Wexler and B.J. Winick, 3-16. Durham, NC: Carolina Academic Press, 1996.

Ungerson, C. "Gender, Cash, and Informal Care: European Perspectives and Dilemmas." *Journal of Social Policy* 24, 1 (1999): 31-55.

United Nations Development Programme. "Human Development Report 1996." New York: Oxford University Press, 1997.

Usher, Dan. "The Value of Life for Decision Making in the Public Sector." In *Ethics and Economics,* ed. Ellen Frankel Paul, Fred D. Miller, and Jeffrey Paul, 168-91. Oxford: Basil Blackwell, 1985.

Van de Veer, Donald, and Christine Pierce. *The Environmental Ethics and Policy Book.* Belmont: Wadsworth, 1994.

VanRoijen, Leona, Marc A. Koopmanschap, Frans F.H. Rutten, and Paul J. van der Maas. "Indirect Costs of Disease: An International Comparison," *Health Policy* 33 (1995): 16.

Vriend v. *Alberta,* [1998] 1 S.C.R. 493.

Waldron, Jeremy. "When Justice Replaces Affection: The Need for Rights." In *Liberal Rights: Collected Papers (1981-1991),* 370-91. Cambridge: Cambridge University Press, 1993.

Walker, Lawrence. "Sex Differences in the Development of Moral Reasoning." *Child Development* 55, 3 (1984): 677-91.

Walker, Margaret Urban. "Moral Understandings: Alternative 'Epistemology' for a Feminist Ethics." In *Explorations in Feminist Ethics: Theory and Practice,* ed. Eve Browning Cole and Susan Coultrap-McQuin, 165-75. Bloomington: Indiana University Press, 1992.

Ward-Griffin, C., and P. McKeever. "Relationships between Nurses and Family Caregivers: Partners in Care?" *Advances in Nursing Science* 22, 3 (2000): 89-103.

Waring, Marilyn. *What Men Value and What Women Are Worth.* Toronto: University of Toronto Press, 1999.

Weaver, Sally. "First Nations Women and Government Policy, 1970-92." In *Changing Patterns: Women in Canada,* ed. S. Burt, L. Code, and L. Dorney, 92-150. Toronto: McClelland and Stewart, 1993.

Webb-Dempsey, J., B. Wilson, D. Corbett, and R. Mordecai-Phillips. "Understanding Caring in Context: Negotiating Borders and Barriers." In *Caring in an Unjust World: Negotiating Borders and Barriers in Schools,* ed. D. Eakerich and J. Van Galen, 85-112. Albany: SUNY Press, 1996.

Welle, Patrick G. "Public Policy and the Quality of Life: How Relevant Is Economics?" *Atlantic Economic Journal* 27, 1 (1999): 91-114.

West, Robin. *Caring for Justice.* New York: New York University Press, 1997.

Weston, Samuel. "Toward a Better Understanding of the Positive/Normative Distinction in Economics." *Economics and Philosophy* 10 (1994): 1-17.

Wexler, D.B. "An Orientation to Therapeutic Jurisprudence." *New England Journal of Criminal and Civil Confinement* 20, 2 (1994): 243-57.

–. "The Development of Therapeutic Jurisprudence: From Theory to Practice." University of Virginia Institute of Law Psychiatry and Public Policy, October 1997.

–. "Therapeutic Jurisprudence: An Overview." *Thomas M. Cooley Law Review* 17 (2000): 125-34.

Wexler, D.B., and B.J. Winick. *Essays in Therapeutic Jurisprudence.* Durham, NC: Carolina Academic Press, 1991.

–, eds. *Law in a Therapeutic Key: Developments in Therapeutic Jurisprudence.* Durham, NC: Carolina Academic Press, 1996.

White, Julie Anne. *Democracy, Justice, and the Welfare State: Reconstructing Public Care.* University Park: Pennsylvania State University Press, 2000.

Widom, S.P. *Victims of Childhood Sexual Abuse: Later Criminal Consequences.* Washington, DC: US Department of Justice, Office of Justice Programs, National Institute of Justice, 1995.

Wilber, Charles K., ed. *Economics, Ethics, and Public Policy.* Lanham, MD: Rowman and Littlefield, 1998.

Wildavsky, Aaron. *Speaking Truth to Power: The Art and Craft of Policy Analysis.* New Brunswick: Transaction Books, 1987.

Williams, Wendy. "Equality's Riddle: Pregnancy and the Equal Treatment/Special Treatment Debate." In *Feminist Legal Theory: Foundations,* ed. K. Weisberg, 128-55. Philadelphia: Temple University Press, 1993.

Wilson, Madam Justice Bertha. "Will Women Judges Really Make a Difference?" Paper presented at the Fourth Annual Barbara Betcherman Memorial Lecture, Osgoode Hall Law School, York University, 8 February 1992.

Winick, B.J. "The Jurisprudence of Therapeutic Jurisprudence." In *Law in a Therapeutic Key: Developments in Therapeutic Jurisprudence,* ed. D.B. Wexler and B.J. Winick, 645-68. Durham, NC: Carolina Academic Press, 1996.

–. "Introduction: The Approach of Therapeutic Jurisprudence." In *Therapeutic Jurisprudence Applied: Essays on Mental Health Law.* Durham, NC: Carolina Academic Press, 1997.

–. "Therapeutic Jurisprudence and the Civil Commitment Hearing." *Journal of Contemporary Legal Issues* 10 (1999): 37-60.

–. "Applying the Law Therapeutically in Domestic Violence Cases." *Kansas City Law Review* 69, 33 (2000): 33-91.

Wyatt, G.E., D. Guthrie, and C.M. Notgrass. "Differential Effects of Women's Child Sexual Abuse and Subsequent Sexual Revictimization." *Journal of Consulting and Clinical Psychology* 60, 2 (1992): 167-73.

Yamamoto, Eric K., and Susan K. Serrano. "Healing Racial Wounds? The Final Report of South Africa's Truth and Reconciliation Commission." *When Sorry Isn't Enough,* ed. Roy L. Brooks, 492-500. New York: New York University Press, 1999.

Young, Iris Marion. *Justice and the Politics of Difference*. Princeton: Princeton University Press, 1990.
–. *Intersecting Voices: Dilemmas of Gender, Political Philosophy, and Policy*. Princeton: Princeton University Press, 1997.
Zweibel, Ellen B. *"Thibaudeau* v. *R.*: Constitutional Challenge to the Taxation of Child Support Payments." *National Journal of Constitutional Law* 4 (1994): 305-50.
Zweibel, Ellen B., and Richard Shillington. *Child Support Policy: Income Tax Treatment of Child Support and Child Support Guidelines*. Toronto: Policy Research Centre on Children, Youth, and Families, 1993.

Index

64-67; redress packages, 74-80; redress
process, 73-74; responsiveness (care
ethic), 70-72; social justice, 79-80;
social policies, 62, 73, 80-83. *See also*
child sexual abuse; institutional child
abuse; redress and compensation
justice, social. *See* social justice
justice ethic. *See* liberal justice ethic

Kant, Immanuel, 95
Kittay, Eva Feder, 110, 129
Kohlberg, Lawrence, 7-8
Kymlicka, Will, 16-17, 19, 25. *See also*
liberal justice ethic

LaForest, Gerard (Justice), 56
law, psychological aspects, 62-64. *See
also* jurisprudence, therapeutic
Law Commission of Canada, 62
Law v. *Canada* (Minister of Employment
and Immigration), 58-59
L'Heureux-Dubé, Claire (Justice), 52-54
liberal justice ethic: anti-statism, 43;
autonomy, abstract, 5-6, 22-23, 37,
120; care ethic, 11, 14-26, 29-32, 59-
60, 127-28; empathy, 20-21; equality
rights, 42-44; jurisprudence, therapeutic, 62-63; litigant and judge
relationship, 51-52; overview, 4-7;
rights and responsibilities, 21-26;
social contract theory, 83; social
justice, 30-31, 36; social policies, 30-
32, 83-84, 92-93, 110-12, 127-28. *See
also* care ethic; liberal paradigm
liberal paradigm: commodification,
83-84, 92; home care policies, 110-12.
See also care ethic; liberal justice ethic

market norms and values. *See*
commodification; economic costing
maternal work, 12-13. *See also* care
theorists, first generation; women
McLachlin, Beverly (Justice), 52-54
Minow, Martha, 44, 64
monetary valuations. *See* commodification; economic costing
moral development theory (Kohlberg,
Lawrence), 7-8
morality. *See* care ethic; ethics and
economics; liberal justice ethic
morbidity and mortality rates, 86, 99.
See also economic costing
mothering. *See* maternal work

National Council of Welfare, 3
National Forum on Health, 122

needs. *See* interdependence, human
neoclassical economics, 92-93
Noddings, Nel, 12, 13, 17

Okin, Susan Moller, 14, 19-20
Ontario Mental Health Supplement, 67
"original position" (John Rawls), 14,
19-20. *See also* care ethic; liberal
justice ethic

pain and suffering, compensation for,
90, 102-3. *See also* intangible losses;
quality of life
policies. *See* social policies
pollution, economic valuation, 97. *See
also* environment, quality and safety of
poverty. *See* child poverty
"primary goods" (John Rawls), 15-16,
24. *See also* care ethic; liberal justice
ethic
privatization of caregiving. *See* deinstitutionalization
providers of care. *See* home care
psychological losses. *See* intangible
losses; pain and suffering
public spending. *See* social expenditures

qualitative measurements, 98. *See also*
economic costing
quality of life, economic costing, 87-88,
97, 104, 146n38. *See also* intangible
losses; pain and suffering
quantification. *See* commodification;
economic costing

Radin, Margaret Jane, 89, 102
rape victims, 100. *See also* intangible
losses
Rawls, John, 14-16, 19-20, 23-24. *See
also* liberal justice ethic
recipients of home care. *See* home care
redress and compensation: background,
64-67; care ethic, 61-62, 67, 70-73;
child sexual abuse survivors, 61, 64-66,
74-81, 98; financial compensation
awards, 74-76; intangible losses, 102-3;
non-monetary issues, 76-80; social
justice, 80-81, 128
Rehabilitation Act (US), 57
remedial jurisprudence. *See* jurisprudence,
therapeutic
reparation. *See* redress and compensation
residential schools. *See* child sexual
abuse; First Nations: children;
institutional child abuse
responsiveness (care ethic): health care

Printed and bound in Canada by Friesens

Set in Stone by Brenda and Neil West, BN Typographics West Ltd.

Copy editor: Joanne Richardson

Proofreader: Jillian Shoichet

Indexer: Susan Safyan